HENRY WILLIAM BIGLER

Henry William Bigler from *Century Illustrated*, ca. 1887. Courtesy of the Bancroft Library, Berkeley, California.

Henry William Bigler

Soldier, Gold Miner, Missionary, Chronicler
1815–1900

M. Guy Bishop

Utah State University Press
Logan, Utah
1998

For Kathy,
and for our children,
Angela, Monica, Adrienne, Michael, Marinda,
Andrew, Matthew, Melissa, and Aubrianna.
Each of you deserves to have your name in this book.

Utah State University Press
Logan, Utah 84322-7800

Typography by WolfPack
Cover design by Michelle Sellers

Library of Congress Cataloging-in-Publication Data

Bishop, Michael Guy, 1951–
    Henry William Bigler: soldier, gold miner, missionary,
chronicler, 1815–1900 /M. Guy Bishop.
    p. cm.
    Includes bibliographical references.
    ISBN 0-87421-253-7 (cloth: acid-free paper)
    ISBN 0-87421-254-5 (pbk: acid free paper)
    1. Bigler, Henry William, 1815–1900. 2. Pioneers—West (U.S.)—
Biography. 3. Mormon missionaries—West (U.S.)—Biography. 4.
California—Gold discoveries. 5. Farmington (Utah)—Biography.
I. Title.
F593.B65 B57 1998
978'.02'092—ddc21
    [B]   98-25354
                                                             CIP

Contents

Illustrations

INTRODUCTION

*U*nintentionally, Henry William Bigler was present when gold was discovered at Sutter's Mill in California in 1848. It was Bigler who wrote down the event in his private journal to resurface nearly fifty years later and provide a first-hand account of James Marshall's earth-shattering find. Henry Bigler's place in history is not really the result of an accident, however. Inadvertent, yes, but Bigler's status was earned by his diligent recording of the facts as they happened. During his participation in the march of the Mormon Battalion (1846–47), Bigler kept a detailed record. Henry Bigler's life story, at least as he would have preferred to have it told, was found not in the march of the battalion or at the gold discovery. For him these were mere sidelights.

The core of his life and values is found in his commitment to his religion. Henry Bigler was a devout Mormon—a humble, caring man whose primary concerns were more for his family and his beliefs than for worldly fame or recognition. While the historical world is most familiar with Henry Bigler as a volunteer soldier marching to California during the Mexican-American War or as the man who recorded the discovery of gold in 1848, there is more to Bigler's life than these more well-known events. In 1857 as he was about to leave a wife and small family to serve his second proselyting mission to the Sandwich Islands in seven years, Henry Bigler expressed to the privacy of his diary how hard this calling was for him. The most telling words were that he was willing to do it "however great the cross." This phrase was a clear expression of

Henry Bigler's core value. Bigler was a Mormon, a member of the Church of Jesus Christ of Latter-day Saints, and that fact determined his orientation to life, his approach to the opportunities and challenges he encountered, and the point of view that is faithfully rendered in the voluminous journal that records his participation in such momentous events of western American history as the march of the Mormon Battalion, the settlement of Utah, and—the event that earned him a permanent footnote in history—witnessing the discovery of gold at Sutter's Mill and the beginning of the California gold rush. Without an understanding of his quiet yet burning zeal, his indomitable devotion, and his unwavering commitment to the cause of Mormonism, much of his behavior would seem puzzling, even tinged by pathos.

This 1857 mission was an example. Henry Bigler was then forty-two years old. Two years before he had completed a mission to Hawaii that had lasted nearly five years. Even earlier, he had accepted two other proselyting calls within seven years of his conversion in 1837. His church service, on missions and with the Mormon Battalion, led Bigler to postpone marriage and a much-desired family until he was forty years old. The 1857 mission took him away from his wife and child for seventeen months. His first wife died in 1874, leaving him with three dependent children and a married daughter. He remarried three years later, fathered six more children, and helped rear an adopted son.

Although he settled down to spend nearly two decades as a farmer in Farmington, Utah, Henry spent the last twenty-four years of his life in relative poverty in St. George, Utah. There he gave his highest priority in his time and efforts, not to earning a living or establishing his family in comfort, but to serving without remuneration in the St. George Temple as an ordinance worker. In that role, he selflessly assisted those who were having sacred rites performed for themselves or, by proxy, for departed loved ones.

In short, though the strength of Bigler's motives may be mysterious, those motives themselves are not. He identified his personal interests completely with those of the church he loved and served from conversion until death. No effort was excessive, no sacrifice too extreme for Henry Bigler. He represents something of an American paradox. A strong, even vivid individual, almost archetypically

American in some ways, his selflessness counters the lonely anomie of the national character. He was a "true believer" who found only continuing reasons to believe, never disillusionment in the cause to which he committed himself.[1]

Bigler has been best known for two years (1846–48) of his long life: his marching to the Pacific shores with the Mormon Battalion and his diary notation of the discovery of gold in California. In 1962, Erwin G. Gudde edited and published the diaries covering that period as *Bigler's Chronicle of the West*. Although Gudde's portrait of Bigler is colorful and carefully researched, he rather dismissively comments that Bigler's "only claim . . . to a niche in the history of the American West rests on the fact that he became, more or less accidentally, the chronicler of certain events during the decisive years of 1846, 1847, [and] 1848."[2] This assessement, however, is too limited. Although Bigler's presence at Sutter's Mill may be termed an accident of history, his priceless record of the gold discovery was not. He kept an almost daily account of the Mormon Battalion's painful progress across half of what is now the United States. While in John Sutter's employment, Bigler used his moments of leisure to write an autobiography that dealt with his years before the battalion experience. Many years before Gudde's assessment, H. H. Bancroft had judged Bigler "a cool, clear-headed methodical man [who] kept a journal, in which he entered occurences on the spot."[3] This biography expands both Gudde's limited portrait of Bigler's life and also Gudde's limited assessment.

In addition to Bigler's role in documenting the discovery of gold and the Mormon Battalion's activities, he was among the first ten LDS missionaries to Hawaii. He not only preached the first Mormon sermon on Maui but chronicled the colorful history of that place and time in Mormon history. He recorded the plodding life of a Utah farmer and family man; then, at the completion of the Mormon temple in St. George, Utah, in 1877, the first since the Mormon exodus from Nauvoo, Illinois, in 1845, he quietly broadened the sphere of his religious duties to include regular participation in its ordinances.

Bigler's journals exist in five separate documents or document groups which are preserved in three archives in two states:

1. Most important in terms of volume and coverage are four pocket-sized, leather-bound daybooks and diaries and nine large, bound journals (measuring approximately 8.5 x 11 inches), containing almost daily entries between 1846 and 1900. They are currently housed at the Henry E. Huntington Library in San Marino, California. They had come perilously close to being lost as unimportant; but in 1936, Utah historian Juanita Brooks discovered several of Bigler's daybooks and an autobiography in a larger volume in the possession of some descendants in the St. George area. Bigler's daughter, Myrtle Ivy Bigler Branson, had already used one journal as a scrapbook, pasting newspaper clippings over its pages. Immediately recognizing their historical value, Brooks began working to preserve the documents. She offered them first to the Bancroft Library; when it showed no interest, the Huntington, where Brooks was a research fellow, accepted them. These thirteen items are:
    - Book A. A retrospective autobiography and journal (large-size format) with a diary continuing thereafter with dated entries covering the period from 1846 to 1899.
    - Book B. A daybook (approximately 100 pages) with dated entries from 10 October 1849 to 15 November 1850.
    - Book D. A daybook (approximately 240 pages) with dated entries from 31 March 1853 to 20 March 1857.
    - Book G. A journal (approximately 200 pages) with dated entries from 14 May 1857 to 13 January 1859.
    - A diary/daybook (over 100 pages) with dated entries from 14 October 1877 to 17 January 1887.
    - Journal, miscellaneous entries (approximately 50 pages), 1888–89.
    - Notepad (approximately 50 pages) containing miscellaneous entries, copies of letters, etc., ca. 1891.
    - Daybook (approximately 50 pages), ca. early 1890s.
    - Daybook (approximately 50 pages), 1892–93.
    - Memorandum/letter copybook (50 pages), 1893–94.
    - Memorandum/letter copybook (50 pages), n.d.
    - Miscellaneous journal/notebook (approximately 50 pages), ca. 1890s.

- Miscellaneous journal/notebook (approximately 50 pages), n.d.

2. In 1890 California historian John S. Hittell presented Bigler with a large, new journal in which he wrote a retrospective autobiography, incorporating entries copied from his original pocket diaries, then continued with daily entries. This journal is undated but, from internal references, was written and compiled about 1898. It is in the Historical Department Archives of the Church of Jesus Christ of Latter-day Saints, Salt Lake City, Utah. It covers from about 1815 to 1899; it is retrospective for 1815–46, with dated entries for 1846–99.

3. Bigler told his story to Hubert Howe Bancroft in 1872 in a long autobiographical letter followed by dated entries covering August–September 1848, laboriously hand-copied from his daybooks. This version, with the pages bound together and titled "Diary of a Mormon in California," is retained by the Bancroft Library, University of California at Berkeley.

4. A typescript covering 8 February 1846 to 3 November 1850 titled "Henry Bigler's Journal Book A: Autobiography of H. W. Bigler" is in the Special Collections and Manuscripts Department, Harold B. Lee Library, Brigham Young University, Provo, Utah. It also includes "Diary of Henry W. Bigler, Volume II, 1848," which covers 23 July 1848 to 26 September 1848, and "Diary of Henry W. Bigler, Volume III, 1849–1881," which, contrary to the title, covers 8 October 1849 through 15 November 1850. After this point, Bigler began using the smaller daybooks, preserved at the Huntington Library and the LDS Historical Department Archives.

5. A published version of Bigler's California experience appears as "Diary of H. W. Bigler in 1847 and 1848," *Overland Monthly* 10 (September 1887): 233–45. Extracted from Bigler's original diary, Book A, and edited by John S. Hittell, it provides a readily accessible version of the gold discovery. The original diary extract is housed at the Society of California Pioneers, San Francisco.

Bigler's accounts lack the glamor of a dissenter or a scoundrel. Rather, his life provides a microcosmic view of nineteenth-century Mormon society through the eyes of a lower-echelon member. His was not the view from the mountain top of a city builder and theology maker like Joseph Smith or Brigham Young. Rather, he was a foot soldier for his faith, steadily and steadfastly doing his duty. Bigler's life history offers a window through which it is possible to understand the experience of many of his contemporaries, few of whom left records as detailed and consistent as Bigler's. This experience includes not only the difficult and routine life of Utah pioneering but also the commitment, faith, and self-sacrifice that characterized a host of lesser-known Mormons whose individual experiences have been lost in historical obscurity.

Henry Bigler did not make doctrine or challenge it. His worldview reflects the positions held by Joseph Smith and elaborated by Brigham Young. Although there is only sketchy evidence that Bigler knew Joseph Smith personally, he was obviously in Brigham Young's trust. On several occasions, Young personally placed his confidence in Bigler's ability to get a job done.

There is a respectful distance between Bigler and the heads of the Mormon hierarchy, yet he was "family." Bathsheba Bigler Smith, one of Henry Bigler's closest cousins, was married to LDS apostle George A. Smith. As a missionary in the Sandwich Islands, Bigler formed a close and cordial friendship with George Q. Cannon, which he retained while Cannon became an apostle and later a counselor to Brigham Young in the church's First Presidency. In St. George, Bigler worked closely with apostle Wilford Woodruff, then president of the St. George Temple and later president of the church.

Bigler's written record offers an unsophisticated mirror of his activities and thoughts, convincingly sincere in intent and formidable in sheer volume. He is not presenting himself for public scrutiny nor bolstering a publicly held position—either his or the church's, although he unintentionally does both. In the simplicity, even ingenuousness, of his far-from-fluent prose, Bigler communicates a combination of fervor and quiet honesty that is, in the end, irresistible.

At least I found him so. In the mid-1980s, I ran across the Henry William Bigler Collection in the Mormon File at the Huntington Library. Since Bigler was distantly related by marriage to my wife, I decided to take a look at his papers. What I found caught my attention almost immediately—thirteen daybooks and journals and an autobiography/journal telling much about mid-nineteenth century California, the American West, and Mormonism from the perspective of an everyday participant in this pageant.

As I struggled to become intimately acquainted with Henry Bigler, many scholarly and personal debts accrued. While it is impossible to name all who have rendered assistance during the research and writing of this biography, some must be recognized. When I sought their opinions regarding my nascent thoughts for a Bigler biography, Charles S. Peterson and Martin Ridge, two eminent historians of the American West, encouraged me to push forward. Later, both men read and offered comments on early drafts of the manuscript. The History Division of the Los Angeles County Museum of Natural History—my employer during the years this book was researched—provided travel funds, professional encouragement, and a congenial work place. Particularly helpful and always encouraging were Harry Kelsey, then the chief curator of the History Division, Don Chaput, and Tom Sitton. The staffs of the Huntington Library and the Historical Department of the Church of Jesus Christ of Latter-day Saints, holders of the majority of Henry Bigler's papers, were most helpful. Peter Blodgett, curator of western Americana at the Huntington Library, and James L. Kimball and Ronald O. Barney of the LDS Church Historical Department deserve special recognition.

Newell G. Bringhurst, Roger D. Launius, and Stanford J. Layton each read the entire manuscript and offered helpful suggestions. Linda King Newell has gone the extra mile throughout to bring this project to fruition. The Mountain West Center for Regional Studies at Utah State University provided funding for editorial assistance from Lavina Fielding Anderson. Also, I appreciated the encouragement of John R. Alley, executive editor of the Utah State University Press, who saw this project through to its conclusion. I am grateful for all of this professional support. Any errors which may remain are mine alone.

Most importantly, I give my heartfelt thanks to my family. My parents, George and Bernice Bishop of Bountiful, Utah, were always supportive. I am grateful to my wife, Kathy, and our children, who have shared their lives with Henry Bigler and me for the past several years. They all have earned the right to have this book gratefully dedicated to them. I hope that they find in it some worthwhile compensation.

All quotations are cited exactly as rendered in the original without editorial interpolations except where necessary for clarity. Portions of various chapters have appeared in different form in *BYU Studies*, *California History*, *Dialogue: A Journal of Mormon Thought*, the *Journal of Mormon History*, and the *Hawaiian Journal of History*.

THE MAKING OF A MORMON
1836–38

I remember the first time I heard the name of Mormon,
Mormonites, Latter-day Saints, they sounded to me strange, this
was in the summer or fall of 1834.[1]

*T*he Monongahela River of northern West Virginia was, in the
late eighteenth century, a great aorta, pumping settlers and
supplies to the western slope of the Allegheny Mountains and
channeling its corn and timber to markets in Pittsburgh and other
population centers. Settlements sprang up along its path, and one
of them was Shinnston in Harrison County, founded on the
Monongahela's west fork, about forty-five miles east of the Ohio
River and seventy-five or eighty miles south of Pittsburgh. The
Bigler family settled here soon after the American War for
Independence, about two miles outside the village in hill country.
A generation later, it was still primitive.[2]

Henry William Bigler, the grandson of those original settlers,
was born there in 1815. The American branch of the family had been
founded by his great-grandfather, Holland-born Mark Bigler, who
had first sought better fortunes at Frankfurt, Germany, then sailed
for the New World in 1733. He was twenty-eight and unmarried,
one of the thousands of western Europeans who wandered away
from southwestern Germany, parts of Switzerland, and the Rhine
River Valley during the eighteenth and early nineteenth centuries.
Bigler landed at Philadelphia and, within five years, had married
and settled in Lancaster County, Pennsylvania, sixty-five miles to

the west. He and his wife moved at least twice more; they were living in Bucks County in southeast Pennsylvania by 1752 and were located in Carroll County, Maryland, when Mark, a successful farmer, died in 1787, leaving behind twelve living children. Habitual movers like Mark Bigler were found across the frontiers of America. By the mid-eighteenth century a "voracious land hunger" filled the frontier. Nowhere was it stronger than in southern Pennsylvania.[3]

Blocked by the Appalachian Mountains from an easy move to the West, many turned toward Maryland, Virginia, and North Carolina in search of new opportunity. Mark Bigler's second son, Jacob, married a "tolerable handsome" redheaded woman of Dutch and Welch parentage named Hannah Booker (or Booher) and moved southwest to the new frontier settlement of Shinnston, where they joined a handful of like-minded pioneers who were claiming the territory for Virginia, for the United States of America, and, primarily, for themselves.[4]

The town was named for Levi Shinn (1748–1807), a New Jersey Quaker, who explored the area in 1773, then settled it three years later. By 1786 when Jacob and Hannah Bigler arrived, Shinn's fine two-story house, gristmill, and store were prominent community structures.[5] In 1793 Hannah Bigler gave birth to her sixth child, a son named Jacob after his father. The younger Jacob (1793–1859) grew up along the West Fork River learning the skills of a woodsman and a farmer. In May 1814 he married a local girl, Elizabeth (Betsy) Harvey, daughter of Basil Harvey, who was a "preacher and a professor of religion"—likely of a Christian primitivist or Baptist persuasion. Jacob and Betsy, as Henry described them, "were poor but honest and religiously inclined."[6] On 28 August 1815, Henry William Bigler was born and possibly named after Jacob's brother Henry. Four sisters followed: Polly (b. 1818), Hannah (b. 1820), Emeline (b. 1824), and Bathsheba (b. 1826).

Henry was eleven years old when his mother, suffering from tuberculosis, gave birth to a daughter, Bathsheba. Betsy was unable to nurse the child properly, and the baby refused to accept a bottle. When little Bathsheba was fourteen months old, Henry stood by helplessly with the rest of the grieving family while the baby "breathed its last" in the lap of Betsy's mother. From her sickbed, Betsy, weeping, embraced her dead child, giving her a parting kiss.[7]

Five weeks after baby Bathsheba's death, Betsy followed. Henry sorrowfully recalled, "She died in the early part of the evening; us children were sleeping in our trundle bed, father came and wakened us and told us our mother was Dieing." The death of his mother and little sister profoundly affected twelve-year-old Henry. For the rest of his life, he manifested a great deal of compassion for the suffering and showed an unusual kindness for animals as well.

Realizing that her own death was rapidly approaching, Betsy had encouraged Jacob Bigler to marry Sarah (Sally) Cunningham— a young woman still in her teens who had been assisting the family during Betsy's protracted illness. Within a year of Betsy's death, Jacob Bigler, with his children's approval, did so. In addition to mothering Betsy's four, Sally gave birth to five more children: Adam (b. 1828), Jacob (b. 1830), Mark (b. 1832), Andrew (b. 1834), and Mariah (b. 1843).[8]

In the main, then, Henry Bigler grew up in a stable family, absorbing frontier skills from childhood, learning wilderness survival from his father and grandfather, and proudly claiming to be "a chip off the old block." When his father gave him a fine rifle, seventeen-year-old Henry felt like "Daniel Boon the old Kentucky pioneer." Admittedly "fond of hunting," Henry took to the woods with this rifle. One summer day as he lay in wait for some deer at a salt lick, the young hunter was surprised by a bear. "It was the first I had ever met in the woods," he recalled, and "my hair fairly stood erect." Remembering what his father had taught him, Bigler rested his rifle on the side of a tree, took steady aim, and fired, then tracked the wounded animal until the next morning. He proudly took home the skin and a forepaw as a souvenir.[9]

Bigler learned the rudiments of reading and mathematics at home, probably from his mother. Even though education trailed behind the priorities of farming and home building, his parents somehow succeeded in instilling an appreciation of education in their son. Western Virginia lacked free public schools until 1829, and Henry recalls learning only "spelling, reading, writing and learning to cipher [multiply] as far as the Rule of three" from a Methodist minister named David Masters in a one-room school with split-log benches.[10] Masters's curriculum did not include grammar, and Henry Bigler's journal offers ample proof of his backwoods southern accent as well as his poor spelling. Until mid-life he wrote *women* as *wimin*, *where* as *whare*, and *few* as *fiew*.

Henry has left no record of specific religious affiliation on his family's part, but Levi Shinn, a descendent of the community's founder, preached Betsy Bigler's funeral service. He was of the "New Lights"—a Baptist schism that had grown out of the exuberant revivalism of New England's Great Awakening and been transplanted to the southern back country by the late eighteenth century. New Light Baptists clung tenaciously to the doctrine of baptism by immersion, enjoyed camp-meeting-style revivalism, and stressed such Christian primitivism precepts as plainness in dress and complete reliance upon scriptural precedents.[11]

In western Virginia where the Biglers lived, fundamental, unorthodox Christianity was popular. By the 1830s, the Methodists, the Presbyterians, and the Baptists dominated the trans-Allegheny frontier, with Baptist and Methodist circuit riders enthusiastically preaching the gospel throughout the region.[12] Betsy Bigler's father, Basil Harvey, was just such an evangelist.

The most noted religious dissenter in western Virginia was Alexander Campbell (1788–1866), a one-time Baptist who hoped to reestablish primitive Christianity as he saw it outlined in the New Testament. His Disciples of Christ believed that primitivism was the sole acceptable form of worship. While the Biglers may not have been professing members of any sect, it may be significant that Betsy Bigler received a New Lights' funeral, rather than the rites of an established church.

When Henry Bigler was nineteen, he began to learn of Mormonism. Although it was not an enthusiastic religion like the New Light Baptists or other Christian primitivist denominations, Mormonism had some similarities with the doctrines Bigler must have heard in his childhood home. Mormons baptized by immersion. They looked to ancient precedents for religious authority. And Mormonism had a distinctive millennialist bent of its own. However, Joseph Smith, its founder, was not interested in raising up another sect to compete in the maelstrom of religious pluralism then sweeping America. Instead, Mormonism saw itself as the one true religion and thus stood foursquare against pluralism.

Bigler's first exposure to Mormonism came during 1834 when a neighbor in Harrison County, Virginia, returned from a trip across the Ohio River with tales of a new religion led by a Joseph Smith, a self-professed prophet. Possibly this neighbor had encountered Mormon converts in Cabell County, Virginia, just east of the Ohio River, where missionaries had preached with some success in 1832. Young Henry ingenuously reports in his retrospective autobiography that he "listened attentively to his [the neighbor's] statements but said nothing although I felt what he said might be true but I disliked the name of their Prophet [because] there was a man living in our neighborhood whose given name was Jo who was forever picking quarrels and wanting to fight somebody at every gathering he chance[d] to be to."[13] Possibly the slightly built Bigler had fallen victim to this bully.

The first "Mormonite" preachers arrived in Harrison County during the fall of 1834. Lorenzo D. Barnes and Samuel James were, according to Henry Bigler, "smart preachers [who] had the scriptures at their tongues end and seemed to know the Bible by heart." Among their fifteen converts was Henry's stepmother, Sally Bigler.[16] Jacob Bigler wrote to church headquarters at Kirtland, Ohio, and obtained a copy of the Book of Mormon. After reading some of his new book, Jacob declared to his children that "no man of himself ever made the Book." Eighteen-year-old Polly also read the Book of Mormon, felt "it made many passages of scripture plain," and "induced" twenty-two-year-old Henry to read it. He soon became convinced the book was true and sought baptism from local church leader Jesse Turpin in July 1837.[14] By the end of the summer, all of the family were members. Persuasive to them were the Book of Mormon's claims to be a volume of sacred scripture and Mormonism's profession that it restored the original gospel of Christ. Henry Bigler also accepted its warning that the Second Coming of Christ was imminent.

Mormonism was only seven years old at that point. Joseph Smith, Jr. (1805–44) had formed the Church of Jesus Christ (later the Church of Jesus Christ of Latter-day Saints) on 6 April 1830 at Fayette, New York, after a series of supernatural manifestations during the 1820s. Chief among them were his claim of a visitation from the Father and the Son telling him to join no existing church and another visitation from an ancient American prophet named Moroni. This second individual, said Smith, told him to translate a record engraved on golden plates which he would find on a hill near the family farm. It told the history of ancient American peoples, including a visit from the resurrected Christ. In 1829, Smith completed the translation; and on 26 March 1830, the Book of Mormon first went on public sale, giving the church's disciples their popular name, "Mormons" or "Mormonites." Believers, however, usually referred to themselves as "Saints."

This new religion had a simple message: God had called a new prophet and restored the true church of Jesus Christ. The steps necessary to gain salvation, it taught, included faith, repentance, baptism by one holding the proper authority, and the bestowal of the Holy Ghost. An influential early believer was Campbellite minister Sidney Rigdon (1793–1876) of Kirtland, Ohio. When he joined the Mormons, he brought a sizable congregation with him. By 1831, Smith had transferred church headquarters to Kirtland.

Issues like the true authority to act in God's name or the claims to continuing revelation, while paramount in the conversion of Henry Bigler and his immediate family, were also crucial to many Americans of the 1830s or 1840s. Often, early converts to Mormonism, possibly dissatisfied with revivalism and with the contemporary Christian religions, looked for and eagerly embraced such a religious awakening as that which Joseph Smith offered. Joel Hills Johnson, for example, reported that he would "sit up almost all night to read religious tracts [and] also read the Bible with much attention."[15] John Steele, an Irishman living in Glasgow, Scotland, in 1842, heard of the Book of Mormon, obtained a copy, read it, and converted.[16] And Lorenzo Dow Young, in an experience not unlike that of Henry Bigler, heard of Mormonism when his brothers, Brigham and Joseph, excitedly reported their experiences with the new religion in 1831.[17]

Henry Bigler's conviction that he had found the truth was confirmed by a supernatural experience shortly after his baptism which, interestingly, resembles Joseph Smith's initial vision of the Father and the Son. According to Smith's 1838 account, he was praying alone in the woods when "thick darkness" and an evil power threatened to overwhelm him; he was delivered from this spiritual oppression when he saw "a pillar of light exactly over my head, above the brightness of the sun, which descended gradually until it fell upon me." In this light, Smith continued, he saw God and Jesus Christ, who told him that no existing church met with their approbation.[18] Bigler, who did not record his own manifestation until about 1898, may have been influenced by Smith's account; still, it offers much insight into the sources of his strong commitment to Mormonism:

> Shortly after I was confirmed by the laying on of hands and while at secret prayer next morning in the woods the Holy Spirit came upon me in so powerful a manner that I sprang to my feet and shouted for joy but before jumping up and while praying, my eyes being shut, I saw a light that rested on me from behind and a stream of a fog like appearance shot out of my mouth and as I jumped up I thought an angel was surely present and at the same time my tongue seemed to move and talk of itself and I felt light as a feather. I spent most of the day alone in the woods and at night while at secret prayer had prity much the same manifestations as in the morning.[19]

Bigler's commitment, rooted in his initial belief and nourished by such experiences, would grow stronger with each passing year. It was a faith that both lifted his heart and wrenched it. For example, soon after his baptism, Henry tried to share his newfound belief with his grandfather, Basil Harvey, the itinerant preacher. Harvey, however, refused to listen to the missionaries or read the Mormon scriptures. He informed Bigler, "If I was to find the Book of Mormon in my house I would burn it." The old man then charged, "If your mother had been alive, you never would have joined the Mormons." Henry does not record his immediate response, but a year later he dreamed that Harvey, then dead, came to him "in a fright" because he was in "great trouble" for not listening to the gospel. "Since then I have been baptized for him," wrote Henry with sober satisfaction.[20]

The family's conversion to Mormonism ended three generations of geographical and social stability. Twenty-year-old Polly Bigler died in April 1838, "a good girl," wrote Henry, "and beloved

by all that knew her."[21] Two months later, in June, a group of
Virginia converts migrated to Far West in Caldwell County,
Missouri. The Bigler contingent was a large one, consisting of
Jacob and Sally, twenty-three-year-old Henry, eighteen-year-old
Hannah, fourteen-year-old Emeline, and the four children of the
second marriage, ranging from ten to four. (The fifth child,
Mariah, was born near Nauvoo in 1843.) This was the first of many
such displacements in response to a prophet's voice for Henry
Bigler, but it was a community near the brink of disaster that wel-
comed the Virginians that summer.

According to an 1831 revelation of Joseph Smith, Jackson
County, Missouri, was the site of both the biblical Garden of Eden
and of the future temple to which Jesus Christ would return at his
Second Coming.[22] A small group of the Saints had arrived in 1831
to establish a communitarian colony; but their exclusivist economic
policy, Northern politics, and communal social customs quickly
brought them into conflict with the older residents of Jackson
County.[23] These Missourians resented the Mormons' claims of
being God's chosen people, doubted the apocalyptic future outlined for their real estate, and feared an abolitionist agenda. Just
eleven years earlier, Missouri had entered the Union as a slave state
and Jackson County was a hotbed of proslavery sentiment. These
fears seemed confirmed when the *Evening and Morning Star*, the
Mormon newspaper published at Independence, Missouri, printed
an ill-advised editorial in June 1832 inviting free blacks to investi-
gate Mormonism. By the end of 1833 the Missouri Mormons had
been forcibly driven from the county.

After a brief sojourn in Clay County, the unwanted
Mormons moved to less-settled Caldwell County in the northwest
where they founded Far West. After a period that was hardly ten-
sion free, though not marred by open violence, economic reversals
in Ohio coupled with religious persecution forced Joseph Smith
from Kirtland to Far West in January 1838. Thus, the Mormon
prophet was in residence when Henry Bigler and his family arrived
in Missouri.

On their first Sunday in Far West, the Biglers attended a
church service where a "beardless boy" named Erastus Snow was
the first orator. Henry Bigler admitted that the youthful Snow,

later an apostle, had "some preach in him." Then, to their delight, Joseph Smith made some concluding remarks. Bigler admiringly recorded that Joseph Smith was indeed "all that the Elders [in Harrison County] said he was."[24] Smith, over six feet tall and weighing about two hundred pounds, was powerfully built and charismatic. Contemporaries described him as "a plain, honest man, full of benevolence and philanthropy."[25] To Henry Bigler, who was short, slight, and never weighed over 150 pounds even in his prime, Smith's physical presence alone would have been imposing.

Bigler also recorded the presence of other Mormon notables, including Joseph Smith, Sr., father of the prophet, whom he rather fancifully described as "favor[ing] the old patriarch Jacob." Sidney Rigdon, then a counselor to Joseph Smith in the church's First Presidency, was "large" and "rather corpulent" but an excellent orator who spoke "comforting words to us." Quoting Matthew 13:11, Rigdon promised the Mormon faithful, "To you it is given to know the mysteries of the kingdom of heaven."[26]

Later that summer Henry Bigler eagerly accompanied a party led by Joseph Smith to visit Adam-ondi-Ahman, a prospering Mormon settlement in Daviess County to the north. According to Smith, Adam and Eve had made their post-expulsion home in this locale; Bigler and his group listened in wonder as Smith identified a particular spot as the site of Adam's altar at which he offered prayers and sacrifices. "It was in a grove of timber and the stones of which it had been made were in big blocks laying around near each other," Henry wrote, "and where they came from I never learned for I saw no other stones in the country like them."[27]

The Mormons were not long allowed to construct such exotic sacred histories. Contemporary politics pressed in upon them. Hostility mounted in Caldwell and Daviess Counties for several reasons. The local Missourians feared that the Mormons might become violent. Rumors swirled that the Danites (a militant band of Mormons committed to cleansing Mormonism internally and punishing its external detractors) intended to avenge past injustices. The continued rapid growth of the Mormon population in western Missouri brought accompanying political and economic threats. Mormon millennial expectations, while devout, were no doubt indiscreet in anticipating the possession of the whole of Missouri at the Second Coming.

Henry Bigler was living with his uncle, Mark Bigler, who had been baptized in 1834, at Adam-ondi-Ahman when he observed that "the Missourians began to hold meetings and resolutions passed to drive the Mormons out of the state."[28] These initial protests culminated in an armed clash between Missourians and Mormons at Crooked River on 25 October 1838 that left three Mormons slain and one Missourian killed and several wounded. Missouri's governor, Lilburn Boggs of Jackson County, issued an executive order that the Saints "must be exterminated or driven from the state."[29] On 20 October 1838 a loosely organized detachment of state militia whom Bigler termed a "mob army" killed eighteen men and boys, apparently unarmed, at nearby Haun's Mill, then surrounded Adam-ondi-Ahman.[30]

Although he was "lieing sick with ague," Henry Bigler joined the other besieged citizens in battle preparations, but the fight was aborted when Joseph Smith capitulated at Far West. Those at Adam-ondi-Ahman also decided to surrender. The celebrating Missourians, Bigler wrote, "seemed to take delight in shooting chickings, pigs, and hogs belonging to the Saints." Along with other Mormons, Henry received a letter of safe passage out of Missouri; but he hurried to Far West, still under occupation, to be with his family. During the bitter winter of 1838–39, "the whole Church of twelve or fifteen thousand were driven and fled to Illinois."[31]

Henry Bigler's version of the Missouri persecutions of his fellow Mormons, which was not penned until the 1890s, reflects the received Mormon view. For the most part, his was not the perspective of a first-hand observer, and he did not arrive in Missouri until just before the hostilities commenced in earnest. Bigler's account was certainly sympathetic, but he was not an actual sufferer. Furthermore, his account was almost certainly influenced by George A. Smith, a Mormon apostle, church historian, and husband of his cousin, Bathsheba Bigler. Henry Bigler lived with the Smiths for some time after the church's move to Nauvoo, Illinois, and certainly would have had easy access to much of Smith's historical work as it was later published in installments in the *Deseret*

News in Utah. George A. Smith *was* an actual participant in these events, casting them in heroic terms and writing about them with emotional intensity.[32] Henry Bigler revealed some telling details about his method of writing at the time he probably composed this account in an 1891 letter to a friend of nearly fifty years, Alexander Stephens:

> [John S. Hittell] made me a nice present a few months ago of a nice Blank book, fools cap size of 500 pages, ruled & numbered, bound with calf, spring back and on the outside my name in gilt letters . . . I am now writing my own history. I have kep a sort of journal ever since the Church left Nauvoo in 1846, but in writing my history I give some account of the day and time before the Gospel found me . . . this I do for the benefit of my children after I am gone.[33]

For Henry and other mid-nineteenth century Mormons who remained true to their faith, the trials of Missouri fostered a strong sense of group loyalty. Out of the persecution emerged an abiding mistrust of the "justice" of the American legal system. A mutuality of purpose joined with righteous indignation against the rest of humankind (tellingly labeled "Gentiles") to create a strong sense of peoplehood. Joseph Smith and his followers even more clearly rejected pluralism as they solidified their already close-knit community. In Illinois and later in the Great Basin of the American West, this insider-outsider demarcation would increase.[34]

Goerge A. Smith, Mormon apostle and Henry Bigler's relation by marriage. Courtesy of the Archives, Church of Jesus Christ of Latter-day Saints.

❧ 2 ❧

ON THE FORGE
1839–45

*At the close of the meeting we were advised to leave off preaching
and go home for we were more fit to drive oxen.*[1]

*M*ost of the Mormon refugees from Missouri assembled at
Quincy, Illinois, during February 1839, bewildered and
leaderless. Joseph Smith was confined in the log jailhouse in
Liberty, Missouri. They had no shelter and were almost totally destitute. Fortunately, the residents of western Illinois welcomed them
as a downtrodden people seeking to escape unjust persecution and
greatly eased their initial suffering; but this compassion lasted less
than a decade. In western Illinois the followers of Joseph Smith
built Nauvoo, one of the most successful cities of the region during
the period. By 1846–47, the Mormons were again forced from the
state by neighbors who found their beliefs and community intolerable. Today, most Mormons regard the Nauvoo years as a "kind of
verification of [the] religious truth" in which they place their faith.[2]
While Henry Bigler may well have viewed these years in this light,
for him they likely passed as a blur of activity and hard work. He
grew in his faith, but probably had little time at Nauvoo to appreciate the growth. Instead he worked to support his father's family
and to serve his church.

These six years of relative peace were the prime of Bigler's
young manhood—from age twenty-four to thirty. The predictable
pattern would have been for him to marry and establish himself in
a career. Instead, he devoted himself to the needs of his father's

family, interrupting this commitment unhesitatingly when the church called for his services.

At Quincy the Saints, in the absence of Joseph Smith, debated the feasibility of continuing the "gathering" at the risk of irritating their neighbors anew as they had in Missouri. Two prominent leaders, William Marks and Edward Partridge, took the position that a gathering was not expedient. When Brigham Young, the senior of the twelve Mormon apostles, arrived, he proposed that the Saints settle among the companies with whom they had migrated from Missouri. In a 25 March 1839 epistle to the church, written from Liberty Jail, Joseph Smith admonished the Saints at Quincy to "fall into the places and refuge of safety that God shall open unto them."[3] Constrained by poverty and the lack of strong central leadership, the Mormons remained in temporary encampments for several months.[4]

By the time Jacob Bigler and his family arrived in Illinois during the spring of 1839, a rough consensus favoring dispersion dominated Mormon thinking. Consequently, Jacob Bigler rented a farm about fifteen miles to the southeast at Payson, Illinois. Perhaps indicating the dire financial straits in which the Biglers found themselves, Henry did not go to Payson but "stopped in Quincy when a steamboat arrived at the warf the mate wanted to hire a hand offering twenty five dollars I accepted the offer and went on board, my duty was to be night wachman."[5]

Henry Bigler enjoyed his life as a riverboatman. Between rounds, he had free access to the galley, where "I always found plenty of food left from the Cabin table such as cooked fowl, fish, veal, mutton and baked beef."[6] This relish for unlimited food seems to suggest he had been on short rations to that point. These riverboat crewmen, probably from New Orleans, affectionately dubbed the slightly built Bigler "Picayune"—a small silver coin then worth about thirty-one cents. Bigler did not seem offended by the nickname, since, speaking of his physical stature, he referred to himself as "a little man."[7] He had a fine time on the riverboat, but an undisclosed illness sent him home after only a month. After recuperating with his family at Payson, Bigler began working for a farmer near Quincy for about half of what he was paid on the riverboat.

Then Joseph Smith, who had escaped from his captors in early April, rejoined the Saints and reversed the dispersion policy. Soon he was leading efforts to establish Mormonism's new capital, at Commerce, Illinois, northeast of Quincy on the banks of the Mississippi River.[8] As the newly renamed Nauvoo rose, Smith turned his attention to proselyting and sent his Twelve Apostles to the British Isles. They left in July 1839, and mission assignments to a host of Mormon men soon followed.

At Quincy in August 1839 Bigler was called as a missionary, "having been ordained an Elder and Seventy in Far West, under the hands of Brigham Young and Heber C. Kimball."[9] Bigler received his specific assignment several weeks later when he and a younger man, Amos Lyons, were sent to preach in western Virginia.[10] Bigler and Lyons took a steamboat downriver to St. Louis where they encountered their first flat-out rejection. Upon asking for a drink of water at a home and identifying themselves as Mormons, they were taken aback when the woman of the house charged them with being "Latterday devils." They should, she said, be ashamed to preach about "old Joe Smith."[11]

Choosing another house in St. Louis, Bigler and Lyons, who traveled "without purse or scrip" as was common among Mormon missionaries, asked for a night's lodging. Their host not only welcomed them but asked them to preach and assembled several neighbors for the impromptu service. The twenty-four-year-old Bigler spoke first while his companion added some brief remarks. It was not altogether a success. "Both being young in the ministry [and] this being our first attempt at public speaking," Bigler wrote, "the meeting was short," and some members of the audience advised the two "to leave off preaching and go home for we were more fit to drive oxen."[12] By the time Bigler recorded this incident nearly fifty years later, he told the story with a certain wry humor, but it must have stung at the time.

The character of Mormonism, with its unique doctrinal and social beliefs, determined much of Bigler's early missionary experiences. Its rejection of traditional Christianity and claim to exclusively possess Christ's original gospel and authority not unnaturally triggered defensive reactions among those who espoused other beliefs. While some among a missionary's audience believed Joseph

Smith's claims to divine revelation and accepted the Book of Mormon as inspired scripture, translated by a miracle, many more dismissed Mormonism and its prophet as a fraud. Proselyting was a spontaneous, highly personalized activity with missionaries "testifying" from their own experience that they spoke the truth and hoping to win converts based on a combination of their sincerity, the persuasiveness of their preaching, and the operation of the Holy Spirit upon their audience. Joseph Smith urged his missionaries to "preach the simple Gospel," meaning that they were to shun the elaborate oratory of popular clergymen.[13] It was thus relatively easy, even for a novice like Henry Bigler, to preach Mormonism. He had to look no further than his own recent conversion experience and deeply held convictions.

Continuing down the Mississippi by riverboat from St. Louis to Cairo, Illinois, then up the Ohio River, Bigler and Lyons disembarked at Shawneetown, Illinois, and crossed to the Kentucky shore. Battling sickness, fatigue, and unpopularity, the two Mormons reached Jackson County in western Virginia late in the fall. "The way opened for preaching," Bigler observed, "and we baptized a man and his wife." In Harrison County, Virginia, they spent the winter of 1839–40 among Bigler's relatives and friends.[14] They made no converts, although Lyons courted and married a local woman. In the spring Bigler returned alone to Jackson County, where he baptized three before the summer's end. He also "held a public discushion with a Baptist minister who had challenged me to debate on religion he claiming there had been no falling away from the Church since the days of Christ and His Apostles." Bigler triumphantly added that the Baptist "came out of the little end of the horn" in the contest.[15]

He does not record when he returned to Nauvoo, but it was probably a year later, in the late summer or fall of 1841. It is unclear where Bigler's family was living at this time, but they may have moved to Bear Creek about sixteen miles south of Nauvoo, their home by 1845. Again, marriage and professional concerns would have been preeminent for many young men; but Bigler committed his time to church service—at that point, the construction of the Nauvoo Temple.

An earlier temple, an imposing edifice, had been constructed in Kirtland, dedicated to the accompaniment of Pentecostal manifestations, angelic visitations, and supernal heavenly choirs, and then abandoned. It had served primarily as a meetinghouse, but Smith envisioned a series of rites for the Nauvoo Temple which, he taught, would enable devout Saints to assure their own eternal life, as well as salvation for their dead.[16] Bigler spent the summer of 1842 "get[ting] out rock for the Nauvoo Temple."[17] Since he was not a skilled stonecutter, his work was almost certainly backbreaking manual labor. It is not difficult to imagine how taxing this duty was for the slightly built man, but his writings include no complaints.

This temple-centered labor further meant that Bigler was in a position to observe the spectacular development of Mormon theology during 1842–44. Weather permitting, Smith usually delivered lengthy sermons at weekly outdoor preaching services on Sunday and often spoke to midweek gatherings of seventies, elders, and others, expounding and amplifying his developing doctrines. Charlotte Haven, a young non-Mormon visitor to Nauvoo in 1843, recalled going to a Sunday sermon delivered by Joseph Smith. "Such hurrying!" she noted. "One would have thought it was the last opportunity to hear him that they would ever have, although we were two hours before the services were to commence."[18]

Many of Smith's new doctrines were connected with the temple. He established the necessity of universal baptism by recognized authority, the supremacy of priesthood power to "seal" husbands and wives and parents and children, both living and dead, and the establishment of vicarious ordinances of baptism for the dead performed by living proxies. Rather more controversial was his evolving doctrine that God was a glorified man and that some elements of human intelligence were coexistent with God.[19] Many Saints shared the heady feeling that they were a chosen people, learning the "mysteries of the kingdom" as preparation for the Savior's Second Coming. John Greenhow, for example, exuberantly wrote in the *Times and Seasons*: "For in Nauvoo we receive line upon line, precept upon precept, and the great things of the kingdom are unfolded to our understandings that we can grow in grace and knowledge. . . . The dark mantle of error [is] fast vanishing before the rays of truth and righteousness."[20] Mormon apostle and theologian John Taylor wrote of the Nauvoo years, "Many great things have unfolded unto us . . . . The diamond has shone in all its resplendent beauty, and thousands who know how to appreciate truth have been attracted by the precious gem."[21]

Unfortunately, Henry Bigler left no such ringing declarations about his Nauvoo experience, and his extant writings of this period are all retrospective, making it difficult to know exactly what he felt at Nauvoo. However, his continuing faith in Joseph Smith's teachings and the unswerving allegiance he later transferred wholesale to Brigham Young and the Twelve Apostles as successors of Joseph Smith are good evidence that he accepted the doctrines enunciated at Nauvoo. Others, like Stephen Post, who embraced Mormonism in 1835, two years before Bigler, judged the Nauvoo community of November 1842 "dead to the cause of Zion" and drifted away from the Mormon fold while Bigler remained steadfast.[22]

The rapidly evolving doctrines developing in Nauvoo during the early 1840s lie at the root of the schisms that shattered Mormonism in the wake of Joseph Smith's death. Perhaps the most important was a secret doctrine: the restoration of the Old Testament practice of plural wives—polygyny or, as the Saints later called it, polygamy. Henry Bigler does not mention plural marriage directly until years later. He may well have heard rumors, but he was far from the inner circle of Mormonism, had been away preaching for two years, and probably had no direct knowledge of the practice. Joseph Smith taught intimates in his inner circle that he had received these instructions as a divine commandment during the Kirtland era and that the time had come to begin putting the teachings into practice.[23] As Joseph Smith and trusted lieutenants began entering into secret plural marriages, while publicly denouncing rumors of the practice, unrest increased. Charged by foes and former friends with adultery and apostasy, Smith faced public challenges to his leadership. Exacerbating and reinforcing the internal dissent came external hostilities. Nauvoo had emerged as the dominant community in western Illinois, posing a serious political and economic threat to such older towns in Hancock County as Carthage or Warsaw.

A major crisis occurred when John C. Bennett, one-time confidant of Joseph Smith and Nauvoo's first mayor, publicly repudiated Smith and was excommunicated in 1842 for "adultery," although it is not clear how much of his sexual activity was authorized plural marriage and how much was freelance opportunism, which thrived in Nauvoo's environment of secrecy and ambiguity. The *Times and Seasons*, then edited by Joseph Smith, who was routinely issuing denials about polygamy, fulminated: "He professed to be virtuous and chaste, yet did he pierce the heart of the innocent. . . . He professed to fear God, yet did he desecrate his name, and prostitute his authority to the most unhallowed and diabolical purposes; even to the seduction of the virtuous and the defiling of his neighbor's bed."[24] In contrast to this elaborate contemporary justification, Bigler's retrospective summary is simple: "Bennett had belonged to the Church and for his wickedness he was cut off."[25] The angry Bennett wrote a series of exposé of polygamy and Smith's political ambitions for the *Sangamo Journal* in Springfield, Illinois, which was widely reprinted and which appeared as a book the same year. Bennett charged Smith with polygamy, murder, swindles, and a plot to conquer the upper Midwest and found a Mormon empire.[26]

Smith counterattacked at a special conference in August 1842 at which, in Bigler's words, "a goodly number of Elders were called to go on missions to preach the gospel and to rebut John C. Bennetts lies, among the number I was called." Hyrum Smith, Joseph's brother, counseled the departing missionaries to "go wisely, humbly setting forth the truth as it is in God" in hopes of reversing the tide of public opinion.[27] Traveling with two other missionaries, his cousin, Jacob G. Bigler, and Josiah W. Fleming, Bigler started in early September. In Fulton County, Illinois, about sixty miles east of Nauvoo, the group met another Mormon elder, Alpheus Harmon. Since Harmon was without a companion, Bigler joined him.

The frustrations and discouragement of missionary work weighed heavily upon Harmon as they trudged most of the way across Illinois and northern Indiana. When they neared the Indiana-Ohio border in late fall 1842, "Brother Harmon concluded to return home to Nauvoo," Bigler recorded. In a nearby grove of trees, "we blessed each other, shook hands and parted." While

Harmon slowly disappeared in the direction from which they had come, Bigler was overcome by a "lonely feeling for he was good company and I believe a good man," but his autobiography contains no suggestion that he himself considered giving up his mission. Much later he learned that Harmon froze to death in a winter storm while crossing the Illinois prairie on his return to Nauvoo.[28] If Bigler had been with him, he may well have met the same fate.

Under trying circumstances, Bigler pressed eastward "preaching every chance I got," but "the wether began to grow cold and my clothes [were] not good, getting worse of the wear. I commenced to inquire for labor with my hands instead of preaching."[29] By January 1843 Henry Bigler was near Lima, Ohio. Stopping at "a respectable looking house" the cold and tired Mormon elder introduced himself as "a servant of the Lord" and asked for lodging. Upon learning that his caller was a "Mormonite" the man hesitated, then told Bigler he would have to move on. "I turned round on my heels and went out, shutting the door after me," noted Bigler. Then, as he was leaving the yard, the householder "called me back and told me he would keep me and make some inquiries about my people and our religion etc." According to Bigler, his Lutheran host, a Mr. McMelon, hoped to "use up Mormonism in no time" and prove Bigler a false teacher.[30] The two men discussed Bigler's message for the entire evening and attended Lutheran services on Sunday where the Lutheran minister "treated me very courteously," Bigler wrote.[31] Bigler was pleased when McMelon asked him to preach in his home. "That evening the sleigh bells made music to my ears and I had a full house," observed Bigler, much pleased. After so much hardship and rejection, Bigler happily noted, "From thence doors were opened for me to preach and I sent out appointments and made my home at McMelons for some time."[32]

The local people manifested some interest in his message, but a Campbellite minister, "a Mr. Moses Bononi or some such name," would "meet me at my meeting," Bigler complained, "and fight the truth and do all he could to prejudice the people against me."[33] One evening "a party came with tar intending to tar and feather me and ride me on a rail," recalled Bigler. Very apprehensive, he nonetheless continued with his message. At one point as tensions mounted, an armed man, whom Bigler describes only as "a friend," came forward, and instructed the congregation to "behave yourselves and listen to what the man has to say, for if you don't I will use my rifle on the first man that attempts to disturb him." He sat on the table behind Bigler as the sermon continued to a much meeker group.[34]

Bigler preached at Lima until spring 1843, distributing many copies of the Book of Mormon and Apostle Parley P. Pratt's popular tract, *A Voice of Warning.* "A number told me they believed what I preached," he recorded, but "strange to say, not one soul offered themselves for baptism."[35] The reasons for this failure are unclear. Certainly Bigler's energy and sincerity were not lacking. Perhaps the residents of this frontier community simply enjoyed the diversion offered by Mormon preaching during a long, cold winter. Of his time among the people of Lima, Ohio, Bigler remembered, "Although there was considerable prejudice yet I had friends and houses provided for me during the cold winter months."[36]

When the roads were dry enough for travel, Bigler headed for Jackson County in western Virginia, where he had enjoyed some earlier success. During the fall of 1843, he taught school to support himself, preached every Sunday, and also seized every weekday opportunity that presented itself. One woman was baptized. Bigler continued this schedule through the winter of 1843–44 and the spring of 1844.

Then in July, an acquaintance who encountered him in Ripley, the county seat, told him the post office was holding "a paper in mourning" for him. The paper contained the news that Joseph and Hyrum Smith had been murdered by an anti-Mormon mob at Carthage, Illinois, on 27 June 1844. The mild-mannered Bigler's first reaction was rage: "At first I felt mad and could have fought like a tiger." But after the impact of their deaths settled upon him, "I felt like weeping and a feeling of loneliness came over me and could I have been alone it would have been a relief to give vent to my feelings in a complete shower of tears."[37]

The news, it goes without saying, came as a complete shock. Bigler does not mention receiving letters from his family or newspapers from Nauvoo during these years of missionary work, nor does he mention encountering other Mormons. He had no way of tracing the escalating hostility among Mormons and

Illinois residents during the past two years. Thomas Sharp, editor of the nearby *Warsaw Signal*, saw the rising Mormon theocracy as a genuine threat to democracy and countered it with bitter eloquence, joined by other citizens. Warsaw's Congregationalist minister, Benjamin F. Morris, denounced the Mormons: "[They] now have all the power, elect whom they please and have taken the entire government of the County into their own hands. . . . They are insolent, lawless, and unchecked."[38]

The triggering incident had been the Mormon attack on a newly established newspaper, the *Nauvoo Expositor*, in which former Mormons threatened to expose polygamy. Smith had ordered the press destroyed as a public nuisance after the first issue, feeding the fears of those who saw Mormonism as opposed to democracy. Smith was arrested for inciting to riot and, with his safety guaranteed by Illinois governor Thomas Ford, traveled to the county seat of Carthage with his brother Hyrum and several friends where they were jailed to await trial. The guards did not resist when men from the disbanded Warsaw regiment blackened their faces with mud and gunpowder, rushed the jail, killed the Smith brothers, and wounded John Taylor, a future president of the church. A fourth Mormon, Willard Richards, escaped injury.

For a disheartened Henry Bigler the rumors he must have been hearing "concerning the massacre at Carthage jail" were now confirmed.[39] "I felt they were innocent men and was murdered by wicked men and apostates," he concluded a year later.[40] Oddly enough, Bigler did not immediately return to Nauvoo but continued his mission until the spring of 1845. Thus, he missed the period of intense mourning that blanketed Nauvoo and the struggle for succession that followed. Smith had provided for five possible modes of succession but had not designated any one of them clearly.[41] Sidney Rigdon and James J. Strang both professed revelations that would have given them supreme authority in the church; other aspirants emerged and some flourished briefly in the next decade. More successful was the Reorganized Church of Jesus Christ of Latter Day Saints, which established itself firmly in 1857 under Joseph Smith III's leadership.

Although it is probably not possible to accurately reconstruct the actual numbers of 1844 Mormons who joined one of these groups, turned to other Christian religions, or simply lapsed, there is no question that the largest cohesive group to emerge from the confusion of 1844–45 followed the Quorum of Twelve Apostles, led by their senior member, Brigham Young. This group remained in Nauvoo, committed itself to completing the temple, and moved west in a more or less organized fashion in 1846–47. Bigler allied himself, apparently unhesitatingly, with Young's group. He never mentioned his reasons for this stand, but the strong image of doctrinal continuity Young projected may have been a factor. Bigler also had personal associations with several apostles but mentions none with the rival claimants: his cousin Bathsheba had married George A. Smith in Nauvoo in 1841; Young had ordained him to the Melchizedek Priesthood at Far West; and Young and Heber C. Kimball had ordained him a seventy before his first mission. Thus, his ties make such affiliation unsurprising.

Of his life following this second mission, Bigler wrote: "I returned home to my father's house. He was living on Bear Creek 16 miles south of Nauvoo."[42] Shortly thereafter he began teaching at the local school.[43] Despite his own limited education, Bigler took up teaching at least twice more to support himself—in Nauvoo during 1844–45 and again at Farmington, Utah, during the late 1870s. While he never had much of an opportunity for formal schooling and never voiced an opinion about it, Bigler must have believed education to be of value and apparently enjoyed teaching. Once again, he does not mention courtship or any other social activities that might betoken an interest in marriage; but in any case, the respite was brief. The larger currents of Mormon history once again swept Henry Bigler along.

The non-Mormons had hoped that the death of the Smiths would bring an end to the hated religion. When it became obvious that Mormonism would not collapse after the death of Joseph Smith, more vigilante violence erupted.[44] Members living outside Nauvoo were harassed, beaten, and burned out as autumn came. Violence erupted at Bear Creek in September 1845. "I have seen the heavens lit up by the flames of some brother's house [set afire] by wicked men," Bigler indignantly recorded.[45] In another instance he lamented that innocent women and children were driven from their sick beds to "lie and suffer without the aid or assistance of a friendly hand."[46] Although Jacob Bigler's family escaped individual injury, it did not matter. Bigler's perspective was completely radicalized. A consummate insider, he felt personally an injury done to any Saint.

In the face of mounting hostility, Jacob Bigler and his family abandoned their property on Bear Creek and moved into Nauvoo in the fall of 1845, where they became part of a society focused simultaneously on salvation and escape. The Mormons in Nauvoo were hastening to complete construction of the temple in anticipation of receiving the "endowment," a sacred rite that conferred both ritual power and ritual knowledge on the believer, instructed him or her in processes deemed essential for ultimate salvation, and summarized Joseph Smith's theological achievement at Nauvoo. According to this view, godhood itself and postmortal life in the presence of God could be obtained by individuals who had been baptized by one holding the proper authority (the Latter-day Saint priesthood), who had received the temple endowment, and who remained faithful to the tenets of Mormonism.

Smith had first introduced the ordinance of the endowment in May 1842 to selected men of his intimate circle in the upper room of his Nauvoo store, pending the completion of the temple. A later but natural development in this theology of salvation was the view of marriage. A marriage sealed by the proper priesthood authority, taught Joseph Smith, would unite both parties for all eternity, across the barrier of death. This doctrine, known as celestial marriage or eternal marriage, was related to, but not identical with, plural marriage.[47]

By October 1845, the temple was near completion, and soon endowments were being given under the direction of Brigham Young and the other apostles. The officiators in the ceremony were the select group of men and women who had been endowed during Joseph Smith's life.[48] While temple ordinances would eventually take on great significance for Henry Bigler, he mentioned his own endowment almost cursorily: "On the 31st December 1845 I rec'd my endowments in the Nauvoo Temple." We know almost nothing of his personal life during the waning days of Mormon Nauvoo. He was almost thirty-one and, in early 1844, recorded that he "was living with George A. Smith one of the Twelve and was his private clerk."[49] Identifying his cousin-in-law, Bathsheba's husband, by title rather than by relationship breathes Bigler's modest pride in his association with a church leader. Two of his sisters had married: "On November 2nd 1845 Sister Emeline married John W. Hess a very nice young Dutchman [and] Sister Hannah had married Daniel Arnold Miller a widower with several children . . . 29th December 1844." Sally and Jacob's youngest child, Mariah, had been born 13 March 1843 in Hancock County and died in January 1846, not yet three.[50]

Reasons for Bigler's bachelor state remain mysterious. As the marriages of his sisters show, social upheaval did not prevent other unions. George A. Smith had two wives by 1846.[51] Perhaps he felt shy with women except in structured roles. Perhaps he felt unprepared financially to marry. Or perhaps, in assuming totally the role of "true believer," he simply wished the complete freedom to devote himself to the Mormon cause.

Philip St. George Cooke from *Harper's Weekly*, 1858. Courtesy of the California History Room, California State Library, Sacramento.

Santa Fe in 1846. Courtesy of the Bancroft Library.

❧ 3 ❧

MARCHING TO THE PACIFIC
1846–48

*It was against my feelings also against the feelings of my brethren
although we were willing to obey counsel believing all things
would work for the best in the end.*[1]

The cold and miserable exodus from Nauvoo began with the
departure of the first advance company, which included
Henry Bigler, on 9 February 1846.[2] Six days later Brigham Young
bade the city farewell. By mid-May more than ten thousand Saints
had fled Illinois. Individuals returned to claim goods and try to sell
their property over the next several months, but for all practical
purposes, the Saints had abandoned their city by summer. All during the rest of the wintry months and the muddy spring, they
struggled along the thawing prairie tracks until, by June 1846, the
main body of the pioneers finally crossed the breadth of Iowa
Territory.

The traversing of Iowa alone was an epic task. Spring mud
forced the Saints to double- and triple-team their wagons. The toll
on humans and livestock was high. It was "a time of suffering,"
Henry Bigler recalled, without detailing his part in it.[3] The strag-
gling start, problems with organization and provisions, and the
slow progress made Brigham Young and the other leaders reevalu-
ate their hope of arriving near the Rocky Mountains by the end of
the year.

Thus, the Mormons became part of the great movement
westward that characterized the 1840s and 1850s and relocated a

quarter of a million Americans from the settled states of the East and Midwest to the western frontier. The reasons for undertaking such a monumental journey were as diverse as the emigrants themselves. Many were seeking more fertile land to better their lives. Others were drawn by the fascination which the West held in the mid-nineteenth century American mind. It was a place of potential where most believed they might realize their dreams. The Latter-day Saints, however, were not drawn by hope as much as they were pushed by circumstances. Most would have been content with their Zion in Nauvoo, had they been allowed to stay there.

After crossing the Mississippi River, the Mormon emigrants stopped temporarily at Sugar Creek, Iowa. Of these first, harried days Bigler wrote, "President Young called the camp together and commenced to organize companies of hundreds, fifties and companies of tens and gave instructions in regard to our moving, preparing outfits etc." Bigler wrote of the organization of George A. Smith's ten, which included Jacob Bigler's family, "my father to be captain, John D. Chase to be the commissary and myself Clerk." The company had five wagons, nine horses, two yoke of oxen, and a variety of foodstuffs including flour, corn meal, crackers, and dried meat. They also took garden seeds, two plows, spades, axes, hoes, fifty pounds of soap, and "smoking tobacco for Indians."[4]

Bigler's writings of the experience reflect more suffering by the migrating Saints. "This morning soon after our camp broke," he wrote on 8 April 1846, "it began to rain and continued all day at times the rain came down in torrents."[5] While crossing Iowa, the Saints requested and obtained permission from the governor of the territory to establish two way stations—Garden Grove, between the Mississippi and Missouri Rivers, and Mt. Pisgah, about thirty miles northwest of Garden Grove. Mt. Pisgah, a fertile expanse of uninhabited prairie along the Grand River in an area belonging to the Pottawatomi Indians, soon became a beehive of activity. The immigration of thousands of Mormons kept the community in a constant bustle.

The George A. Smith company arrived at Mt. Pisgah by early summer. On 30 June, while searching for missing lifestock, Bigler and a relative, Jesse Martin, were approached by an unknown army officer who asked whether Brigham Young was in the camp. This was the first time that Henry Bigler, as a recognizable individual, became part of the larger drama of western American history. It would, however, not be the last time. Warily, Bigler and Martin conceded there was someone in camp by that name, but just where he was at that moment they could not tell. If not an outright lie, this was at best only a half-truth, for "we knew President Young perfectly well and where his quarters were but did not wish to reveal the location to a stranger with unknown intentions."[6]

However, Brigham Young was pleased to meet Captain James Allen. In January 1846, Young had instructed Jesse C. Little, then president of the Mormon mission in the eastern United States, to negotiate with the federal government for a contract to build forts along the Oregon Trail. Then, on 13 May 1846, President James K. Polk seized a border skirmish between Mexican and U.S. forces near Corpus Christi as an opportunity to declare war on Mexico. He recorded in his journal that he intended "to acquire for the United States, California, New Mexico, and perhaps some others of the Northern Provinces of Mexico."[7] In so doing, he responded to the demands of expansion-oriented Americans in the Mississippi River Valley and the South.[8]

The resulting Mexican-American War (1846–48) was a direct effect of American westward expansion, which one historian has labeled "the Great Surge."[9] Beginning during the presidency of Thomas Jefferson, the federal government started demonstrating that the West was linked to America's destiny. In 1803 Jefferson dispatched Meriweather Lewis and William Clark to the Pacific, officially on a scientific expedition but, in truth, to search for an all-water route to the Pacific.[10] In the following decades Americans would push west across the Rocky Mountains to occupy Oregon and, eventually, California. Westering would affect not only the now-famous like Lewis and Clark, John Charles Frémont, and Marcus Whitman, but also the lowly like Henry Bigler and his fellow Latter-day Saints. The vehicle for drawing Henry Bigler to the West was his devotion to his religion, although judging him by the actions of his forebears, Mark and Jacob Bigler, westering seemed to be in his blood.

Though Little never received much encouragement for the fort proposal, the possibility of recruiting a Mormon expeditionary force seemed more promising. On 13 May 1846, President Polk took the "little-noticed but far-reaching action" of directing Secretary of War William Marcy to send Colonel Stephen Watts Kearney and the 1st Dragoons to occupy the then-Mexican city of Santa Fe.[11]

Captain Allen bore a proposal authorized by Polk. Colonel Kearney, now acting as the general of the "Army of the West," sought to enlist up to five hundred Mormons at Fort Leavenworth, Kansas, to form a volunteer battalion which would join Kearny at Santa Fe, New Mexico, and then march on to the West Coast. Polk's orders to the general stated, "You will have the Mormons distinctly to understand that I wish to have them as volunteers for twelve months, that they will be marched to California, receiving pay and allowances during the above time, and at its expiration they will be discharged, and allowed to retain, as their private property the guns and accouterments furnished to them." Polk, correctly, did not foresee much opposition to American actions in New Mexico and assumed, weather permitting, that General Kearney would press on to the president's intended conclusion—occupying California.[12]

Young immediately saw the possibility of getting several hundred men west at government expense and employed his considerable persuasive powers and prophetic stature to convince reluctant Mormon enlistees to sign up. He accompanied Allen to the Mormon way stations strung across Iowa, promising him "you shall have your battalion [even] if it has to be made up from our Elders," and urged "all the young men to go that could."[13] The apparently large number of the eventual enlistees who were seventies, like Bigler, suggests that a missionary-like enthusiasm, perhaps generated by mission-like assignments, influenced battalion recruitment.

Such strong-arm methods were necessary, since many Mormons did not wish to enlist. Upon learning of the government's request, Hosea Stout observed, "We were all very indignant at this requisition and only looked on it as a plot laid to bring trouble on us as a people."[14] Apostle Wilford Woodruff "had reason to believe them [the soldiers] to be spies," although he does not specify why.[15] Henry Bigler, looking back on this event nearly fifty years later, expressed mixed feelings: "It looked hard when we called to mind the mobbings and drivings, the killing of our leaders, the burning of our homes and forcing us to leave the States and Uncle Sam take no notice of it and then to call on us to help fight his battles to me was an insult." Yet when Brigham Young threw his weight behind enlistment, Henry Bigler swallowed his personal outrage and became "willing to obey counsel believing all things would work for the best in the end."[16] It was the pattern he had followed up to that point, and it was the pattern he would follow to the end of his life.

According to Bigler, on 12 July 1846 Willard Richards, a counselor to President Young, promised the new recruits "if we were faithful in keeping the commandments of God not a man shall fall by an enemy."[17] Fortified by the encouragement of the church hierarchy, the recruitment of Mormon soldiers moved ahead. The process took about two weeks; but by mid-July, a battalion, made up of companies A, B, C, D, and E, numbering over four hundred men, was formed. Bigler "attached" himself to Company B as a private, under the command of forty-six-year-old Kentuckian Jesse D. Hunter. His brother-in-law, John W. Hess, was a private in Company E, and his twenty-two-year-old sister, Emeline Bigler Hess, went along as a laundress.[18] At Young's insistence, each of the companies was commanded by a Latter-day Saint and the forty-two-dollar clothing allowance per man as well as a portion of each's pay went directly to the soldier's family. He had also managed to get Allen's promise to ask Polk to let the main party winter on Indian lands until they were ready to go west.

Several members of the First Presidency and Quorum of the Twelve instructed the commissioned and noncommissioned officers they had selected, admonishing them to "be as fathers to the privates, to remember their prayers, to see that the name of the Diety was revered, and that virtue and cleanliness were strictly observed."[19] On 21 July 1846, the battalion departed after a grand farewell at Council Bluffs, headed for Fort Leavenworth, about two hundred miles to the south, where they would receive supplies.

From the very outset, the general health of the troops was poor. Henry Bigler and several of his messmates were suffering from "the ague" (malaria). His condition was so severe that Sergeant Daniel Tyler of Company C and battalion historian noted, "Henry W. Bigler was shaking terribly with the ague."[20] Despite his poor health, Bigler kept a fairly regular account of his battalion activities from early July 1846 on. Not only was he plagued by malaria, but the separation from loved ones pained Bigler as well. He later lamented, "I bid my folks farewell and did not see them again for nine years."[21] Other members of the battalion felt equally melancholy. William Hyde, a sergeant in Company B, mourned, "The thoughts of leaving my family at this critical time are indescribable. They are far from the land of their nativity, situated upon a lonely prairie with no dwelling but a wagon, the scorching sun beating upon them, with the prospect of the cold winds of December finding them in the same bleak, dreary place."[22]

The battalion reached Fort Leavenworth on 1 August, and the men drew their issues of arms, ammunition, supplies, equipment, and clothing allotment of forty-two dollars. Most of this cash was, according to Bigler, "sent back to our families [in Iowa] to help support them." Additionally, Bigler noted, "We also donated of our mite to Elders then on their way to England on missions." Bigler's pay, as a private, was seven dollars a month.[23]

The battalion was at Fort Leavenworth nearly three weeks making final preparations for their march to California. Many of the men, like Henry Bigler, were still trying to shake off nagging sickness. On 1 and 4 August, Bigler suffered further attacks of the ague which were relieved only after a priesthood blessing—a Mormon rite of faith-healing that combined anointing with oil, the laying on of hands, and prayer.[24] Even so, his bouts with fever and chills continued intermittently until November. On 12 August, Companies A, B, and C took up the march toward Santa Fe under very difficult conditions. "The road was a foot deep with sand and dust," Bigler wrote, "the weather very warm and water scarce."[25] Two days later the remaining companies left Fort Leavenworth. Then, on 23 August, battalion commander James Allen died.

The journey from Council Bluffs to Fort Leavenworth had been a harsh one. The new soldiers were exposed to intense heat during the day and pouring rain on three of the nights. When they finally arrived at their destination, a few of the men decided to celebrate. At Fort Leavenworth, these men got drunk; one was actually put in the guardhouse.[26]

According to Daniel Tyler, the remaining officers "agreed that Captain [Jefferson] Hunt should assume the command of the Battalion."[27] Hunt, captain of Company A, was the ranking Mormon, and the men were dismayed when the commandant of Fort Leavenworth appointed Lieutenant A. J. Smith as colonel pro tem until the battalion joined Lieutenant Colonel Philip St. George Cooke at Santa Fe. "The right of command," Henry Bigler believed, "belonged to Captain Hunt [but] was confered on Lieutenant Smith because he was a West Pointer."[28] The men agreed to Smith's leadership only after their own officers advised submission.

Under the disconcerting circumstances confronting the men of the Mormon Battalion—sickness, hardship, and lack of control—the consolations of religion were even more important than usual. For example, on 20 August 1846, Bigler recorded this encouragement:

> About 5 this P.M. the Battalion was called together and addressed by several of our officers namely Captain Hunt, Daniel Tiler [Tyler], Levi W. Hancock and William Hyde. It was a good meeting, they stired up our minds to a rememberance of our duty to God, the mission we was on and the sacrifice we had made to go at the call of our country. The goodness of God was in this very move and remember that we were Elders of Israel etc.[29]

The Mormon soldiers naturally felt attached to their own officers and were further united by mistrust of the U.S. Army's "Gentile" officers. Unaccustomed to military life and serving, in most instances, only because Brigham Young had requested it, the force consisted of very reluctant soldiers. Smith seems to have been professional and competent, committed to reaching Santa Fe as soon as possible, but overly harsh in discipline. He seems to have had little appreciation of the psychological differences between the Mormon recruits and more typical soldiers, nor does he seem to have made any effort to break down the barriers that sprang up all too readily and intensified almost automatically.[30]

Thus, by September, when the shortness of rations and increasing incidents of sickness had slowed the march almost to a crawl, Bigler found Smith's efforts to push the battalion on toward Santa Fe comparable to the acts of an uncaring tyrant. He wrote, "Smith . . . began to show his love for the Mormons by ordering all the sick [whom he considered to be shirkers] out of the wagons and swore if they did not walk he would tie them fast to the wagons and drag them."[31]

Nor were sickness and short rations the soldiers' only adversaries. Two weeks earlier, on 19 August, the already weary recruits were blasted by a severe summer storm with cascading rain and hail. The violent winds capsized tents and overturned wagons. "I very seldom ever witnessed as heavy a gale of wind," observed Bigler. Although little actual damage was sustained, "we all received a pelting from the hail that fell."[32]

Some illness—given the inclement weather, the stress of the march, inadequate food, and borderline dehydration from inadequate water—was probably inevitable; but it was certainly a lethal coincidence that the surgeon assigned to the company was Dr. George B. Sanderson of Platte County, Missouri. Henry Bigler's assessment of Dr. Sanderson, correct or not, summed up the general Mormon view of the man: "[He] was a Missourin, did not belong to our people, and had been heard to say he did not care a damn whether he killed or cured."[33] Not one Mormon Battalion diary has a positive or even a neutral statement about him. Sanderson was universally loathed for his brutality and feared for his violent "treatments"; and when a rumor circulated that he was a former Missouri mobber, Bigler and the other Mormons had no trouble believing it.[34]

Both Joseph Smith and Brigham Young subscribed to faith healing and botanical remedies, the so-called "Thompsonian medicine" of which apostle Willard Richards was a practitioner. The main ailment of the troops was "the ague" (malaria); in the absence of quinine, faith-healing and herbs would certainly have been more efficacious—or at least, less damaging—than the standard treatment of the mid-nineteenth century: arsenic and calomel, both of which Sanderson administered forcibly and liberally.

Two members of the battalion were dead by the time they reached Santa Fe in October 1846, and Sanderson was almost universally blamed. Henry Bigler recorded on 17 September 1846:

"Before taking up the line of march we had the painful duty of burying Brother Alva Phelps of Company E and it was believed that doctor Sanderson's medicine killed him."[35] Three men died in November when the battalion was moving through New Mexico. James Hampton "had been sick for sometime but not thought to be dangerous," recorded James Pace, a lieutenant in Company E. " . . . He received a doze of medison from the *Doctor* & was taken worse instently."[36] Despite his continuous bouts with the ague, Bigler avoided medical treatment and probably shared the feelings of Henry Standage of Company E, who wrote on 12 September: "I can thank God that I have been preserved from the hands of the Dr. and have not been compelled to take *CALOMEL.*" David Pettegrew of Company E prayed, "Oh Lord! Deliiver [*sic*] us from the hands of Doctor Sanderson."[37]

Until early September, sick troopers like Bigler had been able to refuse Sanderson's medicine, professing they would rather leave their bones to bleach on the prairie. Smith and Sanderson responded, on 3 September, by ordering the sick to walk, report for treatment, or be dragged behind the wagons.[38]

Sergeant Nathaniel V. Jones of Company D, a New Yorker in his mid-twenties, attempted to ease the situation by telling Smith that Mormon religious beliefs discouraged the taking of medicine. Lieutenant George Dykes, also of Company D, later corrected Jones's statement saying "there was no such religious scruples," and that the church authorities themselves often took such medicine. This contradictory exchange between these Mormon leaders seems to have made matters more difficult for the sick. According to Daniel Tyler, the intial effort by Jones to bring more humane treatment was "turned to evil" following Dykes's contradictory statement.[39]

On 3 October a dispatch arrived from Kearney instructing Smith that the battalion had to be in Santa Fe by 10 October or the government's agreement with the Saints would be abrogated. Almost immediately, Smith decided to leave the weak and sick to bring up the rear and pressed forward with the healthier segment, including Bigler. They finished their seven-hundred-mile forced march in just under two months, reaching Santa Fe on 9 October 1846. Sanderson, rather than remaining with the sick detachment,

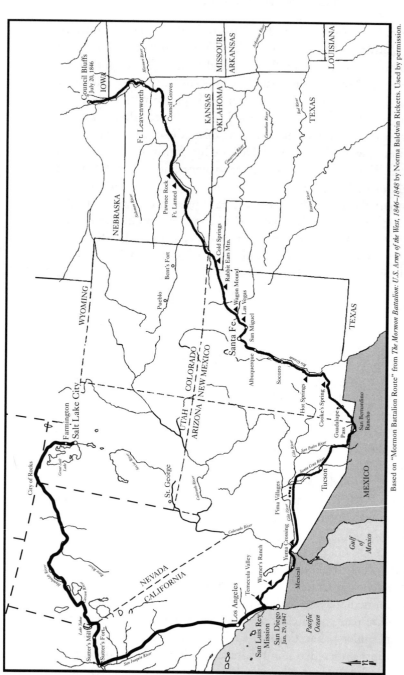

Based on "Mormon Battalion Route" from *The Mormon Battalion: U.S. Army of the West, 1846–1848* by Norma Baldwin Ricketts. Used by permission.

Henry Bigler's West
and the
Trail of the Mormon Battalion

— Bigler's Route with and after the Mormon Battalion March
▲ Camp Sites

accompanied Smith. Tyler noted with disdain, "The fact of Dr. Sanderson leaving the sick behind while he proceeded on with those who were healthy, is fair indication of the interest he took in attending to the duties of his office," then commented wryly, "but the sick did not complain."[40]

Upon inspecting the battalion at Santa Fe, Lieutenant Colonel Philip St. George Cooke found the Mormon Battalion to be "486 strong, but about sixty are invalids, or unfit for service." Furthermore, in his opinion, he had inherited a poorly trained lot. "The battalion were never drilled," complained Cooke, "and, though obedient, have little discipline."[41] Cooke proved to be a skilled yet understanding military officer whose leadership was generally appreciated by the Mormon Battalion. One of his first acts was to order James Brown, captain of Company C, to lead the sick, the infirm, and the laundresses to Fort Pueblo, Colorado, for the winter. From there, Brown's group, joined by a party of Saints from Mississippi, traveled together, joining Brigham Young's vanguard at Fort Laramie in early June 1847. This detachment, which numbered 86, "embrac[ed] only a few efficient men," two officers, and most of the female laundresses.[42] "In the detachment I had a dear sister and brother in law," lamented Bigler. "I felt lonesome after they left for I missed their company very much."[43]

Cooke led the stripped-down battalion—four hundred men and a few accompanying women—out of Santa Fe toward California on Monday, 19 October. Their road for three hundred miles lay southward along the Rio Del Norte. Progress was slow over the sandy roads. They had adequate and ample river water, but, wrote Bigler, "grass [was] scarce and the teams soon began to fail." The men were now relegated to "scanty" provisions. Soon after leaving Santa Fe, Bigler observed in mid-October, "we were reduced to three quarter rations."[44] Soon this was cut further to half and, finally, to quarter rations.

Fortunately for those who could afford it, the first part of their journey took them through Mexican villages at regular intervals whose inhabitants were anxious to trade with the Americans. The Mormon soldiers bought or traded for wood, corn, beans, fruit, goat's milk and cheese, the "finest onions" Bigler ever saw, and two items discouraged by the Mormon health code—wine and tobacco. Henry Bigler does not say whether his personal purchases included these items.

On 31 October 1846 when the battalion would have been near the Mimbres River in New Mexico, Bigler recorded an unexceptional but typical day:

> Clear, about 8 we were on March, went 15 miles and campt, had a first rate camping place. The road today was good with one or two exceptions. We past 2 little Spanish towns, one however was nearly as large as Santafee. I do not get the names of the various little towns and villages owing to my not understanding the Spanish language and it is only a few of the command that do hence I do not pretend to give names.[45]

This monotonous but relatively easy stretch ended quickly. By mid-November 1846, the battalion was heading out into the stark desert of southwestern New Mexico. Their water was limited to occasional shallow springs or intermittent rain fall. Bigler seemingly found the poor food as bothersome as the shortage of water. On 15 November he noted, "Some of the boys brought in an ox that gave out yesterday." The hungry men quickly slaughtered the beast and meat was issued. But Bigler disappointedly found the meat "jelly-like."[46]

It is difficult to place responsibility for supply shortages in any single place. Perhaps the initial requisition at Fort Leavenworth was inadequate. Cooke's eagerness to press on to the Pacific was at least partially to blame. With the ever-sure wisdom of hindsight nearly fifty years afterward, Bigler wrote, "I have ever since thought it was very unwise to have left Santa Fe with only 60 days rations instead of 120 as advised by the guide."[47] In any case, he found the short rations unnecessary: "The country appears to abound with game, such as deer and antelope," he observed on 19 November. "I believe we might have plenty of wild meat if the Colonel would permit a few hunters to go out."[48]

On 3 November, concerned by the slow progress and the short supply, Cooke reduced daily rations to "9 ounces of flour and 10 ounces of pork" per man, a measure that he estimated would provide eighty-six days' worth of food. Only three days later,

Robert Bliss, also of Company B, reported the rumor that "we expect it will take us at least 120 days to go to the Pacific Ocean."[49] Although neither Bliss nor Bigler comments on the impact of these estimates, the discrepancy between supplies and need must have been hard on morale. What must Bigler have thought about the prospect of dying in a western desert while serving a government which had repeatedly ignored the Mormons during the vigilante atrocities of Missouri and Nauvoo?

At Cooke's command, the men supplemented their rations by slaughtering weak draft animals occasionally. "When a poor ox gives out he is kild and brought into camp for the soldiers to eat and we luxuriate on beef soup," wrote Bigler appreciatively on 14 November;[50] but Henry Boyle, a Virginian like Bigler, commented disparagingly on two oxen butchered that same day: "Such beef the wolves would scarcely partake of." On 3 December, Boyle complained, "We are on half rations & have been for some time & we feel hungry all the time."[51]

The extremes in desert temperature were an additional hardship. For example, Cooke noted on 19 November, "After a warm day, the sun blistering the face, water froze last night an inch thick." The next day, he added, "water froze in my hair this morning whilst washing."[52]

Although the obstacles of fatigue and inconvenience must have seemed overwhelming at times, Bigler was a faithful diarist. On 16 November, he described the scene in southwestern New Mexico: "Clear and cool and the top of the mountains is covered with snow that fell yesterday. Marched today about 15 miles and campted. Some grass and little water but no wood for camp use except some fine brush. The country has rich soil but no timber. At this encampment it is reported there is good indications of gold. Some say copper is discovered here." They were, apparently, in New Mexico's Pyramid Mountains by 16 November when he noted optimistically: "I find it not so windy here in the mountains as it was before reaching Santafee. The teams I think are looking better although the grass in this country appears dry but I find by examining it the stakes are jucy and it is believed that it does not rain much here and consequently the grass cures on the stalks and becomes very much like good hay and the cattle and mules like it and seem to do well on it."[53] Now that they were leaving the desert, forage for the livestock improved appreciably.

Near the year's end, the battalion got its first—and only—taste of quasi-military action. On 11 December 1846 near the San Pedro River east of Tucson, scouts startled a herd of several hundred wild cattle along the bluffs overlooking the river. They stampeded toward the wagons at the scouts' rear; and, as E Company's Henry Standage put it in his diary that evening, "the brethren had quite a battle with the bulls today."[54] Bigler's account records: "A number of wild cattle, I believe mostly bulls, came running from the west and ran through our ranks plunging their horns into two team mules, goring them to death almost instantly and running over men."[55] One bull tossed Amos Cox of Company D several feet in the air, gashing a wound in his thigh four inches long and three inches deep. Sanderson competently sewed it shut, and Cox was still living nearly forty years later.[56] Lieutenant George Stoneman, a regular army officer, received an accidental gunshot wound in the thumb, and two other men suffered minor injuries.

An immense black bull charged one Mormon soldier, Corporal Lafeyette Frost of A Company, who stood his ground and coolly dropped the animal when he was only ten paces away. Cooke praised Frost as "one of the bravest men" he had ever seen. Levi Hancock, battalion chaplain, lauded him in a poem, "The Bullfight on the San Pedro":

> But Corp'ral Frost stood bravely by,
> And watch'd the bull with steady eye;
> The brute approach'd near and more near,
> But Frost, betray'd no sign of fear.
> The colonel ordered him to run—
> Unmov'd he stood with loaded gun;
> The bull came up with daring tread,
> When near his feet, Frost shot him dead.[57]

This colorful incident was much celebrated, all the more so because it was virtually the only dangerous action of the entire campaign. About twenty bulls were killed. In all likelihood, the men feasted that night on fresh meat.

Ten days later Bigler was the leading character in a "rather humorous incident" involving a mischievous mule that persistently stole grain from another animal. Exasperated, Cooke commanded Bigler, his orderly for the day, to load his gun so he could shoot the beast. Recognizing the mule as the property of one of his comrades, Bigler discreetly charged the weapon with powder but did not load any shot. Cooke walked ten feet from the mule, aimed, and fired. The mule stood unmoved. The colonel looked daggers at the orderly, threw the gun to the ground, and stormed off to his tent while the troops stifled their laughter.[58] Fortunately for Bigler, Cooke let the incident pass without retaliation.

By early January 1847 they were at the Colorado River, which Cooke termed "the most useless of rivers."[59] Near present-day Yuma, Arizona, the Mormon Battalion entered Mexican California on 10–11 January 1847. Bigler did not record his thoughts on the occasion, but he was probably relieved at this landmark of their progress. Their situation was far from good. "We are all weary & fatigued[,] hungry, nearly naked & barefoot," wrote Henry Boyle on 16 January. A short time later on 22 January when Bigler appraised their location as sixty miles from San Diego, he wrote, "Where the Colonel intends to march us is unknown to me as yet, but I think the feelings of the Battalion is they are in hopes he will march them to Sandiego as they are tired and I may say wore out and wish to go into quarters as soon as they can."[60]

On 25 January 1847, Cooke recorded that he had ordered the battalion to San Diego "as the War was probably to an end in this country."[61] What Cooke may have known at this time about the progress of the war is unclear, but Andres Pico, commander of the Mexican forces in southern California, had surrendered to U.S. Lieutenant Colonel John C. Frémont near Los Angeles on 13 January. The Mormon soldiers knew that San Diego had a harbor and, according to Bigler, indulged themselves in the "fond hope there is something to be had to eat."[62]

Two days later on the afternoon of 27 January, the soldiers mounted one of the hills near the mission community of San Luis Rey (just east of present-day Oceanside, California) and halted involuntarily, stunned by the magnificent view of the "calm unruffled sea. . . . I never shall be able to express my feelings at this enraptured moment," wrote Henry Boyle in his diary.[63] Equally at a loss for eloquence, Bigler "felt to rejoice that we were so near our journeys end." With the eye of a farmer, Bigler also noted that the countryside was "alive with herds of fat cattle, cows and young calves. . . . Wild oats grow all over the whole country and the hills and valleys look like one vast region of green oats."[64]

Such favorable assessments by many veterans of the battalion helped motivate the founding of a Mormon colony at San Bernardino, California, in 1851.[65] Henry Bigler does not say whether he entertained hopes of settling in this rich area, then or later; but Church commitments far from the American West kept him heavily involved during the 1850s.

On 29 January, the weary Mormon soldiers "came in sight of the long talked-of San Diego."[66] In concluding his official report, Cooke wrote:

> History may be searched in vain for an equal march of infantry. Nine tenths of it has been through a wilderness where nothing but savages and wild beasts are found, or deserts where, from want of water, there is no living creature. There, with almost hopeless labor, we have dug wells, which the future traveller will enjoy. With crow-bar and pick and axe in hand, we have worked our way over mountains which seemed to defy ought save the wild goat, and hewed a passage through a chasm of living rock more narrow than our wagons. . . . Thus, marching half-naked and half-fed, and living upon wild animals, we have discovered and made a road of great value to our country.[67]

At about the same time, Robert Bliss was writing in his diary: "We have endured one of the greatest journeys ever made by man"; he attributed their survival to "the faith and prayers of the Saints."[68] Not surprisingly, Bigler's writings for this date reflect his assessment of the country rather than thoughts on their journey. Near the San Diego Mission, where they camped, he observed "fine gardens, three large vineyards, palmetotrees, pomgranates, dates [and] other kinds of tropical fruits."[69] After two days in the San Diego area, the battalion was ordered by Cooke to backtrack thirty-one miles to San Luis Rey, a fortifiable position midway between San Diego, which required no pacification, and Los Angeles, where a Mexican countermove, if it came at all, could logically be expected.

San Diego in 1846. Courtesy of the Bancroft Library.

Mission San Luis Rey. Courtesy of the California History Room, California State Library, Sacramento.

San Luis Rey traced its history to 1795 when Governor Diego Borcia issued orders to locate a mission between San Diego Mission (1769) and San Juan Capistrano (1776). Three years later, a site with "good timber, plenty stones [for construction], firewood, and good pasture" was located, the mission was named, construction began, and the mission fathers began Christianizing the local natives.[70] For reasons unclear to the battalion soldiers, but very possibly due to the war still flaring in the area, they found the mission abandoned. "The Indians now have it all their own way," Bigler wrote. "[They] worship the Great Spirit in their own way."[71]

Garrison duty at San Luis Rey initially consisted of cleaning up the town square and repairing the building comandeered as the barracks. Bigler described the mission community as "a handsome situation" for the tired soldiers and "one of the pritiest sights we had ever seen, the church white almost as the driven snow." His only complaint was "plenty of fleas" in the barracks. Time passed peacefully and pleasantly. At San Luis Rey the men drilled regularly in weather which Bigler described almost daily as "beautiful & fair" or "cleare & fine."[72] Anxious to maintain discipline now that the grueling march was over, Cooke focused on attire and grooming. An order on 5 February stipulated that the garrison soldiers must wash their clothes, cut their hair, and shave. The command to shave was particulary irritating. The men had hoped to return home sporting their beards.

The Mormons used their more leisurely schedule to hold regular Sunday services—a practice which they had had to abandon on the march. On 21 February, "Elder [Daniel] Tyler preached to the Brethren on the necessity of remembering their covenants, especially those who have clothed themselves with the garments of salvation." This reminder was aimed at those who, like Bigler, had been endowed in the Nauvoo Temple. Due to the large number of seventies in the battalion, special meetings of this quorum also convened when circumstances permitted.[73]

On 15 February 1847, Company B, Bigler's company, moved to San Diego to garrison that area, where they remained until 9 July. The other Mormon companies moved from San Luis Rey to Los Angeles, where they garrisoned the newly constructed Fort Moore, named for Captain Ben Moore, who had been killed in the Battle of San Pasqual in December 1846.[74] In San Diego, Bigler helped dig wells for some local citizens, and some skilled masons from the battalion raised the first brick house in San Diego—possibly the first in California. At least once he "went a fishing down to the ocean and caught some verry curious fish." On July 4th Company B celebrated American Independence Day by firing five pieces of artillery, then parading with the muskets. The enthusiastic citizens, wrote Bigler, "brought out their wine and 'aquadiente' [brandy] all we wanted to drink and a hundred times more."[75]

Other than the fleas ("last night the fleas came verry near taking the fort"), Bigler enjoyed life in California. The construction projects brought him extra money which he invested in a horse and a packsaddle, obviously in preparation for the trip to Utah.[76]

San Diego appears to have been something of an idyllic interlude, unmarred by unseemly behavior on the part of the troops. The Los Angeles detachment of the Mormon Battalion, in contrast, adjusted over-enthusiastically to the prevailing mores for a religious group, possibly because of greater idleness or greater temptation. Henry Standage disapprovingly called the *Californios* in the City of the Angels "a very idle, profligate, drunken, swearing set of wretches. The conduct of the Spaniards in the grog shops with the squaws is really filthy, even in the day time"; and Mormon leaders had been forced to chastise their troops for "drunkenness, swearing, and intercourse with the squaws."[77] James Pace, an officer in Company E, admitted that "drunkenness was common with sum of the Mormons" and that during one "lamentable" night, "the screams & yells of drunken Mormons would have disgraced the wild Indians mutch moor a Laterday Saint."[78]

The military conquest of California was, however, clearly over; and on 4 July, Company B received orders to "march forthwith to the City of Angels" for release from service. Henry Bigler wrote with pleasure: "As our time was now drawing to a close . . . we expect to leave for our friends somewhere in the mountains." Naturally, no word had followed them across the continent, and speculation about where the Saints had settled included northern California, British Columbia's Vancouver Island, or along the Bear River in Utah. But, as Bigler wrote, "the truth is we do not know where President Young and the Church is!" On 12 July, near San

Juan Capistrano, Bigler happily wrote, "Tonight I stand guard for the last time for Uncle Sam, I hope." Four days later, they reached Los Angeles and, on 16 July, were mustered out. Bigler rejoiced, "Once more I feel free." They could not leave immediately, for their pay had not reached them. While they lingered, Colonel Jonathan D. Stevenson, the commandant of the southern military district in California, tried to persuade the Mormons to reenlist. "Uncle Sam is beating up for volunteers," Bigler wrote, "[and] a good many has already reenlisted." He, however, felt no temptation to follow suit.[79]

Instead, he patiently waited and assessed the city:

> The Pueblo or more properly De Los Angeles is quite a place . . . Los Angeles is situated on the San Pedro river [actually the Los Angeles and San Gabriel rivers] about 30 miles from the ocean. Most of the people of Los Angeles appears to be wealthy. They have fine vinyards and fruits of most all kinds, pears, figs, and lemons, the pears are already ripe and for six and quarter cent I can get 20.[80]

Their pay arrived on 18 July and two days later Bigler was designated one of ten scouts for the larger battalion party. He had been a member of the Mormon Battalion for almost a year. He provides no reflection on his experience, then or later; and in some respects it had very little effect on him. No doubt he gained at least minimal military skills, learned to get along on the march, cooperated with his messmates cheerfully, saw first-hand the arid Southwest, and associated with another culture—the Hispanics of New Mexico, Arizona, and California. These can all be counted as advantages, but his experience did nothing to strengthen his attachment to the government of the United States or its officials. On the contrary, he had found the officers unsympathetic, harsh, and prompted by motives other than the well-being of the men.

Furthermore, Bigler's motives in enlisting were very different from those of most volunteer soldiers. He was not lured by the prospect of adventure, travel, booty, or glory on the field—nor even by patriotism. He had joined only because his ecclesiastical leader had requested it; and faithful to the pattern that characterized Bigler's entire life, he suppressed personal desires when his religious duty called. He embarked on this distasteful task as a religious duty, endured its hardships sustained by a religious consciousness, and left it feeling that he had done his duty. His participation not only showed his devotion and willingness to sacrifice but also strengthened is bond with other like-minded Mormons. He was only thirty-one, but for the rest of his long life, he remained unfailingly willing to subject his individual will to the presumed needs of the collective whole.

The exodus from Nauvoo to Utah was an ordeal that tested the mettle of most Mormons, finding many wanting. This section of Henry Bigler's journey had left him only more strongly committed to Mormonism.

DONNER PASS
Donner Party Campsite

Johnson's Ranch

Sacramento River

North Fork
American River

LAKE TAHOE

Sutter's Fort

Sutter's Mill

Consumnes River

SAN FRANCISCO BAY
San Francisco

Mokelumme River

Stanislaus River

SIERRA
NEVADA

Tuolumne River

Merced River

San Joaquin River

Monterey

COASTAL

Kings River

MTS.

San Luis Obispo

Kern River

PACIFIC OCEAN

TEHACHAPI
MTS.

Santa Barbara

CALIFORNIA

Los Angeles

San Luis Rey Mission

Henry Bigler's Trail of Destiny
San Diego to Sutter's Mill

San Diego

Based on "San Diego to Sutter's Mill," by Jeanne Gunther, from *The Gold Discovery*
Journal of Azariah Smith, edited by David L. Bigler. Used by permission.

n

❦ 4 ❦

SUTTER'S MILL
1848

This day some kind of mettle was found in the tail race that . . .
looks like goald.[1]

*H*enry Bigler had no desire to linger in California, once the
battalion soldiers had been mustered out and received their
pay. On 20 July 1847, he recorded, "The discharged members of the
battalion held a meeting and organized companies for the journey
to Salt Lake, with chiefs of hundreds, of fifties, and of tens. I
became one of ten pioneers who were to go in advance, find roads,
and select camp grounds."[2] This position was far from ceremonial.
"We hardly knew what course to take," confessed Bigler in his
journal on 21 July 1847. "We had no guide, except an old
[California] map, not half the rivers and creeks marked on it."[3]
They initially believed that the church could be found where "we
then called 'Beare River Valley'" which feeds the Great Salt Lake in
northern Utah.[4] Bigler does not say why they expected to find the
Mormons at this location, but it is possible that they had heard of
the area from old mountain men for whom it was always a favorite
haunt.[5] Guessing that the Latter-day Saints were in the vicinity of
the Bear River and Great Salt Lake, the group opted for a route
which included the fort of Swiss immigrant Johann Augustus
Sutter on the Sacramento River. For Henry Bigler and several
other members of the battalion, it was a trail of destiny. The lack of
sure knowledge did not distract the Mormons from their desire to
get to the Salt Lake Valley, however.

Bigler does not record the size of the group that left for the Mormon settlement in the Great Basin in July 1847 nor where they camped the first night. On the second night, they stopped at the rancho of General Andres Pico, the defeated *Californio* general.[6] This rancho was located near the San Fernando Mission northwest of Los Angeles. Bigler's colleague Robert Bliss revealed the cultural prejudice which was virtually the nineteenth-century norm, describing Pico as "an Intiligent man above the common Spaniards"; and Bigler described Pico as "handsome, well dressed, and affable."[7] Graciously, Pico welcomed these American soldiers, allowed them to camp for the night near his ranch, and sold to them "some excellent wine and pears."[8]

Due to their lack of a guide and the inadequacies of their map (which Bigler complained was "no good"), after twenty-two days of travel they had made less than three hundred miles and were in the vicinity of the San Joaquin and Merced Rivers.[9] There some Indians told them of some other Americans settled nine or ten miles further north along the San Joaquin River. Bigler and his associates speculated that these settlers "must be families of the Saints who have come around the Horn in the Ship Brooklyn."[10] Bigler was referring to the New Hope settlement on the north bank of the Stanislaus River near its junction with the San Joaquin.[11] However, there were other Mormons in the vicinity as well. The Indians could have been speaking of the camp belonging to Thomas Rhoads on the Cosumnes River some forty or fifty miles east of Sacramento.[12]

Approximately 230 Latter-day Saints, under the leadership of Samuel Brannan, had sailed from New York City in December 1845 and landed at Yerba Buena (San Francisco) 29 July 1846. While some members of this party sought work in the San Francisco area, Brannan dispatched others to found an agricultural community. By January 1847, Brannan reported glowingly to Brigham Young: "We have commenced a settlement on the river San Joaquin, a large and beautiful stream emptying into the Bay of San Francisco. . . . About twenty of our number are up at the new settlement, which we call New Hope, ploughing and putting in wheat and other crops."[13] Brannan wanted to persuade Brigham Young to settle the main Mormon group in his New Hope, even making the long trek northeast to intercept Young west of Fort Laramie, Wyoming, during the last week in June 1847, but to no avail. Embittered by the refusal, Brannan returned to California and eventually severed his ties with the church.[14] Around 21–22 August 1847, Andrew Lytle and a scouting party of the battalion veterans located what was, in all likelihood, the Rhoads settlement on the Cosumnes River. At least Bigler reported that "some of the people he [Lytle] visited with were 'Mormons.'"[15] Two days later, still on the Cosumnes, they met "several American families" who, Bigler said, gave them some longed-for information: "They told us that the twelve apostles with 300 pioneers had reached Salt Lake Valley."[16] Now, at last, they knew where they were headed. Bigler's party reached Sutter's Fort, about seventy miles northwest of New Hope, on 26 August. By coincidence, Sutter had formed a partnership that very day with James W. Marshall to build a sawmill on the American River, a decision highly significant to Bigler. "A good many Mormons here," Sutter wrote in his diary the following day.[17]

Johann Sutter (1803–80) had arrived in Mexican California during the late 1830s from Switzerland, avoiding a debtors' prison and an angry wife. In 1839 he convinced Governor Juan Bautista Alvarado that he, Sutter, could act as a semi-official representative of the Mexican government in the unsettled and only partially explored interior of northern California in exchange for the right to occupy a fifty-thousand-acre tract of land near the confluence of the Sacramento and American Rivers.[18] Sutter, styling himself the guardian of this corner of the Mexican frontier, founded a fort as the basis of New Helvetia. With a diversified economic base that came to include cattle ranching, fur trapping, and farming, the one-time Swiss debtor was soon on the road to financial success. He had enough provisions to sell some to travelers like the Mormon Battalion company, his blacksmith shod their horses and mended trail-worn equipment, and those in the fort passed on more accurate information about routes and passes over the Sierra Nevadas than the Mormons had previously had.

This took a few days, and when the Mormons were ready to leave, some of the men who lacked good outfits—and even some whom Bigler felt were "tolerably well prepared"—decided to winter at the fort rather than attempt a Sierra Nevada crossing with

Johann Augustus Sutter. Courtesy of the California History Room, California State Library, Sacramento.

winter approaching.[19] The fate of the Donner Party the previous year was a caution they took seriously. Their exact numbers are not known, nor is the size of the party that continued. But Bigler was among the travelers who set out on 27 August.[20] The following day, he privately observed his birthday: "Today I am 32 years old," he wrote, adding in his typically self-effacing manner, "I am grateful to an all-wise Providence that my health is good, that I am on my way home, and that everything is as well with me as it is."[21]

With appreciation, but also with apprehension, he wrote of the towering western rampart: "The mountain was a sight to look upon. I think it must be a mile high." A more ominous reminder was a trailside grave with a wooden headboard that read simply, "Smith. Died Oct. 7th, 1846." On the sixth day of travel, his apprehension manifested itself in virtually the only fanciful passage in his writings: "We are now surrounded by lofty mountains covered with a heavy forest of pine timber and the whole country looks dark and dismal and I think if there is any witches and hobgoblins anywhere in the world they must be in these mountains"[22]

The party reached the summit on 4 September, after eight days of steep climbing up over what is now Donner Pass through snow "three feet deep" in some places. Hurriedly they descended the east slope, following a branch of the Truckee six or eight miles "to a shanty built last winter by the emegrants." Inside were "the skeletons of several human beings." The next day, a hunting party stumbled upon "a shanty with the dead lieing about it undisturbed by wild beasts. . . . From the best information I could get they were Missourians emegrating to California last season, about ninety souls."[23]

Bigler's party had come upon the lake camp of the Donner Party. These snowbound travelers had erected three makeshift shelters along present Donner and Cold Creeks—the Breen, Graves, and Murphy cabins. While it is not clear which structures the Mormon party had stumbled upon, ten members of the Donner Party starved or froze to death there between 9 December 1846 and 19 March 1847 at the lake camp, their corpses cannibalized by some of their comrades.[24] The Mormon party hastened quickly away from "this painful looking place" and on to Donner Lake.[25]

At this point, they were approximately 550 miles from the Salt Lake Valley, opposed primarily by the arid desert, their own fatigue, and their ignorance. Without reliable maps or information, the party did not know how far to go or where, exactly, to look for Brigham Young. Then on 6 September, the fourteenth day of their journey, they encountered Sam Brannan. Disgruntled from failing to convince Young to bring the Saints to the West Coast and hurrying back to California to oversee his own interests, he painted a discouraging picture of prospects in the Great Basin. Bigler, obviously troubled, recorded: "Sam Brannan says the Salt Lake country is no place to live and he thinks the Mormon Church will be established in California."[26]

Accompanying Brannan was Captain James Brown, leader of the Mormon Battalion's sick detachment; and fortunately for Bigler's peace of mind, Brown was bearing authoritative instructions from Brigham Young to the Mormon veterans in California. Young's epistle, as Bigler related it, "advised all who had no family in Salt Lake and no considerable stock of provisions, to work in California through the winter." While he longed to be with the main body of the Saints, the unattached Bigler obeyed without hesitation: "About thirty of our party, including myself, following the advice of the epistle from the heads of the Church, gave our hands and parting blessings to the others who went forward, while we returned to California."[27]

The Brannan party backtracked quickly and, only eight days later, on the afternoon of 14 September, reached Sutter's domain. Work had not yet begun on the Sutter-Marshall sawmill; but Sutter needed timber for a new gristmill and its three-mile millrace dug. He offered to hire all of the Mormons at twenty-five dollars per month or twelve and a half cents per yard on the millrace. The men discussed this offer that evening, decided it was "fair and liberal," and struck an agreement with Sutter the following day on the per-yard rate, with Sutter furnishing provisions. The entire company labored on the ditch until 27 September. That day, Bigler noted, "James W. Marshall came to our [cabin] and said that he was a partner with Sutter in building a sawmill up in the mountains on the South Fork of the American River, and he wanted four of us to go up there with him. Israel Evans, Azariah Smith, William Johnson, and I, . . . went with him, traveling with an ox team."[28] Neither Sutter nor Marshall ever explained why these four were chosen; the assignment may well have been made at random. But whether by chance or not, the assignment put Bigler on the site of the discovery of gold.

Like the Mormons, James Marshall was a California war veteran who had also stopped at Sutter's Fort in search of work.[29] An adequate supply of lumber had always been a pressing need for Sutter. Realizing that his holdings further up the American River were well wooded, he apparently decided to send Marshall to seek a mill site. Marshall chose a spot on the South Fork of the American River some thirty miles above the fort, a place called Culumah (later Coloma) by the local natives.

When the party of four Mormons and Marshall arrived on 29 September, they found several other battalion veterans who had stayed to work for the winter. Towering mountains, covered with a dense growth of pine and oak, flanked the south side of the river and provided ample habitat for game and predators. Bigler, the western Virginia backwoodsman, must have felt quite at home. The only lodging available was a double log cabin. Peter L. Wimmer (or Weimer), Marshall's construction assistant, occupied one end with his wife, Jennie, at least one child, and Wimmer's aged parents. Jennie Wimmer, "the only white woman here," cooked for the mill hands, reported Bigler. While the Wimmers' religious persuasion is unclear, the grandparents, according to Kenneth Davies, "definitely were Mormons." Bigler and his three companions took the other half of the cabin and set to work "getting out mill timbers, erecting the building, making a dam, and digging a race." Bigler had an especially enjoyable assignment— camp hunter. For this job, "Marshall pays the same wages as for work at the mill, and he sends an Indian with me to carry home my deer," wrote Bigler with obvious pleasure. "Sutter had neglected to send provisions and we should have been on short allowance but for my game." His success with his rifle assured adequate supplies to feed the party and supplemented the rather monotonous diet of unbolted flour and pork or mutton.[30]

By late December 1847, six Mormons were working at the mill site: Alexander Stephens, James S. Brown (not the battalion's Captain James Brown), James Barger, William Johnson, Azariah Smith, and Henry Bigler, along with Californians James Marshall,

Peter Wimmer, Charles Bennett, and William Scott. The other battalion members had been transferred to Sutter's gristmill.

Over time, each man developed a more or less permanent assignment. Marshall was foreman; Wimmer supervised the Indians who were digging the race; Bennett was head carpenter with Scott as his assistant; Brown and Barger labored in the saw pit to supply the carpenters with lumber; Bigler did miscellaneous chores around the site when he was not hunting; and Stephens, Johnson, and Smith worked as teamsters, felled trees, helped dig the mill race, and laid the foundations for the mill structure.[31] Christmas Day was marred by an altercation between Jennie Wimmer and the Mormon workers, an open conflict that had begun smoldering several days before when Sutter's holiday gift of twelve bottles of brandy arrived, six for the Mormon workers and six for the Wimmers. The Mormons had not only drunk their own portion, but the Wimmers' as well. Mrs. Wimmer lost her temper, and the workmen responded in kind, accusing her of "always [keeping] back the best parts of the victuals for her favorites."[32] These ill feelings were exacerbated by close quarters in the double cabin, the inclement weather, Marshall's absence, and, very likely, the veterans' homesickness and melancholy.

On Christmas morning, Mrs. Wimmer took further offense when some of the workmen were slow to respond to her breakfast call and threatened them with no food at all. Bigler penned a comic verse giving his version of the altercation:

> On Christmas morn in bed she swore,
> That she would cook for us no more,
> Unless we'd come at the first call,
> For I am mistress of you all.[33]

The Mormons spent this day of freedom from labor by climbing a mountain on the north side of the river where they rolled stones down into the water, delighted when they surprised a number of deer. Afterward they held religious services. Bigler offered a prayer, they sang a hymn, and Bigler, possibly the most experienced orator of the group, preached a sermon. William C. Grant, a gold seeker on the American River in 1849, hearing the story of this Christmas discourse, reportedly called it "the first sermon ever preached in El Dorado." Upon returning to camp, the men learned that Mrs. Wimmer had relented handsomely, preparing not only meat and bread, but also pumpkin pies for them.[34] The holiday thus apparently ended with increased goodwill on both sides; however, when Marshall returned from Sutter's Fort on 15 January, Bigler and his colleagues obtained his permission to build a separate cabin about a hundred yards from the American River mill site. Six days later, the Mormons "[had] built a snug little cabin near the mill and were living in it" wrote Bigler.

The heavy rains that month worried Marshall, who inspected the tail race daily. He ordered that the gate at the head of the tail race be left open each night, hoping that the water flow would help deepen the ditch. According to Marshall's 1857 account:

> I used to go down in the morning to see what had been done by the water through the night; and about half past seven o'clock on or about the 19th of January—I am not quite certain to a day, but it was between the 18th and 20th of that month—1848, I went down as usual . . . near the lower end [of the mill race], . . . upon the rock, about six inches beneath the surface of the water, I DISCOVERED THE GOLD. I was entirely alone at the time. I picked up one or two pieces and examined them attentively.[35]

Marshall collected four or five more particles of gold and showed them to William Scott at his carpenter's bench. He and Scott then showed the specimens to Azariah Smith, William Johnson, James Brown, and Henry Bigler.

Nearly forty years afterward, in 1887, Bigler recalled the following particulars "which are as fresh in my memory as though they happened last week":

> On January 24th while looking at the race, through which a little water was running, [Marshall] saw something yellow on the bedrock. He sent an Indian to Brown for a plate, whereupon Brown said, "I wonder what Marshall wants with a tin plate." Just before we quit work for the day Marshall came up and told us he believed he had found a gold mine. Nothing more was said on the subject, as no one considered the matter worthy of attention.[36]

The flow of events from the moment of the find is hazy. Neither Bigler's day book nor a later version written by Brown

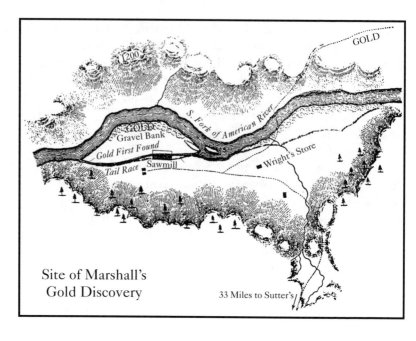

Site of Marshall's Gold Discovery

GOLD

S. Fork of American River

GOLD
Gravel Bank
Gold First Found

Tail Race   Sawmill

Wright's Store

33 Miles to Sutter's

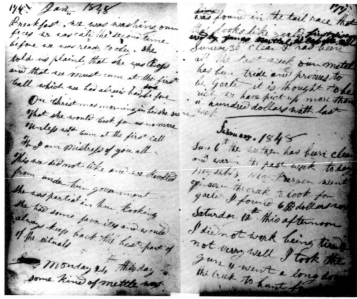

Page from Henry Bigler's diary recording James Marshall's discovery of gold. Courtesy of the Society of California Pioneers, San Francisco.

made any mention of Scott's involvement. Bigler's later (1887) account mentions Marshall sending an Indian to the workers at the top of the race, while Marshall's own account does not.[37] James S. Brown and Bigler claimed that Marshall called for a tin plate,[38] but since Marshall knew nothing about "panning" for gold at this time the story may well be apocryphal. Of all the supposed first-hand accounts of the actual discovery of gold, only Henry Bigler's 1848 account has withstood the test of historical scrutiny. On the following Sunday, 30 January, six days after the historic find, Azariah Smith noted: "This week Mon. the 24th. [date was inserted at a later time] Mr. Marshall found some pieces of (as we all suppose) Gold."[39] The Mormon workmen, skeptical from years of hard circumstances and bad luck, discounted Marshall's claim, especially since no one else had seen evidence of gold; but he must have described it in a manner which seemed convincing to Bigler. At least Bigler gave the event enough credence to make a one-sentence note in his diary: "This day some kind of mettle was found in the tail race that . . . looks like goald," he wrote on 24 January 1848. It is the only record made on the very day the gold was found. Thus Henry Bigler became somewhat of an "accidental" participant in the drama of American history. He did not find the gold, he was not with Marshall in the mill race that fateful morning, but he recorded the only near-immediate account of the discovery.

That evening Marshall had Brown and Bigler dam up the top of the tail race so Marshall could "see what is there in the morning."[40] In the privacy of his own cabin, Marshall studied his metal closely. He hammered it and found it malleable. He heated it in the fire and observed that it did not readily melt or change color. He compared it with a gold coin in his possession. He began to feel quite certain there *was* gold in the tailrace.

The next morning he went to the lower end of the now-empty ditch, picking up several more particles of gold as he went. He put about a spoonful of the gold on the crown of his hat as proof and hurriedly returned to the mill declaring "Boys, by G-d I believe I have found a gold mine." Now, the other men excitedly went to Marshall's "mine." First, James Barger picked up some gold particles, then Bigler used his jackknife to dig some out of a crevice in a rock.[41] Having extracted a promise of secrecy from the mill hands, Marshall dashed off to Sutter. Perhaps doubting Marshall's claims or hoping to temper his excitement, Sutter wrote cryptically in his diary: "Mr. Marshall arrived from the mountains on very important business."[42] Then the two men administered every test they knew to the metal. Satisfied about the nature of his find, Marshall returned to the mill site four days later.

On 30 January Henry Bigler observed, "Our metal has been tried and proved to be gold."[43] A few days later, Sutter arrived. Marshall and the Mormon laborers planned a practical joke. As Bigler described it:

> Marshall came to our shanty and told us that Sutter had arrived and was at the other house, and he added: "Now boys, we all have a little gold and I move that we all give some of it to Bigler so that when he goes in the morning to shut off the water, he can sprinkle it on the bedrock where the old man will find it when I take him down to the race; and he will get so excited that he will treat us all round out of the bottle he always carries with him." This suggestion was agreed to with a hearty laugh. The gold was contributed and put in the race before breakfast, and while we were still at the table in our shanty we saw the captain, a well dressed old gentleman, hobbling along with a cane between Marshall and Weimer [sic]. We went out; he shook hands with us all; spoke to all affably, and invited us to go with him prospecting.[44]

Unfortunately for the pranksters, Wimmer's son had already found the plant. The ruse was still successful, since Sutter, viewing what the boy held, exclaimed "By Jove, it is rich!" But the disrupted scheme cost the Mormon miners the gold which they had each contributed.[45]

Realizing the potential damage of a hasty announcement, Sutter extracted a solemn promise from the Mormons that they would keep quiet about the gold and finish the work on the mill.[46] Although the workers kept their promise during the week, they spent Sundays hunting gold. On 6 February, possibly the first chance they had to do so, James Barger and Henry Bigler "visited the creek opposite the mill to look for gold" and dug six dollars worth out of the rock cracks with their jackknives. Bigler, by his own admission, was now smitten by the "gold bug" and apparently became very proficient at prospecting, because Barger joked that "Bigler could see gold where there was'nt [sic] any."[47] These two Mormons were, in all likelihood, El Dorado's first prospectors because, unlike Marshall's accidental find, Bigler and Barger went looking for gold.

The next Saturday afternoon, smitten by gold "on the brain," Bigler fabricated an excuse to prospect. On 12 February, "I took my pan and went down the creek pretending to hunt for ducks, but in reality to look for gold. About half a mile down the creek I discovered some rock on the opposite side that indicated gold. I took off my shirt and pants, crossed over and soon picked up $21.50 worth lying in the seams of the rock." The next day, Sunday, he returned to the same spot and picked up at least an additional half-ounce of gold dust. Not only was he one of the first prospectors, but, Bigler believed, he was also the first claim jumper, as he remorsefully noted, "it is on Sutter and Marshall's claim."[48] By 12 February Bigler was calling this area "Capt Sutters and Mr. Martials land" for they had arranged to lease ten or twelve square miles of the surrounding territory, doubtless including mineral rights, from the local Indians for three years.[49] Unfortunately for the two expectant millionaires, Richard B. Mason, military governor of California, refused to confirm the treaty because the United States and Mexico had not settled affairs in the region and he felt that he had no authority to act on the matter.

Slowly but inevitably, word of the discovery at Sutter's Mill began to reach the world beyond Coloma. Charles Bennett, who was dispatched to Monterey with the petition to Governor Mason, had left hints of Marshall's find along his trail. On 11 February Jacob Wittmer, a teamster from the mill site, purchased a bottle of liquor in a grocery at Sutter's Fort and paid for it with gold. Then, on 20 February, Henry Bigler wrote a letter to three messmates from the battalion—Jesse Martin, Israel Evans, and Ephraim Green—who were working on Sutter's grist mill and told them of the gold. Naively, Bigler swore them to secrecy because "Mr. Marshall did not want it known until further development, not knowing how extensive it was."[50] When the three returned to Sutter's Fort several days later, they told Sam Brannan about the gold and the secret was soon public knowledge.

On 22 February, Bigler again shirked his camp duties to seek gold. "This morning I started out to hunt for ducks, but soon changed my notion, and made my way to my gold mine." Recklessly wading across an icy stream, he chilled his feet, "so I tried to strike a fire, but my hands were so benumbed I could not hold the flint and steel. I tried to catch fire from my gun, but my powder had got wet and I could not set her off. I was then obliged to dance and jump about, and while doing so could see the yellow pieces lying on the rocks." After he got warm, he picked up over twenty dollars worth of gold. Suspicious at his absence and lack of game, the other Mormons questioned him until he admitted his prospecting adventures and called for a makeshift scale: "My yellow game was weighed . . . and declared to be worth $22.50 cts." Bigler good-humoredly recorded. The others were amazed; he was the first to see gold outside the mill race.[51]

While Bigler was certainly bending the letter of the agreement with both Marshall and Sutter, his eagerness to enrich himself was natural. He would have been superhuman or totally lacking in imagination not to see the gold as an opportunity to escape the poverty he had been born into. Between 19 March and 12 April he reportedly found at least seventy-seven dollars worth of gold as an occasional prospector.[52] In contrast, as Sutter's full-time laborer, he earned at best thirty or thirty-five dollars per month.

By mid-March 1848, the sawmill was operational; but Sutter's workers were deserting him. On 28 April, Sutter noted in his diary "Knight and Nash left for the gold mines" with several more following within a few days. Three weeks earlier, on 7 April, Bigler and two Mormon workmen left Coloma to settle their wages for the past six months with Sutter, passing the deserted and partially finished grist mill on their way. It was a mute witness to the overwhelming lure of gold. Of this attempt at payment, Sutter wrote on 11 April: "Settle Accounts with a good Many people. Stevens [sic], Brown & Bigler left for the Sawmill."[53] Sutter could not settle in cash, but Bigler returned to Coloma with over $475 in goods—cloth, flour, coffee, and sugar.

As early as April 1848, while Sutter's workmen still monopolized prospecting on the American River, hopeful gold miners began to trickle into the Coloma country. In May 1848, Bigler took out a claim to one square mile of land near Coloma, where he laid the foundation for a house, clearly with some intention of remaining in California for at least a while. Within the month, however, he changed his mind.

On 1 June Bigler noted about his claim, "I have no idea that I can hold it. The miners pay no attention to Sutter and Marshall's claim. People come in so fast that the banks and ravines are filled with mining camps."[54] He was clear sighted enough to realize that his claim would be jumped as heedlessly as their's. Instead, he turned his thoughts once again to the body of the Saints—and his own family—settling their own territory in the West. Whatever gold fever may have possessed him in May was short-lived.

Although Bigler's firm commitment to Mormonism—including the principle of gathering—no doubt strengthened his resolve to leave the heady atmosphere of the gold field, history supports his wisdom. Certainly, some great fortunes were made; but they were also lost, and many more men never came close. The great discovery, which made Sutter such glittering promises, ruined his thriving empire. His fort, once such an important fixture in northern California, soon became but a way station on the road to the mines. As months of toil and investment at Coloma seemed about to bear fruit, he had to close his mill. No wages, however high, could keep carpenters or mill operators at work.

Gold fever swept the rest of California during the summer and fall of 1848. It hit first at San Francisco and Monterey in August 1848, later draining Santa Barbara and Los Angeles. By 7 December word of the discovery had reached Washington, D.C. The excitement quickly swept the Atlantic seaboard, New England, the Ohio River valley, cascaded up and down the Mississippi, spread into Canada, and eventually stirred interest in western Europe, Australia and the Sandwich Islands, and even parts of South America. Argonauts came over land and by sea. The population exploded seemingly overnight: at the beginning of 1849, exclusive of Indians there were some 26,000 persons; by the year's end there were probably near 115,000.[55]

Bigler was not there to see it. In company with an unspecified number of Mormons who had also been in Sutter's employ, he started for Salt Lake City 17 June 1848 over the Salt Lake Cutoff and reached Utah on 28 September with his goods.[56] They must have proven as valuable as cash in the pioneer community. "Here I found my Sister Emline," Bigler joyously noted. Her husband, John W. Hess, had returned east to help his widowed mother across the plains.[57]

Thus, Bigler turned his back on the gold field, leaving California for the same religious reasons that had taken him there in the first place and returned him there for the winter. Chance had placed him in a historic place at a historic moment, giving him a permanent footnote in history as the man who dated the discovery of California's gold.

Bigler does not say what he anticipated in his future. Surely it was to settle down in one of the Mormon agricultural communities that were springing up in the Great Basin, find a wife, and raise a family. Ironically, even these modest ambitions would be postponed again and then again as he faithfully responded to the call of his leaders. Even more ironically, the first call would send him back to the gold fields from which he had so resolutely turned away.

Sutter's Mill. Courtesy of the California History Room, California State Library, Sacramento.

⁅ 5 ⁆

RELUCTANT ARGONAUT
1849–50

*I walked back and forth across my floor and give vent to my
feelings in a flood of tears, everything I looked upon seemed to
sympathise with me and said go in peace, only be faithful and all
will be well with you.[1]*

*H*enry Bigler's diary entries for the weeks immediately following his return to Salt Lake City were concerned largely
with the mundane tasks of earning a living and finding a place to
stay but still breathe a perceptible kind of happiness that he was
back among his people.

The rawly new Great Salt Lake City by 1848 had a population
nearing four thousand people. All around, Bigler noted the bustle
of community building: "working roads in to the canyons, getting
out timbers, making adobes, preparing to build houses," digging
irrigation ditches, erecting barns and fences, establishing schools,
and planning a temple. Brigham Young had chosen the temple site
on his first morning in the valley. Some were already raising frame
houses.[2]

Happily, Bigler found he was not forgotten. As a veteran of
the Mormon Battalion, he began to enjoy a respect which would
follow him for the rest of his life, wherever he made his home
within Mormondom. For example, Bigler discovered that George
A. Smith, by then an apostle for ten years, had kindly set aside some
city property for his father. "It was situated in a very nice part of the
city on City Creek," Bigler noted, "2 blocks west from the Temple

Block." For Henry, Smith had reserved a lot "somewhere in the south part of the city, some distance from the Temple Block and on rather low land." From the description, this land was probably boggy and therefore less desirable. Henry's father was not expected in the city for at least one more year, and a prime lot near the temple standing vacant would have been a tempting acquisition for others. "I liked the lot for it was near where the Temple would eventually stand," recorded Bigler. "I gave up the lot intended for me and took the one designed for Father."[3]

Bigler built a cabin, began working, and renewed his socioreligious ties with the Thirtieth Quorum of Seventies. Revealingly, in December 1848, a meeting of the seventies called for volunteers to serve as missionaries to the Pacific Islands. Among those expressing a willingness to take up such a mission was Henry Bigler.[4] Almost certainly he did not want to leave Salt Lake City so soon, but his willingness to step forward is a solid reminder of his bone-deep commitment to the church. No call was forthcoming at that time.

As winter swung toward the spring of 1849, the golden lodestone in California drew thousands from all over the world, influencing the Mormons in Utah as well. The Mormons had several choices—aggressive participation to win a share of the potential wealth available on the Pacific shore? studied indifference? or something in between?

Some Mormons wanted to join wholeheartedly in the gold rush, but Brigham Young's public position was active opposition to Mormon gold seeking. In winter sermons, he condemned it—urging, persuading, promising, and even threatening to keep the Saints as a unified body. "You will do better right here than you will by going to the gold mines," Young told his followers in the Salt Lake Valley. "Those who stop here and are faithful to God and his people will make more money and get richer than you that run after the god of this world."[5] As a rather humorous example of how seriously some Latter-day Saints took Young's counsel, Bigler records trying to purchase some building materials with his California gold dust. The merchant sturdily replied, "I wants none of your gold," and Bigler was forced to go to another source for the product.[6]

Since its settlement, Great Salt Lake City had lacked a monetary system. Originally the Mormon pioneers employed a simple barter procedure, but the arrival of the California gold dust brought by Bigler and his companions held promise of remedying this situation. However, gold dust was not the most practical medium of exchange. Instead, Brigham Young and the community leaders issued paper currency backed by the gold. The first bill, issued in one-dollar denominations and bearing the signatures of Young, Heber C. Kimball, and Thomas Bullock, began to circulate in January 1849. Some months later, a stamp was secured that allowed the pioneers to coin gold pieces ranging in value from $2.50 to $20.00.[7] To continue this system, Young quietly sent apostle Amasa M. Lyman and Mormon frontiersman Orrin Porter Rockwell to California during the spring of 1849. Their task was described as a "mission": they were to preach, look after church interests on the West Coast, bolster the faith of the Mormons known to be in California, and collect any past due tithing from Mormon miners and merchants in the gold fields.[8]

This collection of tithes, however, brought back less than five thousand dollars for church coffers when the missionaries returned in July 1849, and Brigham Young, while continuing to publicly condemn those pursuing worldly wealth, began to consider other means which might allow the Mormon community to benefit from the gold rush while still retaining its group integrity. The idea of calling "gold missionaries" of unimpeachable loyalty and obedience was a logical one. "The Lord will open up the way for a supply of gold to the perfect satisfaction of his people," announced Young.[9]

In October 1849, Brigham Young put his plan into action but distanced himself from publicly sanctioning it by adding an intervening layer. He authorized several prominent Mormon men to sponsor gold missionaries to go to California. These missionaries would mine on behalf of their benefactor for shares of the take. In theory, this would provide additional income for select church leaders who would then funnel the much-needed gold dust into the Salt Lake Valley economy.[10]

At least four missionaries and sponsors have been identified: George Q. Cannon, sponsored by John Taylor; James Keeler, sponsored by Thomas Callister; William Farrer, sponsored by Joseph Horne; and Henry Bigler, sponsored by John Smith. Smith, the sixty-eight-year-old uncle of Joseph Smith, Jr., the father of George A. Smith, and the father-in-law of Thomas Callister, was then serving as Salt Lake City Stake's first president and later would become church patriarch.[11] On 8 October 1849, Henry Bigler soberly recorded in his journal a visit from Uncle John, who had headed the company in which Bigler had left Nauvoo. Brigham Young had counseled Smith to "fit out some person and send him to California [to] get some of the treasures of the earth to make himself comfortable in his old age."[12] Bigler reluctantly but predictably accepted: "I hesitated, [but] when he explained to me what the President had said and the counsil President Young had given to him in relation to sending a man to the mines etc. After I had consented to go I could not help feeling sorrowful and a reluctance to go for I feel attached to this place and to this people for they are my brethren and dear friends."[13] Bigler apparently considered their agreement fair: "The bargain between me and Father Smith is this. He to [bear] the expense of fitting me out for the gold mines, and after arriving there I am to be saving and prudent and after all the expenses was paid I am to have half the gold."[14]

Grieving but dutiful, Bigler sold his wheat crop, paid his debts, and arranged to join a California-bound company led by apostle Charles C. Rich. On 10 October, the evening before departure, Uncle John Smith "laid his hands on my head and blest me and also Brother Keeler in the name of the Lord."[15]

This arrangement offered Henry Bigler a chance to build up some capital, but he was still an intensely reluctant argonaut. On the afternoon of 11 October, while waiting at home for James Keeler to pick him up, Bigler's suffering was intense: "At this moment I experienced what I shall not attempt to describe," he wrote in his diary. "I walked back and forth across my floor and my feelings were spent in a complete shower of tears." However, when Keeler drew up in front of the house, Bigler "hastened to the [window] curtains . . . hastily wiped away every tear and went out."[16] Bigler's reluctance was quite a reversal for the man who just one year earlier had slipped away from Sutter's Mill at every

John Smith, Mormon church patriarch, uncle of Joseph Smith Jr., and sponsor of Henry Bigler's gold mission. Used by permission, Utah State

opportunity to prospect. He does not expand on the reasons for his reluctance besides his deep satisfaction at being with the body of the Saints, but surely his knowledge of the potential hardships of mining influenced him as well.

The trail to California was well traveled that fall. Addison Pratt and Hiram Blackwell, two proselyting missionaries bound for the South Pacific, left on 2 October. Apostle Rich, James S. Brown, and F. M. Pomeroy, traveling by horseback, departed on 8 October. Mormon Battalion veteran and skilled trailblazer Jefferson Hunt was guiding a large train of about 250 gold seekers to California, which Bigler joined. They departed from Salt Lake City on 11 October 1849.

During the first two days of Bigler's and Keeler's trek, it "rained like Sam hill," in Bigler's homely phrase, and left the tops of the surrounding mountains snowcapped. It was a warning that October was late in the year to start a journey that involved mountain passes. At Provo they caught up with Rich's party of three, who had been joined by Pratt, Blackwell, and two additional companies. One was a party of twenty Mormon packers led by James M. Flake, and the second was a group of fifty Gentile packers captained by O. K. Smith, of Chenango County, New York, both bound for the gold fields. Flake, a North Carolinian of Bigler's age, had, like Pratt, left Salt Lake City on 11 October with his party of twenty young men, including two more of the gold missionaries, George Q. Cannon and William Farrer. This combined group chose Flake as their captain with Charles C. Rich to advise him. Given the status accorded to an apostle, it is likely that Rich was actually in charge of the party.[17]

On the night of 15 October Bigler had a dream which so profoundly influenced him that he wrote it down the next day in his journal: "I dreamed I was not going for goal[d] but was going to the Islands on a mission to preach the gospel."[18] Just why Bigler had the islands of the Pacific on his mind is unclear. Perhaps, although his journal does not record it, he still remembered the mission for which he had earlier volunteered; perhaps the presence of Blackwell and Pratt influenced him; perhaps he was unconsciously contrasting his present reluctance with the unwavering resolution with which he would have accepted a proselyting mission. Or perhaps it was a genuine premonition of the future.

On 20 October near the Sevier River southwest of Provo, Bigler and Keeler were once again reunited with the faster-moving Flake and Smith packers. Charles Rich was further ahead as he pressed hard to get to his mission in California. It was a dry, desolate country they were traversing, and water was a constant problem. By 24 October they had caught up with Hunt's large train. It has not been possible to reconstruct the exact numbers in the party, but estimates place its size somewhere between three and five hundred men, 113 wagons, and about fifty packers. Motivated by both religious and secular hopes, Easterners and Midwesterners, Mormons and Gentiles, they pushed into the desert.[19]

Dissension about speed promptly became an issue. The pace Jefferson Hunt set was much too slow for his party. The O. K. Smith group was also in a great hurry. In southwestern Utah the company split up on 16 November. Some travelers chose to remain with Hunt on the Old Spanish Trail—a longer but proven route— while O. K. Smith, professing to have a map that showed a cutoff, led off another group. Smith claimed that he had received the map from an old mountain man named Barney Ward. There was, in fact, a fur trapper named Barney Ward who had made the desert crossing from Los Angeles to Santa Fe a number of times, and he is known to have claimed that a short-cut existed from southern Utah to Walker Pass in the Sierra Nevada. Where Smith may have met Ward is not clear; none of the Mormon diarists with the party mention Barney Ward, either in Salt Lake City or at any stop on the route south.[20] Bickering and contention were rife in the party, nor were the Mormons immune. On 30 October, Bigler recorded in his diary that "Bro. Rich requested the Camp to come together. He told us he wanted that we should have order and understanding." Rich also counseled the men to observe their prayers and thus live a more righteous life even while in the wilderness.[21]

Rich and Flake, as leaders of their combined group of about twenty-five gold missionaries, determined to accompany Smith. Bigler wrote in his diary for 31 October 1849, "We expect to leave the spanish trail and take the cut off and travil a more direct west *without a gide or trail* and be in the mines in about 20 days."[22]

Bigler and Keeler had to abandon their wagon and transform their teams into saddle horses and pack animals.

Why the usually prudent Charles Rich decided to part with Hunt and accompany O. K. Smith and the Gentile gold seekers was unclear. Perhaps the danger did not seem so great at that point. Jefferson Hunt, who had been over the trail once, obviously felt strongly that there were dangers in an untried trail, but he does not seem to have made strenuous efforts to persuade Rich to stay with the party. Instead, he simply stated that he had contracted to guide the party to California and was staying with the route he knew. Possibly a stronger stand by Hunt might have influenced Rich's decision, although it likely would not have swayed O. K. Smith or the other Gentiles. Bigler does not comment on how he felt about the change. Whatever his personal feelings, he loyally followed decisions made by others.

After being plagued by dryness, the travelers were afflicted with violent rains on 1 November, their first day of separate traveling. Bigler spent most of the night huddled around a small fire in a vain attempt to keep warm. The following day continued wet and cold. Two days later, near the present Utah-Nevada border the party laid over until noon to rest the animals and the men. Bigler took advantage of the pause to carve his initials and the date "on a rock close to our camp."[23]

On 8 November lack of water became a problem. One member of Smith's company approached the Mormons and offered to "pay any price for a drink of water." None was for sale. Bigler had drained his canteen by the afternoon and felt "exceedingly thirsty" until Charles Rich persuaded him to share his water.[24]

The terrain also roughened. On 16 November, they were in the Pahroc Range, about twenty miles west of present-day Pioche, Nevada. Bigler wrote:

> When we left camp this morning it was expected we soon would come to a valley but as yet there we are still in the Kanyon surrounded by high mountains. The Kanyon is narrow and in places dangerous for our animals to travel. There was one place today that one false step would [have] plunged a horse hundreds of feet down the mountain without any possibility of saving life. Towards

Historians J. Roderic Korns and Charles Kelly point out Henry Bigler's initials carved into the rock at Beaver Dam Wash. Used by permission, Utah State Historical Society, all rights reserved.

evening it commenced to rain. . . . Tonight I stand guard and the rain pours down and bids fair for a wet dismal night.[25]

Within a few days, Bigler would have welcomed another downpour. On 9 November, one of his two pack animals collapsed from thirst and exhaustion; he loaded his whole outfit on the remaining animal and continued on foot, sending James Keeler on with the rest of the party. "I was soon left behind without any arms and no one knew I was so far behind," he recorded of that long day. Futilely scratching holes in the sand, Bigler tried to find water, then turned some bullets over in his mouth in an attempt to encourage saliva. He was nearing collapse from fatigue and potentially fatal dehydration when he spotted one of his fellow Mormons, Joseph Cain, backtrailing to find him. A tin cup glistened in the sun as Cain raised his hand to wave. Bigler gratefully "Clened the Canteen of evry drop" of "the best water I ever drank."[26]

On 16 November, Rich became convinced that trying the cut-off was a mistake and advised returning to the Old Spanish Trail. The Mormons as a group willingly obeyed, Bigler commenting with obvious concern for the rest of the party: "Bro. Rich . . . give his opinion of the route, that it was his mind not to go that way any further that he should make for the spanish trail. Smith said he would continue his course across the mountain if he perished and we never herd from him again we mite know he was dead, had died with his face westward and not before he had eaten some mule meat, too." Two days later, Bigler pessimistically added, "Capt. Smith is a goner if he don't beat down south on the Spanish trail."[27] Smith's stubbornness yielded twenty-three days later; and after several more days of wandering in the desert, he led his party safely back to the Old Spanish Trail. Although their suffering was great, no lives were lost.[28] At least 107 members of Jefferson Hunt's original wagon train, in contrast, ill-advisedly struck off into Death Valley near Cedar City.

By early December, Bigler, Hunt, and other Mormon Battalion veterans reached familiar country near Cajon Pass—the gateway to southern California. Early winter storms had already begun and Bigler, who left the main body to hunt deer, was lost in a sudden blizzard. God, he recorded gratefully, "guided me by his spirit" back to the main party.[29] At about this point, the Flake-Rich company, including Bigler, separated from the Hunt party and pushed on hastily toward Los Angeles.

Within four days the party reached the Chino ranch of Isaac Williams, where Bigler and other veterans had stayed for several days the previous year. Williams, an American fur trapper, had come to California in 1832, become a citizen of Mexico, married the daughter of Antonio Maria Lugo, a wealthy *Californio*, and, in 1841, took over the Lugo ranch at Chino. Williams discussed selling his property to Charles Rich for a Mormon outpost in southern California. The asking price, according to Bigler, was two hundred thousand dollars.[30]

Though Williams was absent on a trip, he had always been friendly to the Mormons, and his clerks distributed flour and fresh meat to the weary travelers without charge, pending Williams's return. In return for the kindness, the Mormon travelers did some work for Williams while they waited for the weather to clear up. Henry Bigler greatly appreciated this rest stop since he had caught a bad cold due to the cold and rain that resulted in one of the sinus infections to which he seemed susceptible. He was still ill with "a severe pane" in his left eye on Christmas day, 1849, when Williams treated his guests to a feast of roast beef, baked duck, potatoes, and plum pudding. Bigler's ailment left him "weak and feeble" for several days after Christmas, but he continued as one of the work party.[31]

The topic of a proselyting mission had come up twice during the journey. James Brown had invited Bigler on 18 November to accompany "him & Bro. Pratt to the islands saying that Bro. P. wanted me to go and that he had heard Bro. Pratt ask Bro. Rich how he would like to swap off one of his men for Bro. Blackwell and Bro. Rich had said if it was agreeable between the parties he had no objections."[32]

Pratt had become increasingly disenchanted with Hiram Blackwell, who had a persistent tobacco problem. Blackwell had promised to forsake the vice but failed to do so. In late October 1849 after having caught Blackwell smoking, Pratt wrote, "I determined to say nothing more about it but leave him in California"—which is what ultimately happened.[33] This invitation offered the opportunity to fulfill a literal dream, confronting Bigler with two

honorable alternatives. His reluctant refusal, "I did not like to con-
sent to go," reveals his commitment to his primary responsibility.[34]
Then on 31 December, Addison Pratt asked Bigler if he would be
willing to go to the islands. Bigler did not refuse this time, but
"told him I should if that was their council."[35] There is no record of
whether Pratt and Brown approached other gold missionaries, but
their persistence with Henry Bigler says much about how they
judged his ability. Apparently Rich did not issue a calling at that
point, and the subject dropped though it did not die.

In mid-January the Mormons started north, part of a massive
influx of gold seekers that boosted California's population from
about fourteen thousand in 1848 to just under a hundred thousand
by the end of 1849.[36] The 1849 traffic had been relatively small and
limited largely to local, internal movement by those who were
already in the area. The great flood of migration was triggered by
President James K. Polk's January 1849 announcement of the strike.
The first wave of overland argonauts could not leave until the spring
thaw, which meant they reached California during the late summer
of 1849. But ships embarked around the Horn as early as February,
reaching California in significant numbers starting in late summer.
The many men and some women came from all sections of the
United States, western Europe, Latin America, and Asia.[37]

Henry Bigler began his gold mission in the Mariposa mines
of central California—probably at Mormon Bar. This site, located
on Mariposa Creek, a mile southeast of present-day Mariposa in
east-central California, was probably discovered by Mormons from
the battalion in 1848, then abandoned as these men returned to Salt
Lake City. Bigler had not worked at the creek earlier but probably
knew about it. In his retrospective autobiography, he mentions
working in the Mariposa mines only once; in all likelihood, he
quickly moved north to American River, now swarming with miners, entrepreneurs, and camp followers.[38] Camp towns named Slap
Jack Bar, Murderer's Bar, Rough and Ready, Spanish Diggings,
and Rattlesnake Bar dotted the foothills of the Sierra Nevada
where Bigler had hunted in solitude the previous year.

Bigler and his companions reached these mines by the end of
February 1850, but he then let his diary lapse for nearly seven
months. When he resumed writing in September of 1850 he

noted, "I have exposed myself much boath to indians and wether more then I ever want to do again, liveing out in storms of snow and rain without shelter. Some of my brethren have died . . . most all of the brethren have been sick haveing been much exposed working in the water up to their arms and necks building dams to get a little gold."[39]

At that point, Bigler was working on the middle fork of the American River at Slap Jack Bar. He would stay there until October and had possibly been there during the spring and summer of 1850 as well. The whole region was alive with miners in 1849 and 1850, and this fork produced an estimated seventeen million dollars worth of gold by the end of 1850. But Bigler and his companions "made but little, the expenses over run the gain."[40]

Then in late September, apostle Charles C. Rich arrived at Slap Jack Bar and suggested that several of the men serve proselyting missions to the Sandwich Islands (Hawaii). Rich believed they could live more inexpensively there while mining was curtailed during the winter than in California where the gold rush had greatly inflated the cost of supplies. Therefore, it would, in the words of Henry Bigler, "be like killing 2 birds with one stone" for the men to go to the islands.[41]

Bigler does not say who was in the Mormon party at that point, but the others called to the Sandwich Islands included Thomas Whittle, Thomas Morris, John Dixon, George Q. Cannon, William Farrer, James Keeler, and James Hawkins. Bigler was "tired of mining and of the country and long to be at home among the saints."[42] He added sadly, "I have taken from the earth $836 dollars, this would appear as though I aught to have lots of money but I have none."[43] He borrowed some money—he does not say how much—to send Uncle John Smith a hundred dollars via Amasa Lyman who was returning to Utah, and paid $83.60—as an honest Mormon tithing of 10 percent—to Rich and Lyman for himself and Smith. Bigler could not remember all of his expenses, but he itemized some. He had spent eleven dollars for a fifth share with four other Mormon miners to buy a washing machine "for cleaning or washing gold."

After he moved to a different site, he paid forty dollars for his own washer. A pick and shovel cost ten dollars, four wash pans, eight. His clothing, "as near as I can recon[struct]," had come to ninety. A scale to weigh the gold dust cost twelve dollars and blankets cost ten. The inflation of these prices can be marked by his estimated living expenses at Slap Jack Bar: twelve dollars a week. At the Mariposa mines, he had lived on nine. Once, when he was too sick to work, Bigler had had to hire a man to labor in his stead constructing a dam at the cost of seventy-five dollars. He listed a few miscellaneous items, adding apologetically that he could not give "an exact account of every particle that went through my fingers."[44]

With the other Hawaii-bound gold missionaries, Bigler continued to mine along the American River until late October 1850 and sent an additional $240 back to Uncle John Smith. When the party left, they spent several days near Sacramento searching the gold fields for Hiram Clark, the newly designated mission president. They were unable to locate him; but Hiram Blackwell, whom Pratt and Brown had left behind, joined them there.[45]

On 29 October 1850 as they waited in San Francisco for their ship to sail, Bigler recorded another significant event in California history. "A great day here today, [as] the Citizens Celibrate the admission of Callifornia into the Union." The festivities started with an artillery salute, a parade, speeches in the main square, and general merriment. "Everything went off verry well until dusk," noted Bigler. Then, "the steamer *Sagamore* burst hur boilers and blowed everything all to attoms." The following morning, Bigler and some of the other Mormons, drawn by morbid curiosity, went to the dock to view the carnage left by this locally built steamer. The entire cabin and wheelhouse had been blown away, and eighty people were believed killed.[46]

Clark, who had been recovering from an illness in Sacramento, reached San Francisco on 8 February; and the missionaries sailed aboard the British vessel *Imaum of Muscat* bound for the Far East with an intermediary stop in Honolulu. Unfavorable winds stalled departure until 22 November.[47]

爲 6 爲

THE SANDWICH ISLANDS
1850–54

*I thought how different it was when we landed here in 1850
ignorant of the language and among strangers . . . but now we
were surrounded by thousands who seem to love us and are Saints.[1]*

*M*ormons were latecomers to the Hawaiian Islands.
Discovered by British sea-captain James Cook in 1778 and
named for his patron, the Earl of Sandwich, Hawaii rapidly
became a popular stop with sailors and whalers. By 1850 Protestant
evangelists sponsored by Boston's American Board of
Commissioners for Foreign Missions (ABCFM) had been in the
islands for two decades.[2] The first missionary party, which included
ordained ministers Hiram Bingham and Asa Thurston, and thirteen other persons, sailed from Boston in October 1819 aboard the
brig *Thaddeus*. Full of zeal but ill-prepared for what awaited them
in a strange new land, the missionaries arrived off the west coast of
the island of Hawaii on 30 March 1820. There they learned of the
death of Kamehameha the Great, who had unified the several
island kingdoms by 1805, recognized the value of friendships with
the *haoles* (foreigners), and even elevated some to positions of
power and wealth within his kingdom.

His successor and son, Liholiho, was wary of the potential
threat to his power posed by the white newcomers. He gave
Bingham and Thurston permission to establish a mission station
on Hawaii; but when they tried to do the same on Oahu, he
demurred. He did not want to let the intruders out of his sight,

fearing lest they attempt to seize Honolulu.[3] Dealing with a monarch they considered capricious was complicated for the missionaries by struggles with the language and massive cultural shock. They were offended by the "lewd" hula, casual public nudity, and such examples of polygamy and incest as the king's marriage to five wives, including two former wives of his father and his own half-sister.[4]

With unremitting zeal, the New Englanders worked to Christianize the natives and, by the summer of 1827, numbered about fifty-seven thousand converts.[5] At this point, their religious hegemony was challenged by a party of French Catholics—six members from the order of the Sacred Hearts of Jesus and Mary—and several agriculturalists. The New Englanders launched a prompt crusade against what they called "idolatry," encouraged the harassment of priests, and looked away from injustice inflicted on Catholic converts.[6] It was a holy war, waged simultaneously against the natives' polytheistic traditions and another Christian denomination which seems lamentable from a twentieth-century perspective. Although the Catholics did not retreat and made steady progress of their own, Calvinist successes were considerable by the time the Mormon missionaries arrived in 1850. The mighty Congregationalist Kawaiahao Church had been dedicated eight years earlier in Honolulu.

The voyage to Hawaii had not been pleasant for the Mormons. "Bros. Hawkins and Dixon were vomiting as hard as they could," noted George Cannon, and "as soon as they got through with the bucket I was on hand [and] it came up pretty freely."[7] Bigler had the luxury of complaining in his diary about poor food and sleeping conditions, since he and Thomas Whittle escaped seasickness. On 12 December when the *Imaum of Muscat* dropped anchor in Honolulu harbor, Henry Bigler and his friends hurried to a temperance hotel to celebrate their safe passage with a well-cooked meal. Bigler's first impression of Honolulu was concise: "The town is pretty and wears a tropical look."

The next day, the company walked up the Nuuanu Valley northeast of Honolulu, paused to take much-needed baths at beautiful King's Falls, then found a secluded place a mile further on for the religious ritual of dedicating their new mission. They erected a rude altar and sang hymns. Clark led them in a prayer imploring God to bless their efforts, then John Dixon spontaneously spoke in tongues, which James Hawkins interpreted as a prophecy that "a good work should be done" by the group. The religious observance comforted and encouraged them all. Bigler summarized: "We felt well and rejoiced feeling that the Lord was with us."[8]

Two days later, a Sunday, Bigler and a few companions attended Congregationalist services at King's Chapel in downtown Honolulu. Bigler was both impressed and discouraged at hearing the New Englander preach "in the native language," of which they understood "not one word."[9] Since the Mormons planned to proselyte among Caucasians, however, the language problem did not seem serious.

They designated Honolulu, which had the largest white population, as mission headquarters. Clark took it as his assignment with Thomas Whittle, and the remaining elders drew lots, a New Testament custom, to go two by two to the other islands. Bigler drew Molokai as his assignment and Thomas Morris as his companion; Clark, however, advised Morris to remain in Honolulu to earn some money so Bigler accompanied Cannon and Keeler to Maui.[10] As a result, Bigler developed a significant relationship with Cannon that would continue to impact his life for years to come.

Lahaina on Maui's west coast, the island's principal town, had long been a favorite retreat of native royalty; but by 1850, it was a well-established whaling port, dominated by Protestant missionaries and Yankee whalers. Calvinist mission stations had been established at Lahaina (1823), Wailuku (1832) about fifteen miles to the east, and Hana (1837) on the far eastern tip. The missionaries also operated Lahainaluna School, a boys' high school and seminary, two miles east of Lahaina. The American Seaman's Friend Society added a harmonizing religious note with its Seaman's Bethel Chapel, operated for the spiritual welfare of itinerant sailors in Lahaina.[11]

The three Mormons arranged to rent a "native house" for a frugal four dollars per week, then sought opportunities to preach. Since all three of them kept diaries, it is possible to reconstruct their activities in great detail. On Sunday, 22 December 1850, they called on James Young, governor of Maui. He was the son of John Young, an English seaman who became a friend and officer of

View of Honolulu, Paul Emmert, lithograph, 1853. Hawaiian Historical Society collection.

Kamehameha, and a native woman. Bigler, Cannon, and Keeler boldly requested permission to hold meetings in the royal palace, then vacant. Young promised to check into it but evaded a direct answer. Cannon believed the governor "dare[d] not to grant us any favors" due to the strength of the Calvinists on Maui; but Young did, in fact, pass on the request to the Minister of the Interior at Honolulu, explaining that "it was not for me to give out the Government's place. I was only the Caretaker."[12] Since no answer from the minister has been preserved, the result still appears to have been negative; but without waiting to learn it, the missionaries asked the Reverend Townshend Elijah Taylor, pastor of the Seaman's Chapel, for the use of his pulpit on the same day, 22 December.

Taylor, who was married to a daughter of Asa Thurston and had been stationed in Lahaina for two years, hesitantly agreed. That very afternoon, perhaps not wishing to allow Taylor to change his mind, the Mormons held their first preaching service. Bigler, the oldest and most experienced of the three, gave the first Latter-day Saint sermon ever delivered on Maui. He mentions nothing about it in his diary; however, James Keeler wrote, "Br. B. got up and told them that he would read a chapter in the acts of the apostles . . . then spoke on the first principals of the gospel of Christ." (Mormonism's "first principles" are faith, repentance, baptism by immersion, and the conferral of the Holy Ghost, the latter two ordinances being performed by proper priesthood authority.) After Bigler's sermon, noted Cannon, a listener asked what "additional light" the Mormons added to known religious teachings. Bigler quickly responded that Mormonism had "the authority as they had anciently and there were Apostles and Prophets" as in the days of Jesus Christ.[13] This claim to have restored the original church established by Christ was always the crux of the Latter-day Saint claim to legitimacy and, in this case, effectively answered the questioner.

Thanks to this sermon, wrote Cannon in his diary the next day, "we are beginning to be known." But Taylor did not let them use his pulpit again, and Young continued to hedge on the palace's availability. "From what I have been able to observe," wrote Cannon rather astutely on 4 January 1851, "I think the [Congregationalist] Missionaries have all the power here in the Government."[14]

The next Sunday, the Mormon missionaries heard the Reverend Dwight Baldwin preach at his "fine stone church" in Lahaina. Baldwin, who had come to the islands in 1830, had been stationed on Maui for the past fourteen years. Bigler was impressed by the outstanding native choir, which "almost raised the roof of the meeting house."[15] The contrast between the Congregationalist achievement and Mormon aspirations must have been painfully obvious.

Since Lahaina's Caucasian population was small and indifferent to the Mormon message, the missionaries realized that they must teach the native Hawaiians if they hoped for a more cordial reception. "It [was] true that we had not been particularly told to preach to the natives of these islands," Cannon observed, "but we were in their midst, [and] had full authority to declare unto them the message of salvation."[16] But to take this bold step they must learn the language. Although none of the Mormons ever said as much, the clear success of the Congregationalists may also have influenced their decision.

Be that as it may, by 19 January, the decision was made. Bigler, Cannon, and Keeler embarked upon an intensive study of Hawaiian. Within three weeks, twenty-three-year-old Cannon began to grasp the language, particularly, he reported, after a "miraculous" experience. One evening while attempting to converse with some Hawaiians, he felt "an uncommonly great desire" to understand them, felt a "peculiar sensation" in his ears, and could thereafter understand the language. Bigler and Keeler, who were present, reportedly expressed a belief that Cannon had received the gift of tongues, as promised believers in the New Testament.[17] Whether by a miracle or simply as the result of hard work, Cannon became so proficient that he later translated the Book of Mormon into Hawaiian.

For Henry Bigler the language came much more slowly. Although he apparently had been struggling with the language since January 1851, Bigler first mentioned his difficulties with Hawaiian in a letter to fellow missionary William Farrer on 26 June 1852: "I am increasing in the language thank the Lord." A year later, he lamented privately in his diary: "I never can speak fluently [and] I cannot understand readily what a native sayes when speaking."

Obviously his slow progress was not from lack of desire. He so grieved, sometimes, that it seemed "as if my heart strings would burst." He concluded that "to get this language quick it requires young elders say from 20 to 25 or 6 years of age . . . the youngest have always went a hed & I think it is a hard task for old heads to get it."[18] Bigler was then thirty-six.

By mid-January 1851, the missionaries' funds were exhausted. They decided that each man should "shift for himself" and selected districts by drawing lots. Bigler got the southern portion; but as he was leaving, the other Mormons stopped him with the happy news that they "had got a place for all of us free of charge and to be fed for nothing besides." A native woman, Na Lima Nui, offered them food and shelter and language instruction, an invitation the three Mormons accepted as providential.[19]

Despite this good fortune, the soul-wrenching trial and disappointment continued. Some elders on other islands left their mission, not only discouraged by the lack of results and the difficulty of the language but also feeling that they had fulfilled Rich's instructions of seasonal preaching to the Caucasian population. The sorely disenchanted Mormon missionaries were John Dixon, who had been laboring on Kauai, and Clark's companion, Thomas Whittle. On 24 January 1851, Clark recalled Cannon to Honolulu to act as his companion; but when he saw Cannon's proficiency in Hawaiian, he told the young man to return to Lahaina and sent along William Farrer, a thirty-year-old native of England, as Bigler's new companion.[20] Hiram Blackwell, who had been working with Elder Hawkins on the island of Hawaii, left a few weeks later. Each of these three cited Charles Rich's charge about spending the winter in Hawaii to justify their departures. By that fall Bigler and Farrer had relocated to Oahu, leaving Cannon and Keeler on Maui. Hawkins was apparently alone on Hawaii.

Less than a month later, on 21 February 1851, Clark came unexpectedly to Maui to urge the four missionaries to join him in a more promising field. He told them he had recently baptized a printer named Blake, from the Marquesas Islands northeast of the Society Islands group. The two had decided to return—Blake to print Mormon tracts and Clark to proselyte. "We listened to his talk," wrote Bigler, "but could not coinside with his views and said we were sent to these Islands and to no other."[21] Clark left alone—there is no record that Blake accompanied him; and by April 1851, only Bigler, Cannon, Keeler, Farrer, and Hawkins remained in Hawaii.[22]

Elder Phillip B. Lewis, forty-seven years old, and several new missionaries arrived at Honolulu in September 1851. Lewis had been called by apostle Parley P. Pratt, then the supervisor of all LDS Pacific missions, to serve as the new mission president. By February 1853 Bigler happily reported the arrival of "several Elders from Utah," including Francis A. Hammond, John S. Woodbury, William McBride, Ephraim Green, James Lawson, Reddick N. Allred, Edgerton Snider, Thomas Karren, and Benjamin F. Johnson.[23]

The combination of departures, mobility, and intensive language study which reduced the Mormon missionaries' public profile led the Reverend Dwight Baldwin to conclude that the Mormons had conceded the field: "When the Mormons first came to Lahaina . . . they made great efforts among foreigners only—but never made but one convert. From that time on, for nearly one year, they disappeared from Lahaina, working in the region of Wailuku, Kula, Koolau, etc." Baldwin wrote off the few converts as a "vile sort" who had already been excommunicated from the Congregational Church for living, "as we supposed," in a licentious way.[24] But when Baldwin discovered his mistake, the Congregationalists moved to protect their flock with the same zeal they had shown at the arrival of the French Catholic missionaries.

Behind both the Mormon determination and the Congregationalist protectiveness shines an honorable commitment to their own faiths as the pure gospel of Jesus Christ and a burning belief that the souls of innocent Hawaiians stood in jeopardy—not only from their native religions but also from the "false" doctrines of the other Christian group. From that perspective, the selflessness and sacrifice of both groups command respect. Religious competition, however, is seldom an edifying spectacle, involving as it almost invariably does strong competitiveness, uncharitable claims and counterclaims, and escalations toward force—even violence.

For example, in December 1850, shortly after his arrival in the islands, Farrer harshly criticized the preaching of the Reverend Samuel Chenery Damon at the Honolulu Seaman's Chapel for never explaining "any principle or doctrine" and dismissed it as "a dry mess." On Maui just a few weeks later, Keeler called Baldwin a purveyor of "priestcraft and darkness."[25] Bigler's diary does not contain similar verbal condemnations of the rival missionaries, but given the strongly polarized positions of the times, it seems likely that he would have shared his colleagues' views.

In March 1851, Cannon and Keeler established themselves further east on Maui near Wailuku, a fertile area blessed by constant ocean breezes. The Congregationalist mission station there had been established in 1832 and was currently manned by the Reverend Daniel Toll Conde, a forty-four-year-old evangelist who had been in the islands since 1836. After exchanging social pleasantries, the sparring began. Although the account we have is from Cannon and, hence, one-sided, Conde, formerly a resident of upstate New York, apparently felt well informed about Mormonism and briskly informed Cannon that it was impossible to countenance "anything about revelation these days." At his next Sunday service, which Cannon, Keeler, and Bigler attended, Conde "commenced upon Mormonism," accusing Joseph Smith of being a "notoriously bad character" who pretended to see angels, lived with many wives, and was a "very wicked man." Cannon confronted Conde after the sermon, defended Joseph Smith, and demanded a retraction. The minister refused.[26]

Bigler also tested his mettle against representatives of rival denominations. By September 1851, Bigler and Farrer had moved to the island of Oahu, where they worked separately to increase their productivity. Both men now spoke sufficient Hawaiian that they felt at ease with this arrangement. Bigler lived at Kaneohe, about fifteen miles northeast of Honolulu. Kaneohe, a well-watered and fertile area, was separated from the capital city by the barrier of the *pali*, a precipice off which Kamehameha's army had driven his foes during the 1795 battle for control of the islands. Farrer was usually at Waialua, a farming and grazing district on Oahu's northwest shore. Although about twenty miles apart as the crow flies, meeting required a trek around the entire northern and eastern portion of the island, approximately the route followed today by state highway 83.[27]

In January 1853, Bigler visited Farrer at Waialua and observed that the Protestant and Catholic missionaries had established fine meetinghouses not more than two miles from one another. When the Hawaiians informed Bigler and Farrer that the Catholic priest was claiming the Mormons were afraid to see him, the two elders promptly "gave his holiness a call."[28] The priest, a Frenchman, spoke no English, so the men conversed in Hawaiian. The unnamed Catholic initially treated the Mormons with courtesy, even offering them a meal, but refused to allow them to preach in his meetinghouse.[29]

The next day, Bigler and Farrer called on the Reverend John S. Emerson, who had served at the Congregationalist mission station at Waialua periodically since 1832. A native of New Hampshire, he taught a practical form of religion which incorporated Calvinism with training in advanced agricultural methods. So persuasive a missionary was he that, according to his colleagues, "in no part of the Islands had the people been more in the habit of reading the Scriptures than at Waialua," where they "read the entire Bible through once in [every] three years."[30] He was also a relentless protector of his flock, denouncing Mormonism in the bluntest of terms. When Bigler and Farrer called on him, he received them coldly and charged the Mormons with teaching "a distorted doctrine of the bible and [being] from the devil." He "utterly refused" the Mormons' request to preach in his meetinghouse and "accused us of coming to these islands to divide the Church of Christ."[31]

Undeterred, Bigler recorded in his journal on 4 February: "We held two meetings [and] had full attendance notwithstanding the opposition of the two priests." Within the next two weeks, they baptized six converts. Then the Catholic priest paid them a call. He told the Mormon elders that "he believed we wanted to do right but we were in error and he thought he could convert us and make Catholic priests of us." When that ploy utterly failed, the clergyman went directly to Emerson's house to urge him "to use his influence with the people to warn them about the Mormons."[32] Despite this unusual coalition between Catholic and Congregationalist, Bigler noted with unconcealed satisfaction a few days later that they had established a Mormon branch "rite under the noses of both catholic and protestant priests."[33]

The next conflict occurred in March 1853, when Emerson attacked Bigler on the issue of plural marriage, accusing Brigham

Young of having more than one wife. Bigler denied the accusation, averring that the Mormons were being "basely slandered."[34] The next month, Emerson renewed the attack. This time he confronted Bigler's new companion, Thomas Karren, one of nine missionaries who had been called in August 1852 in Salt Lake City and who had arrived in Honolulu in February 1853. Bigler and Karren called on Emerson on 17 April. Emerson summarized this encounter in his 1853 station report:

> To [Karren] I again put the question, if they did not believe in polygamy & practice it. To which he said yes with great earnestness. He also said it was a doctrine of the Bible, & a practice approved by God, from the time of Abraham & Solomon down to the present time. I then asked the other Mormon [Bigler], who, only one month before, had denied the existence of such a doctrine among them, what all this meant! & what do you think was his reply, "O this is a new revelation, I did not know it before, but you will see more surprising things than these."[35]

This instance is a revealing example of the depth of Henry Bigler's commitment to Mormonism. Bigler had not been in Salt Lake City since 1849 and could truthfully say he had no personal knowledge of the practice of plural marriage which had been publicly disclosed at Salt Lake City in 1852; however, it seems highly unlikely that he had not at least heard rumors of polygamy. Bigler was, by every measure available to a researcher, a man of flawless integrity and unswerving truthfulness in his personal life, yet it seems difficult to escape the conclusion that he was willing to withhold the full truth—as in the initial attack on Brigham Young—then use the principle of continuing revelation as a defense of the church in this partisan attack. He seems to have felt that the good of the church justified less than total candor.

By the end of April, Karren had become "perfectly discouraged" at his seeming inability to learn the language and had returned to Honolulu. Bigler was alone once more. He was sorry to see Karren go for, in Bigler's opinion, Karren, also a Mormon Battalion veteran, was "zealous and good company."[36]

At Kaneohe, Bigler's primary adversary was the Reverend Benjamin Wyman Parker, whom he described as "a bitter opposer against the truth." Parker and his wife had presided over the Protestant mission station at Kaneohe since 1834. In late March, Bigler called on Parker, and they had a heated discussion about polygamy. A few days later, Bigler recorded a dream in which he was molding gold bullets and discussing Mormonism with "Mr. Parker's wife and daughter." The daughter, Mary, must have intrigued the lonely Bigler. In his dream, Bigler asked Mary "if she would like to marry a man who that could make gold bullits." He could not remember the reply.[37] There are no further details about either the dream or the women in Bigler's diary, but perhaps the still-unmarried Bigler wanted to believe that eighteen-year-old Mary Safford Parker was interested in a step that would have moved them into the same religious circle.

On 15 April Bigler returned to Waialua following a brief absence and found a funeral in process for an acquaintance named Koa, who had recently told Bigler that he and his wife "ment to be baptised." Bigler called on Koa's parents and obtained Koa's birth date and place, which he noted in his diary so "when the time cums for this people to be baptised for their dead that he may be remembered."[38]

During the spring and summer of 1853, a smallpox epidemic swept the islands, beginning about May in Honolulu. Bigler first became aware of the disease when Hawaiians at Kahaluu, northeast of Honolulu, expressed fear of him as a carrier of the sickness on 12 July. Clearly, they associated the disease with *haole* immigrants. The following week, he visited the neighboring village of Puheemiki, which had already suffered several deaths and many current cases. At about the same time, he received a letter from William Farrer in Honolulu informing him "the Smallpox [was] so bad that they had not been able to hold any meetings."[39]

Henry Bigler was deathly afraid of the disease and "dreaded to go near where it was." Yet he unflinchingly continued to visit the sick, performing the healing ordinance of blessing by the laying on of hands when requested. On 20 July 1853 he noted in his diary, "Came to Puheemiki learn that the Small pox is bad here, several has died among [them] is one of our sisters, and several natives is lieing low with it." Two days later he wrote a stirring account of the human plight of the victims:

I went to see Sister Dennis [a native woman who belonged to the church] who is very low with the small pox and I never seen any person in all my life hardly that I felt so sorry for as I did hur . . . I am afraid she will never recover she was a awful sight to look at and my soul was filled with pity for hur.

. . . I was called in to look at a sick boy with the small pox. this exceeded anything I have seen yet the stench was all most intolerable and he seamed to be a perfect mass of corruption from head to foot. Poor little fellow how I felt for him.[40]

The smallpox epidemic of 1853 took over 2,400 Hawaiian lives before it finally ran its course. Oahu was by far the hardest hit of the islands. J. W. Smith, a Protestant missionary on Kauai, gratefully reported, "The Small Pox, which produced such frightful ravages on Oahu, passed over us very lightly." Mormon theology remained a comfort to Bigler, despite the frightful suffering he witnessed during this plague. As the incidents cited above demonstrate, Bigler was very moved by the suffering he witnessed on Oahu. Still, his deep faith saw him through the crisis. "Perhaps," he wrote of the LDS victims, "they are taken for a wise purpose in the Lord."[41]

On 7 January 1854 Henry Bigler, for some unknown reason, offered his assessment of the work in the Hawaiian Islands for Brigham Young, Heber C. Kimball, and Willard Richards, then the First Presidency of the church. "Prejudice has been great but it is giveing way and we are gaining influence all the time," Bigler wrote, perhaps out of a sense of obligation or of pride, then added cautiously: "Yet there seems to be much to be done among this people before they are redeemed from all their former practices we did hope that the work could all be done on these islands in a fiew years but it seames that it is only well started."[42]

He does not express any weariness in the work nor any desire to return home, though surely the subject had been on his mind. Most days Bigler's mind was entirely upon the task at hand, yet he occasionally got sidetracked for at least a moment. For example, on 24 July 1853, he observed, "Today all day my mind is in the valley and with the brethren at Lahaina. 6 years ago today since the brethren first entered the Great Salt Lake Valley it was then nothing but a howling wilderness, nothing but the savage, the wolf, the grisley [grizzly bear] could be found and my soul longs to get thare

George Q. Cannon. Used by permission, Utah State Historical Society, all rights reserved.

too."[43] But in typical Bigler fashion, he set these thoughts aside and went out that afternoon with his native companion, Elder Paku, and held two meetings with potential converts. At a missionary conference convened at Honolulu on 24–25 July 1854, Clark's successor, President Phillip B. Lewis, a forty-seven-year-old convert from Massachusetts, offered a motion which Henry Bigler recorded in his diary with understandable joy: "that the following elders be honorably released from this mission to return to their homes in the vallies of the mountains, namely George Q. Cannon, James Keeler, William Farrer, James Hawkins, and myself."[44] Three days later, the returning elders engaged passage for San Francisco on the steamship *Polynesian*. The tickets were fifty dollars each. "We did not have the money," Bigler wrote in his journal, "but we had faith that it would be forthcoming."[45]

So, one year after he had pondered returning to the valley, it became a reality for Bigler. One month earlier Bigler had picked up some mail in Honolulu which certainly moved his thoughts to home and family: "Recd a letter from Geo. A. Smith dated at Salt Lake City April 27th stating that my father and family was well also that Father John Smith was not expected to live."[46] Before adjourning the conference, all the elders retired to a private room to hold a "blessing meeting," laying hands on one another's heads in turn and petitioning God in each other's behalf. Thomas Karren's benediction upon George Q. Cannon especially impressed Bigler, who recorded its promise during the 1890s: "Brother George, the Lord has His eye on you and thou wilt be called to fill an important station in this Church of which you know not, yea a high office in the Church and kingdom of God." At the same time, Bigler also recorded a dream Cannon had reported to him at Slap Jack Bar in 1848. Cannon had seen himself in a room with Brigham Young and the Twelve Apostles, who were about to set him apart to an important calling.[47] This promise was literally fulfilled when Cannon was ordained first an apostle in 1860 and a member of the First Presidency in 1873.

Although Bigler does not say how, the necessary funds for their tickets materialized. As he watched Honolulu disappear behind him in August 1854, he felt satisfied with the time he had spent in the Sandwich Islands. With much effort he had mastered

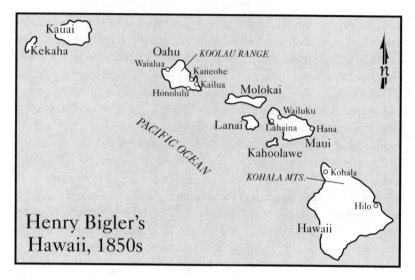

Henry Bigler's
Hawaii, 1850s

a difficult foreign language, and almost three thousand Hawaiians had embraced Mormonism. Yet there had been personal satisfactions that transcended these institutional achievements. As Bigler remembered it over forty years later, "We were followed to the wharf by a crowd of Saints and friends where a long shake of hands ensued, money would be given to us or left in our hands. There were many tears and I confess that the parting struck me in a tender place. . . . We [were] instruments in the hands of God to bring them to a knowledge of the Gospel and now have not only many Saints but friends."[48]

7

MARRIAGE AND RETURN TO HAWAII
1855-58

This morning . . . previous to my departure I laid my hands on my wife and child and little boy and blessed and dedicated them to the Lord after which I immediately left not knowing when I would see them again.[1]

*I*n San Francisco, Henry Bigler and his fellow missionaries reported to Parley P. Pratt, an apostle, then presiding over the missionary work in California and the Pacific Isles. Pratt generously gave them the hospitality of his lodgings while they looked for work to earn outfits to take them back to Salt Lake City. Also in San Francisco was apostle Amasa Lyman, who, along with apostle Charles C. Rich, was then presiding at the Mormon colony of San Bernardino in southern California. He advised them to stay in northern California until spring, when a Mormon company would leave for Utah.

Obediently following Lyman's counsel, Henry Bigler asked advice about work from Moses A. Meder, a Latter-day Saint who had lived in the area for several years. Meder urged Bigler to go with him to Santa Cruz, where he was certain he could find work. "I did so and worked for a man in the lime burning business," Bigler noted. In March 1855, he returned to San Francisco, where Pratt told him that William McBride was leading a company to Salt Lake City by way of San Bernardino. The party of thirty-seven left northern California on 23 April. It was a sweet journey for Henry Bigler—not only a homecoming but a courtship.

The object of his attentions was Cynthia Jane Whipple, the twenty-year-old daughter of Willard Whipple and Elizabeth Barrows Whipple, originally from Jamestown, New York, who had been living in the Santa Cruz area. McBride had baptized Jane in October 1854 at Santa Clara, California. By coincidence, McBride had earlier served in Hawaii with Bigler and perhaps introduced Henry to Jane. Bigler's diary for the winter does not mention her, but on 30 April 1855, as the wagon train rolled out, he recorded, "Captain McBride lead out in front, in his wagon sit Sister Jane Whipple holding a banner, on it these words, 'Latter day Saints.'"[2] That is his only mention of Jane Whipple until 18 November 1855 when, about four months after arriving in the Great Salt Lake Valley, he carefully penned: "I married Cynthia Jane Whipple at the house of Brother Edson Whipple in Provo."[3] Edson Whipple was the bride's uncle. Jane was twenty, Bigler was forty.

Despite her youth, this was a second marriage for Jane. Born at Jamestown, New York, in 1835, she had married Joseph Dikeman and given birth to a son, named Henry Willard for Jane's father, in June 1850 at Bradford, Pennsylvania, when she was fifteen. At that point, she and Dikeman had been separated for some time, possibly even before the child's birth. The fact that she was using her parents' name, despite the presence of her child, indicates her repudiation of her former marriage. When Bigler married Jane, he adopted five-year-old Henry Willard as his own.

Despite Bigler's silence on the subject of "Sister Jane Whipple," the trail gave him many occasions to observe her and little Willard, to offer morning and evening salutations, to exchange a few sentences of friendly conversation, and to offer a hand with the chores. A man traveling alone was not deemed responsible for his own cooking, and Bigler was almost certainly assigned to another family for meals. The Whipple family, with two women to care for only one man and a child, was a logical campfire at which to welcome Henry Bigler.

The company passed through present Las Vegas, Nevada, in late June 1855, where they found "30 brethren from Salt Lake making a settlement." After a few days' rest for the teams and repairs on wagons, they pushed on north, arriving at Salt Lake City by 20 July, where Henry's father was waiting for him. Bigler had not seen his father in nearly nine years and commented, "He looked very natural, did not look so old as I expected but his voice had changed."[4] Possibly Henry expected an older-looking father because he himself had aged considerably due to hard conditions in Hawaii and California.

Jacob Bigler assured Henry that "the folks were all well and very anxious to see me," welcome words indeed after so long and perilous a separation. The entire family had settled in Farmington, a rural village sixteen miles north of Salt Lake City. The father and son spent Saturday night with George A. Smith; on Sunday, Bigler and the other returning Sandwich Islands missionaries spoke. Brigham Young was in attendance and, much to Bigler's delight, "seemed to be pleased with our report and labors." Then, the Biglers went to Farmington, where Henry was lovingly greeted by his kin "who appeared [as] glad to see me as I was pleased to see them."[5] The family now consisted of Jacob and Sally (Henry's stepmother), and his half-brother, nineteen-year-old Andrew. The three older half-brothers, Adam, Jacob, and Mark, had married (with the exception of Jacob) and established their own households. Henry's full sister, Emeline Bigler Hess, her husband John, and their five children, ages one to seven, lived nearby.

For the next four months Henry lived with his parents in Farmington, a period of modest personal rewards for him. Only two weeks after his arrival, on 4 August 1855, he was set apart as one of the seven presidents of his Thirtieth Quorum of Seventies—a significant ecclesiastical calling likely reflecting his success as a Hawaiian missionary. Later that month he accompanied his half-brothers, Mark and Andrew, as they received their endowments in Salt Lake City's Endowment House and witnessed Andrew's marriage to Loretta Smith.[6] Farmington is sixty-five miles from Provo, but Henry found a way to continue his courtship of Jane. Following their November wedding, the new family of three settled at Farmington in Henry's parental home at first, with "Lil," a cow Henry's father gave them, as a wedding gift.

Farmington, in what is now Davis County, was the Bigler family home for the next twenty years. It had been scouted out as a settlement site in August 1847, less than a month after the Mormons' arrival in the Salt Lake Valley. Captain James Brown, an acquaintance of Bigler's from the Mormon Battalion, led the exploring party, a small detachment of Mormon Battalion soldiers bound for California. They reported that although the area had little wild game it appeared ideal for farming and stock raising. Young kept the first wave of settlers in the Salt Lake Valley, but Isaac Haight, a Mormon herder, led a group of families to the Farmington area in October 1848, then returned to Salt Lake City, leaving his brother Hector to become known as the founder of the community. Farmington, as its name suggests, was a desirable location because of its excellent farm land and abundant water supply, a significant resource in a desert. As an additional lure, many returning Mormon Battalion veterans, including Bigler's brother-in-law, John W. Hess, settled in Farmington. Davis County was named, probably in 1849 or 1850, in memory of Daniel C. Davis, the by then deceased captain of Company E of the battalion. By 1851, four years before Henry and Jane settled there, 280 persons, about 65 families, were living in the county.

Henry records little of that first married winter, whether he was contented or disappointed, whether it was easy or difficult to adjust to a wife after so many years of singleness. He must have been pleased when she became pregnant in February, for his love of children was consistent. In May 1856, when Jane was four months pregnant, they went to the Endowment House in Salt Lake City, where Heber C. Kimball, a counselor to Brigham Young in the church's First Presidency, sealed their union past death and into eternity. On the same day, Jacob and Sally Bigler, and Emeline and John Hess, were also sealed.

In September 1856, Henry and Jane rented a farm from Allen Burke in what is now north Farmington, although they apparently still lived with Jacob and Sally. Bigler sharecropped for Burke, who furnished the team, plow, and seed grain. It seems clear from Bigler's temperament and values that he was a hard and consistent worker, but although he may have helped with the harvest, perhaps for a share, he could not plant until the following spring. They were obviously close to poverty, as indicated by Bigler's grateful notation on 6 September 1856: "Today my wife got a check . . . for Fifteen dollars from her Father; it was quite a surprise but an agreeable one for which we feel thankful." In November the

Whipples sent a load of foodstuffs which included coffee, tea, and sugar—luxuries in Utah—along with five dollars cash—for which Henry and Jane were "very grateful."

Possibly the Whipples were trying to ease Jane's circumstances, for on 4 October 1856 she had given birth to Elizabeth Jane, a multisyllabled name that Bigler consistently uses in full for the infant, though when she was eighteen he began calling her by the affectionate nickname "Lizzie." She weighed a healthy nine pounds, eight ounces. As was the custom, the parents took her to Farmington Ward on 5 February 1857, where Bigler gave her a name and blessing.[7] Henry Bigler seems to have enjoyed family life with Jane, baby Elizabeth Jane, and seven-year-old Willard immensely, for he accepted his next church assignment with bitter regret though unquestioning obedience.

On 28 February 1857, only three weeks after the blessing ceremony for Elizabeth Jane, Bigler met Brigham Young on the road between Farmington and Salt Lake City. Young pulled his carriage up next to Bigler's wagon, told him to prepare for another mission to the Sandwich Islands, and asked him to leave the names of other Hawaiian-speakers at his office. This call tore across the domestic tranquility Bigler had recently been enjoying. But, determinedly, Bigler recorded that he still "felt willing to do anything the Lord required . . . however great the cross mite be."[8] Five weeks later at the April semiannual conference, Bigler noted that "88 missionaries [were] called, eleven of them to go to the Sandwich Islands and the balance to go east."[9] Perhaps some solace to the modest Henry Bigler was his designation as leader of the Hawaii-bound elders, a mark of Young's confidence in him.

On the morning of 14 May 1857, wrenched by grief, Henry Bigler bade farewell to Jane, Willard, and little Elizabeth Jane. His Mormon faith gave him a ritual by which to express his concern and call upon God to protect them. "I laid my hands on my wife and child and little boy and blessed and dedicated them to the Lord," he wrote. It was a patriarchal act that must have been bittersweet for him, to whom such family joys were still new; by the same token, Jane and the children must have been comforted by his invocation of divine power to safeguard them while he was absent. Bigler then resolutely walked out, "not knowing when I would see them again, perhaps not for several years." Sobbing, little Willard ran outside after him. Bigler describes the heartbreaking scene: "I had scarcely got out of the yard when I was overtaken by Willard, his little heart was full and [he] wanted to know how long I would be gone and said, 'Pa maby you will die and I will never see you again,' . . . I told him the Lord wanted me to go and that he must be a good boy and pray for me that I mite live and come home a live."[10]

With these tender feelings, Bigler must have sent the child back to the house and slowly walked away, "looking back occasionally to catch a last glimpse of [my] house." Sorrowfully, once he was out of sight of the house, he found "a suitable place for secret prayer," knelt, and uttered another heartfelt prayer for his family's safety and well-being.[11] Jane needed his prayers. Bigler had been able to plant the crops that spring, but he would not be there for the fall harvest. He does not say whether his father and brothers had agreed to take over the sharecropping arrangement on his behalf. Certainly Henry knew he could count on them to see that Jane and the children were not in actual want and Jane's parents had shown themselves interested in her comfort, even from the distance of Provo. There was no way, however, that the mission would not require sacrifice from them all. He comforted himself when he made his journal entry that night by quoting a locally popular verse that defined the difference between a mere Mormon and a true Saint—"a Saint was always on hand to go at every call made by night or day."[12]

The eleven missionaries traveled with some Mormon herders who were driving 622 head of cattle to the Latter-day Saint settlement at Carson Valley. Bigler and his colleagues helped herd cattle and stand night guard. Uncomplainingly, he recorded on 16 May: "I was on gard last night until midnight and went to bed with cold damp feet and Slep vary uncomfortable." Two days later, he "stood gard from midnight to daylight this morning. To day we drove [the cattle] a bout 20 m. and encampted—dureing the afternoon it rained tho not cold I was wet to the hide. Musquetoes plenty."[13]

According to Bigler's diary, the Sandwich Islands missionaries parted from the drovers on 1 July, in western Nevada's Carson Valley, arriving ten days later at Stockton, California, where "we forthwith engaged our passage to San Francisco on board the Steamer Cornelia for $4 each," arriving the following day.[14] On 14 July, he met Jane's father, Willard Whipple, near San Francisco and accompanied him to Redwood City, several miles south of San Francisco. There Bigler met Jane's brother, Orson, for the first time, and the three men rode about five or six miles out of town to visit Eli Whipple, Willard's younger brother, and his wife, Patience. "I found my wife's uncle & family all well," recorded Bigler with obvious pleasure, "and [they] appeared glad to see their new relative."[15]

The next day, Eli took him to visit some of Jane's friends and to Bear Gulch, "where my wife use[d] to live," apparently before moving to her parents' home in Santa Cruz. In his only written reference to Jane's first husband, Bigler revealingly recorded:

> As I looked and pondered I remembered many things she had told me that had transpired where she lived with hur former husband (Joseph Dikeman) who treated hur more like a brutal person than like a kind husband. My heart melted for Sorrow and pity and never did my wife seem half as near to me as she did at this moment. I was oblige[d] to turn and conceal my feelings.[16]

This entry speaks volumes about Henry Bigler—his assumption that a husband should be kind, how thoroughly his young wife trusted and confided in him, and the depth of his tenderness for her. We do not know what attracted her first to Joseph Dikeman, but surely the simplicity, steadfastness, and sheer human decency of Henry Bigler permanently captured her heart.

Then Bigler stayed with Patience and Eli Whipple at Redwood City for three days (18–22 July). On the last day of their visit, Patience Whipple, whom Bigler observed *"has been* a Sister in the Church," asked Henry if Jane was willing for him to have another wife. "I replyed that she was." Patience promptly retorted that "it was polygamy that had destroyed all the mormonism she ever had." She simply "could not believe it." Bigler challenged her to "throw off all prejudice and seek the Lord in humble prayer." Only then, he said, might she know the truthfulness of the doctrine. It seems that Patience Whipple believed Bigler to have taken up his mission to Polynesia in order to search for a second wife. He was deeply hurt by this false accusation. He anxiously sought to set the record straight by telling her, "I was honest and pure before the Lord so far as getting another wife was concerned."[17]

Bigler's staunch defense of Mormonism's "peculiar principle" is significant for two reasons: first, whether Henry and Jane had specifically discussed the possibility of a plural relationship—and it sounds as if they had—Bigler evidently felt that Jane's faithfulness would, like his own, withstand such a test. Second, Bigler never practiced the principle that was Mormonism's preeminent test and validation; thus, faithfulness alone was not the only consideration for Bigler where this practice was concerned. It is an interesting complexity in one whose unflinching obedience never wavered between conversion and death.

From the time the Hawaii-bound elders arrived in San Francisco until early August, all worked hard to save funds for their mission and taught the Mormon gospel part time in the Bay area. Some, if Bigler was typical, also found time to visit friends or relatives. Bigler rejoined his fellow missionaries in San Francisco, where the Sandwich Islands contingent formed teams with the local elders to preach until their ship departed for Honolulu. Bigler worked with an Elder Wandell[18] in the Santa Cruz-Watsonville area. En route from Santa Cruz for San Francisco to board ship, Bigler paused near Santa Clara on 7 August where his 1855 wagon train had camped. Again, the site was precious to him because of its associations with Jane: "I Stopted and took a good look at the old camp ground where brother Parley [Pratt] had organised a company of Saints to go up to Zion under the direction of Elder McBride," he remembered. As he gazed upon the scene, Bigler was overcome by melancholy and withdrew the likeness of his wife from his pocket. He "cast a look but was compeled to close it and proceed on my way." A haunting loneliness consumed him: "There was no Saints there now and Parley had gone."[19]

Bigler actually preceded the rest of his missionary party, thanks to the intervention of his friend and former missionary colleague, George Q. Cannon, who was then publishing the Mormon newspaper, the *Western Standard*, in San Francisco. When Cannon learned that the clipper *John Laud* was scheduled to leave 22 August for Honolulu, Cannon called the Sandwich Islands missionaries together and proposed that Bigler take it so that he would be in Hawaii by 6 October when an elders' conference was scheduled. All agreed to this recommendation, and Bigler departed with the ship, traveling steerage, an arrangement which required him to sleep in the hold and spend his days on deck. As his journal documents, it was not an enjoyable trip:

> Sunday 23d [August]—Sea sick. could not eat.
>
> Monday 24th—A little better drank some gruel and eat a little. it is cold and disagreeable on deck and even in bed all night my legs was cold not having anything to cover myself with except my coat.
>
> Tuesday 25th—Feel better than I did yesterday eat a little codfish and drank some coffee for breakfast . . . I feel lonesome and thought a good deal about home — got out my wifes letter and read it . . . Pea soup, boiled pork and bread puding for dinner. I done tolerable justice to the pea soup.

Even more seriously, Bigler caught a head cold the next week which resulted in a severe infection in his right ear; untreated, it ruptured the eardrum and damaged the auditory nerve, leaving him deaf.

On 4 September, to his relief, "I found the islands were in sight." The ship dropped anchor in Honolulu harbor later that day. Bigler was "still quite deaf" in his ear, which was constantly ringing. Bigler's arrival was not expected, but due to his prior missionary service in Honolulu, he was not at a loss. "I went a shore and found Elders Silas Smith, Pack, King and Partridge living up stairs in our old meeting house," Bigler recorded. Rest and food made him feel much better, but he was disconcerted by his deafness and by how much Hawaiian he had forgotten. On 6 September, his first Sunday in Honolulu, Bigler met with the local Saints and, upon the request of the Elders, rose to speak. "I tried to Speak to the people to tell them about the times in Utah etc., but I found I was deficient having lost so much of the native language." Bigler and the other elders later visited the Seaman's Bethel and heard the sermon of Reverend Samuel C. Damon, whom Bigler had first met in 1850.[20]

On Monday, Bigler walked by himself to a private spot outside the city, where "I poured out my soul to the Lord for his kind protection & blessings since leaving home and for him to still have mercy on me and help me fill my mission . . . and to bless my little family until his servant should return home and meet them again in the flesh to rejoice together and praise his Holy name." Thus, renewed in commitment, he began to proselyte. On 24 September 1857, John S. Woodbury arrived from San Francisco, the only one of the ten remaining missionaries to come by that ship. "I felt disappointed that none others of the elders were along," Bigler wrote. An even worse disappointment for Bigler was that "a male [*sic*] came but I got no letter."21

When an elders' conference met 4 October 1857 at Honolulu, Silas Smith, who had served as mission president since July 1855, was released, and Bigler was nominated as his successor. It is not clear from extant records whether Brigham Young had intended Bigler to become president. Bigler himself makes no earlier mention of a formal calling to the position, though Cannon's desire to have Bigler in Hawaii by the conference may indicate that he also saw Bigler as the president-to-be. Referring to himself in the third person, Bigler recorded without comment that Smith "tendered his resignation and nominated Henry W. Bigler as his successor which nomination was sustained." It was a weighty calling and also a significant honor, but Bigler never revealed any of his feelings upon assuming this office. Choosing to rely upon men of proven ability, he "then nominated Elder James Keeler (who is expected soon from the [West] coast) as his first councillor and John S. Woodbury as his second councillor." The elders then listened to reports from representatives from each island. It became painfully clear that Bigler was taking over an ailing mission; Mormonism in Hawaii had stagnated. Bigler recorded the bleak facts precisely in his journal: total membership stood at 3,192—roughly the same number as when Bigler had left three years earlier. Maui was the stronghold of Hawaiian Mormonism with 1,165 members. Next was the Kohala district on Hawaii with 692. Oahu could claim 371. Hopefully, Bigler speculated that "so many [of the Hawaiian Saints] have moved from place to place since being baptized that they are lost track of and hence are not represented as faithful members."22 This attempt at optimism could not, however, hide his concern. Since 1856 the Mormon ranks had been dwindling.

Particularly disappointing was the situation on Lanai. In August 1854 Elder Ephraim Green had moved to the Palawai Basin on Lanai with the intention of establishing a Mormon community that could act as a temporary local "Zion," or gathering place for the native Saints, a suggestion of Brigham Young's. Matters looked promising that year and the next, since July 1855 saw the high point of Mormon success to that point—4,650 members.[23]

Bigler presided over the strategy session which followed the reports. "The subject of gathering was taken up," he wrote, "and all seemed to feel in consideration of the many failures at Lanai that it would be adviseable to select one or more other places where the Saints may be gathered with less difficulty."[24]

Although Bigler spent much of his time mentally, physically, and spiritually wrestling with what he described as the "dwindled away and withered up" state of Hawaiian Mormonism,[25] the temporary decline in Mormonism's popularity is more accurately seen as a combination of factors. First, Hawaiian nationalism began to reflower during the 1850s, involving a rejection of Anglo-Christian religious values, particularly the Puritanical tenets of Calvinism that forbade drinking, gambling, dancing, and traditional religion. By the late 1860s and early 1870s, much of the restructured Hawaiian society that the Protestant mission had been creating since the 1820s fell into disarray.

To revitalize Hawaiian Mormonism, Henry Bigler suggested a reformation similar to that which had rekindled the fires of commitment among Utah Mormons, 1856–57. As in Utah, the purposes of the reformation would be to stem the tide of apostasy and to rebuild faith among the local Mormons. Church members in Utah had reaffirmed their commitment by openly confessing their sins, being rebaptized, and striving to live religious laws more exactly. The Hawaiian elders, Bigler recorded at the end of that long day's conference, unanimously concluded to "endeavor to introduce the Spirit of the reformation among the native Saints."[26]

No doubt the new president was pleased by this resolve, but his journal the next day includes a note of private wistfulness. He sent "2 little gold coins to [Jane] & our little daughter who is one year old this morning" with the missionaries departing for San Francisco, whom he described as "five spirits bound for their mountain home." He escorted the missionaries to the boat and then returned to the lodgings, feeling "lonesome and homesick." Stoically he added that he felt "oblige[d] to throw it off and not allow myself to think about it."[27]

On Sunday, 11 October, Bigler preached at a meeting attended by fifteen or sixteen, sadly recording that in 1854 this congregation had included over sixty members of good standing. In the past three years, however, the native Mormons had heard many glowing promises about a printing press of their own or a ship that would take them to Utah. Disappointingly, neither of these plans ever materialized, leaving their confidence in Mormonism badly bruised. Furthermore, John Hyde, Jr., a talented British convert who had been called as a missionary in May 1856, had reached Honolulu as an ardent anti-Mormon, probably because of his exposure to polygamy in Utah. He joined forces with the Protestant clergy in Honolulu to attack the Latter-day Saints and published an eighteen-page pamphlet in Hawaiian that circulated widely. At least one prominent native convert, J. W. H. Kauwahi, joined Hyde in spreading disaffection.[28] According to Bigler, "the faith of the native Saints is gone." He felt as if he was "preaching to the walls," local commitment was at so low an ebb.[29]

Not only did he feel responsible for the spiritual life of the struggling mission, but Bigler, as mission president, now had to assume responsibility for its debts as well. On Tuesday, 13 October 1857, he reported: "Made some inquiries for work to rase means to pay off the church debts . . . Elder Woodbury is getting up a school teaching the natives & a few chinese english for the same purpose." Bigler worked at various odd jobs to pay off the Church's debts in Hawaii almost until the day he left the mission in 1858. For example, in 9 December 1857, Bigler wrote, "Today I commenced to work a month for a Mr. William Duncan," "underpinning" or bracing the foundation of Duncan's house.[30]

The hoped-for reformation never caught fire, possibly due to increasing cultural resistance on the part of the Hawaiians. Many of them, doubtless including some former Mormons, now flatly rejected anything associated with Anglo-European dominance. Bigler, with a limited understanding of this profound resistance, regularly wrote the other elders encouraging them to try harder. For example, on 13 and 14 November, he sent Fred A. Mitchell, then working in Kohala, Hawaii, instructions to answer his questions "on the subject of reformation" and similar instructions on how to institute the reformation to William B. Wright on Kauai. But mid-nineteenth century Hawaii was simply not reformation-oriented Utah.[31]

Even as internal forces were checking Bigler's efforts in Hawaii, external events were drawing the curtain on Mormon proselyting in the Sandwich Islands and elsewhere. On 28 May 1857, while Bigler had been crossing western Nevada on his way to Honolulu via San Francisco, President James Buchanan had ordered U.S. Army troops to march into Utah, put down a reported rebellion, and wrest control of the territorial government from a reportedly tyrannical and hostile Brigham Young. In September 1857, Colonel Albert Sidney Johnston had taken command of the 2,500 troops which, by then, had reached the vicinity of Fort Laramie, Wyoming.

As Johnston's army approached, Brigham Young, preaching a stern line of military resistance, mobilized the Nauvoo Legion (Utah Territorial Militia), declared martial law, and ordered the blockade of Echo Canyon. Meanwhile, his people made preparations to defend themselves. On 7 January 1858, Bigler reported local rumors "in a Gentile paper" about the federal government's intent to "crush" the supposed rebellion in Utah and "punish its infamous leaders."[32]

These rumors confirmed an official communication Bigler had already received. On 4 September, Brigham Young had written to Bigler: "The United States evidently have commenced a war with us, and are determined to put an end to us or our religion." The letter closed the mission and ordered all of the elders to return "as soon as possible." Rather surprisingly, however, Young did not cite security but missionary inadequacy as his reasons for closing the mission. He had heard that missionary work in Hawaii was "dead or dying. . . . If there are faithful Saints there they are experienced enough in the work to enable them to stand firm in the faith, while those who are filled with the lusts of the flesh will float off with the current and if at any future time it should be thought wisdom to renew the work there, the Church will flourish more rapidly through the testimony of those who are faithful to their God."[33]

Bigler and Woodbury immediately sent out letters to the presiding elders on each island which contained carefully selected extracts from Young's communique of 4 September. "We wish the mission debt paid up as soon as possible," wrote Bigler and Woodbury. The Mormon elders were told to prepare for a "sudden change of affairs in the mission," but not to discuss this matter in public because it would almost certainly disrupt the effects of missionary work. Without fully acknowledging the rumors of war, they told the Hawaiian elders to "persue a strait forward course until you hear from us again, which will not be long."[34]

It is not clear why Bigler gave his missionaries only partial information, since such a course could only heighten their anxiety. Perhaps his own mixed feelings about abandoning the local Saints had something to do with it. On 27 November, as promised a week earlier, Bigler and Woodbury wrote to the mission leaders again:

We [say] to the Elders one & all, let us wind up our business as soon as possible on these Islands, and then we will call a conference, . . . As you have opportunity it will be well to lay these things before the native Saints and let them know what is up, that this nation is rejecting the message of the Elders and the Lord is going to take his servants from among them. You might translate the copy of br. Brigham's letter and read it to them with such suitable instructions on it as you think proper, also incourage the Saints to wake up & live faithful to their God, and those who are alive to their duties to continue in well doing.[35]

About a week later, on 3 December 1857, he and John S. Woodbury reported somewhat anxiously to Brigham Young:

Upon receiving [Young's November letter] we wrote to all the presiding Elders . . . to wind up and set in order the branches and then turn their attention to raising money and means in some honorable way to pay up the Church debt which is yet due $140.
. . . If you have any counsel for us it will be thankfully received for as yet we have nothing only what we have seen in your letter.[36]

Less than three weeks later, on 23 December, Bigler and Woodbury wrote Brigham Young again: "We are endeavoring to carry out your Counsel to the best of our ability. . . . The work is at a low ebb on these Islands. It seems that those who profess the name of Saints . . . have lost their first love and we can scarcely get them to attend meetings . . . we have been preaching reformation in this place of Sin and corruption but as yet the Saints have not waked up."[37]

Thus, although Bigler may have felt concern about abandoning the Saints, he confirmed to Brigham Young that the spiritual apathy of the Saints was acute and, by inference, that Young's reason for ordering the abandonment of the mission was accurate. Tellingly, neither the first letter nor the second asked Young to confirm the war rumors, even though Bigler's journal during January contained reports every few days about the military situation and he frequently expresses worry about the security of Jane and his children.

Ironically, on 7 January 1858 Bigler reported attending a meeting in which many Hawaiian members confessed their sins and wanted to renew their covenant of baptism. "Some were melted down like children," he noted, "and I felt for them and felt to bless them in the name of the Lord for they manifested a good Spirit." Twenty-two native Saints were rebaptized that day. However, Brigham Young's will coincided with his own; he wanted to be home. That same day, he recorded a newspaper report that the Mormons would soon abandon Utah and move to Sonora, Mexico. Although he does not make explicit mention of his experiences in Missouri and Illinois, no doubt they were on his mind.

On 4 February, Brigham Young, who would have barely received Bigler's and Woodbury's second letter, dictated official instructions which Bigler received on 20 April: "You are all, without regard as to when you were sent [to Hawaii], counselled to start for home." For the first time, Young supplied information about the war: Johnston's army was in winter camp at Fort Bridger, Wyoming, and "we are taking active measures to be in readiness for any movements they may chose to make when spring opens."[38] In the intervening eleven weeks, the Saints had evacuated northern Utah and none were dwelling north of Provo.[39]

Bigler promptly convened a final conference five days later. No one spoke for remaining, but all unanimously agreed "to return home as quickly as possible." Despite reformation efforts, membership stood at 3,068, 124 fewer members than at Bigler's first conference six months earlier. The Maui report that Bigler recorded in his journal on 25 April could have stood as a description of the entire mission: "The majority of the Saints are in a backward state & indifferent to the privileges they enjoy." Both duty and desire were calling them home. With the history of the Missouri and Nauvoo expulsions behind them, fear for their families drawing them on, and with Brigham Young's face-saving lead to follow, the missionaries had few incentives not to paint Hawaiian prospects in the bleakest terms—but reality was certainly bleak enough.

The next important consideration was whether to close the mission or call a local member as president, an option Brigham Young had left open in his letter of 4 February. Bigler polled the other elders. "After some discussion it was moved & carried that only presidents of conferences be appointed," Bigler noted in his record.[40] Consequently, the native congregations on Lanai, Kauai, Oahu, Maui, and Hawaii were left in the hands of trustworthy local leaders until such time as an official Latter-day Saint presence might return to Hawaii.

In accordance with Young's earlier directions, five of the missionaries departed from Honolulu for Utah on 9 December 1857, while the rest concentrated on earning their passage home. On 20 April 1858 Bigler and Woodbury received a letter from Brigham Young dated on 4 February, expressing pleasure "that so many of the Elders had already sailed." He again urged the remaining elders to "start for home as speedily as you can wind up your affairs and obtain passage money." Upon the receipt of this letter Bigler called the elders together and directed that "all the Elders from Utah now on these islands [be] released and return home to the valleys of the mountains." On 29 April 1858 he and Woodbury delivered some parting counsel to the anxious Saints in Honolulu. Privately, Bigler confided that "I felt sorrow for them for they seamed as though they would feel lonesome after we were all gone."[41] That same day the remaining five missionaries secured passage on the bark *Yankee*, due to sail a week later.

Bigler spent his final days in Hawaii trying to clear up the remaining mission debts, attempting (unsuccessfully) to sell their supply of Book of Mormon copies, and making personal preparations. On 30 April, the night before sailing, a local couple named Wing hosted the five departing missionaries at a farewell *luau,* and gave them ten dollars to divide among themselves—a donation which Bigler felt was "vary liberal."[42]

On his way to the wharf the next morning, Bigler stopped by a butcher shop and, out of curiosity, weighed himself. He had not recorded his weight before leaving Utah, but now he weighed a meager 130 pounds. As a final insult, the police, under pretense of searching for some stolen money, rifled their trunks. "Not another man on bord was searched, except one," Bigler recorded indignantly, "and there was some 30 passengers." The captain later said he "did not know our trunks had been searched," which Bigler accepted as a sort of apology, and ordered the steward to give them unlimited sugar in place of the molasses he had provided to sweeten their coffee. Since the steward had made it known that sugar was available at a price, Bigler was again gratified by this mark of respect. They also preached at the request of the passengers, and their message was received cordially. Unfortunately, the captain could do little about their accommodations. Once again, they were forced to travel steerage, "the horriblest stinking place I ever was in," wrote Bigler as they boarded on 1 May. "I had not been there 2 minutes before I was seasick."[43]

The Protestant missionaries noted their departure with satisfaction. The 1858 Congregationalist mission station report from Hana, Maui, declared, "Mormonism is at a low ebb. All its foreign Elders left for Salt Lake." From Hilo, Hawaii, the 1859 annual report read, "As for the Mormons the Salt Lake war seems to have scattered them. I have not seen a Mormon priest or prophet for the past year."[44] Latter-day Saint missionaries would not return to the islands until 1864, but into this vacuum stepped Walter Murray Gibson, a usurper, who assumed unofficial authority over the native Saints in September 1861. Ironically, the very faithfulness of the loyal Saints and their anxiety for the return of Utah elders made them susceptible to his claims. He settled on Lanai, organized the Saints into an unpaid labor force, and concentrated on enriching himself, alternately promising spiritual rewards and threatening damnation to keep the Hawaiian Mormons docile.

When the long-suffering Saints finally sent reports of his conduct to Brigham Young and missionaries again came from Salt Lake City in 1864, Gibson was excommunicated.[45]

The *Yankee* docked in San Francisco on 19 May, and on 21 May, Bigler and Woodbury wrote their last mission report to Brigham Young: "While at the Islands we done our best to carry out your council. The mission debt is paid, the books [Book of Mormon copies and missionary tracts] boath native and English we nailed up in boxes and left them in care of the natives . . . It was the best we could do not being able to obtain a suitable place without paying rent."[46]

While Bigler's second mission to Hawaii was clearly not as rewarding as the first, he had once more shown his willingness to sacrifice personal preference, convenience, and profit at the call of his ecclesiastical leaders. Although he was returning to a turbulent and frightened Utah, the next eighteen years would be the first, and only, extensive period since his conversion that Henry Bigler's life was fully his own.

FAMILY AND FARMING
1859–76

This afternoon my daughter had a fine son weighing eleven pounds. Got a letter from my little boys saying they wanted to come home. I sent them money and told them to take the cars and come home.[1]

aiting for Bigler at the San Francisco post office was a welcome letter from Jane. She reported that "the Soldiers are at [Ft.] Bridger and sware they will be coming in and that the Church has got to leave and is going into the Deserts."[2] Her father had reached Utah "sometime last winter" from San Bernardino and had moved her and the children from Farmington to Provo "about the first of April" in response to Brigham Young's order that the northern counties be evacuated. "I was glad to hear this and learn that they were all well," Bigler noted with obvious relief. According to Jane, "the Church have got to move again that they were preparing for it now."[3]

In May 1858 Bishop John W. Hess of the Farmington Ward, Bigler's brother-in-law, began the evacuation of Farmington. Most of the ward relocated near Juab County's Willow Creek in central Utah between present-day Mona and Nephi, while some residents, like Willard Whipple and his daughter, Jane, went only as far south as Provo or Springville.[4] Echoing the defiant rhetoric of Mormon leaders, Jane told her husband that the Mormons intended to frustrate a plundering army by laying "all the settlements in ashes, and not leave a single thing." Ardently, she closed her letter: "O I shall be glad now when you get home. May you be preserved from your enemies and return in peace is my prayer."[5] Bigler did not give the date of Jane's letter but internal evidence dates it to early April. Although he must have longed to press on quickly to Utah, he had to remain in the San Jose area until August while he earned enough money to outfit himself for the journey.[6]

Polygamy, the rigorous personal rule of Brigham Young, and the harsh landscape of the Great Basin had all operated since 1847 to separate the Mormon wheat from the tares. The military threat of Johnston's army was frightening away still others while creating new solidarity among those who remained. Bigler, as he traveled through California, encountered a significant number of unhappy Saints who had escaped Utah for various reasons. "Verry little of the Spirit of Mormonism" existed among the San Francisco Bay area Saints, Bigler wrote. At San Jose he encountered a man named Beers who, with his brother and their wives, had, in Bigler's words, become "disaffected" and "abandoned" the Rocky Mountain Zion. About twenty-five miles south in Watsonville he met Brothers Lyman Hutchens and John Baldwin. They were, noted Bigler, "in partnership in building a brewery for making beer." Mournfully Bigler repeated his judgment from San Francisco: "Very little of the Spirit of Mormonism seem[s] to be a bout them." Baldwin claimed "he would have to be damned & go to hell" before returning to the Salt Lake Valley.[7]

Also near Watsonville, Bigler met a couple named Wilcox who found fault with Brigham Young. Bigler indignantly recorded Mrs. Wilcox's criticism: "Mormonism was all rite but [Young] was not exactly what he ought to be, . . . a poor person might go to Brigham and ask him for a little sugar . . . for a sick person in the family and like as not they would be told to go to work and get it if they wanted any, that Bro. Joseph [Smith] never done that way, always give to the poor when he had it and never turned them away." Bigler defended Young as "liberal to the poor and sick saints" yet "down on those who are lazy."[8] When he later met another family heading to California, he concluded, without documenting his reasons, that they also "must be disaffected Mormons."[9]

Earnestly Bigler urged repentance and encouraged these one-time Mormons to return to the fold. Just before he left the Bay

Brigham Young, ca. 1860s. Courtesy of the Archives, Church of Jesus Christ of Latter-day Saints.

area, Hutchins and Baldwin assured Bigler that they planned to return to Zion, but they "do not want to go this year." John Baldwin flatly informed Bigler that he did not relish "wading up to his arms in the snow to get a little fire wood" during the winter. Bigler laughed and reminded him, "Brigham said that Salt Lake was the greatest country in the world for makeing Saints."[10]

Such faithlessness deeply saddened Henry Bigler, who willingly embraced the nineteenth-century Mormon vision of Zion. Whatever the personal chafings that had made California more appealing than Utah to these former Saints, he could not understand such thinking. Sacrifice, labor, and obedience to ecclesiastical authority were the cornerstones of Henry Bigler's religion—and his religion was his life. He had no image of an existence apart from the Saints. His willingness to leave his wife and newborn child to fend for themselves for an undetermined period while he preached the gospel of Mormonism in Hawaii was a decision wholly in character with the simple steadfastness of his original commitment. Repeated meetings with those whose commitment seemed very shallow indeed must have puzzled, as well as distressed, him.

By October 1858 when Henry Bigler reached Farmington, the hostilities had all but ended. President James Buchanan had been persuaded to reconsider his punitive military expedition. While still publicly condemning the Mormons as disloyal, Buchanan's official stance became noticeably conciliatory. In truth, the administration had underestimated both the cost of the Utah expedition and the number of soldiers required to regain control of the Mormon kingdom. By spring 1858, Buchanan's administration had lost its taste for a policy of extermination or even forceful punishment of the Latter-day Saints.[11] By summer Jane and the children had returned to Farmington. With relief, Bigler resumed the life he left twenty months before.

His next eighteen years were the core of his life—a life of chores night and morning, of field labor from sun-up to sun-down, of eating meals earned by his own labor at his own table, of evenings seated at his own fireside with Jane and the children, of weekly worship with the Saints of his ward, of the occasional debate or play or musical evening provided by that same ward, of uniting with neighbors to do some piece of bridge building, road repair, or schoolhouse roofing for the good of the community, of occasional trips for needed supplies south to Salt Lake City. And of that quiet, strong core, we know almost nothing. From the record, it looks more like a smooth interlude, almost a blank, between the more exotic episodes of his far-traveling youth—as a soldier, gold miner, and missionary—and the final quarter-century of his life when he gave over his days to the ordinances carried out within the temple in St. George, Utah. For almost the first time since becoming a Mormon, Henry Bigler led a quiet, rather uneventful life that revolved around the peaceful, repetitive, and mundane chores and duties of a Mormon husband, father, and farmer in northern Utah. These must have been deeply happy and contented years for him, despite the problems, sorrows, and worries that shadow even a quiet life.

He seldom kept a daily journal during this period and did not record his farming and occasional school teaching with the meticulous accounting he gave to the Mormon Battalion's march, mining, or missionary activities. Significantly, however, he never lost his attentiveness to family matters. While most of his infrequent writing during these years was limited to one- or two-sentence entries, they told of domestic matters—his joy at the birth of a child, a significant religious event to which he attached eternal consequence, and his sorrow at family tragedies. On these occasions, his usual laconic entries gave way to intensely personal expressions of rejoicing and grief for his children and other family members.

It was a sign of the peaceful, fruitful years ahead that Jane became pregnant immediately after his return. Their son, Charles William Bigler, was born on 30 July 1859, just a month after the death of Henry's father.[12] Eight months after his return, Jacob Bigler called Henry to his deathbed on 22 June 1859 at his home in Farmington. A dedicated Latter-day Saint since his conversion twenty-two years earlier, Jacob had suffered with the Saints in Missouri and Illinois, crossed the plains to Utah at age fifty-four, and, just before his death, requested that Henry's mother, Elizabeth Harvey Bigler, be sealed to him. Apostle Heber C. Kimball had earlier told Jacob he could have this vicarious sealing performed following the completion of a new temple in Utah.

Henry reassured his dying father that the ordinance would be performed and stood proxy for Jacob while his sister, Hannah Bigler
Miller, stood in Elizabeth's place when the sealing was performed
at the Endowment House on 23 April 1869.[13]

Henry and Jane continued to have children at regular intervals of two and a half or three years to join three-year-old
Elizabeth Jane and infant Charles William; Henry Eugene's birth
on 27 August 1862 was linked with another death in the larger family. Henry's deeply loved sister, Emeline Bigler Hess, died on 31
January 1862, at age thirty-eight, leaving nine children. When
Bigler blessed Eugene on 3 September 1862, he prayed: "I bless you
with health that your life might be spared upon the Earth and
grow up to manhood and have the Holy Priesthood to do much
good in helping to build up the Kingdom of God that you may be
an ornament in His kingdom and an honor to your parents."[14] A
similar sense of vulnerability is apparent in the blessing Bigler gave
their next child, Jacob Edwin, born 24 August 1865. On 1
September 1865, Henry Bigler pronounced this blessing on the
child: "Jacob Edwin, my infant son I take you in my arms to bless
you . . . that your life may be spared and preserved from the powers
of Darkness . . . that you may grow up to manhood to help avenge
the blood of the Prophets and to bare the Holy Priesthood & build
up the Kingdom of God on earth."

Eugene and Jacob's blessings were fulfilled, but death struck
the next two children. Bigler does not record his feelings when "a
child a little boy" was stillborn in December 1867, but his anguish is
clear when he recorded the brief life and agonizing death of his and
Jane's last child, Emeline Elvira.[15] She was born 23 April 1869.
Three months and thirteen days later, "this morning about 3 oclock
my little Emline Elvira died! and in the afternoon between 4 and 5
oclock was buried."[16] On 1 May 1869, when she was eight days old,
he gave her a name and blessing, recording his desperate plea to his
God.

> O god my Eternal Father I take this Child in my arms to bless it . . .
> I pray the[e] in the name of Jesus Christ thy Son that thou wilt bless
> it with thy holy spirit and with health that it may live to a good old
> age and not die that its life may be presious in thy sight that thou wilt
> not let the powers of Darkness distroy its tabbernicle but let it grow

and become a mother in israel and thus fulfil the measure of its creation and although thou [Emeline Elvira] mayest be afflicted with
pane and disease yet thou shalt recover and thy life shalt be spared.

Despite Bigler's fervent prayer and the anxious care of both
parents, Emeline died of an ailment Bigler does not name and may
not even have known. Stoically, Jane and Henry shouldered this
new burden. Life on the Utah frontier was fragile; death was a regular visitor in Bigler's world. At this point, his mother, father, three
sisters, and one child were dead.[17]

The ordinance of naming and blessing was the first in a series
of rites that acknowledged the passage of children into the community. It was usually performed in the presence of the ward congregation within a few weeks or months of birth, with the father,
male relatives, and other Mormon men standing in the blessing
circle. An infant's salvation was not jeopardized if it died before
receiving this ordinance, but most families saw that it was carried
out, blessing and naming a weak baby at home. The next important
ordinance in a child's life was baptism by immersion, traditionally
performed within a few months after the eighth birthday and, in
the nineteenth century when ponds, lakes, and rivers were the
usual sites, humanely reserved for the summer months if possible.
This ordinance, though public, was usually attended only by family
members. Confirmation and bestowal of the "gift of the Holy
Ghost," however, usually followed promptly in a sacrament meeting and was again a rite in which the father and a few other male
members of the family and ward participated. The ward clerk kept
records of all these ordinances.

Although there is great modern emphasis on the patriarchal
propriety of a father performing such LDS rites for his offspring as
naming, blessing, baptizing, and confirmation, such was not neces-
sarily the case in the nineteenth century; and during his years in
Farmington, Bigler also called upon friends to perform these
offices. Willard was baptized in Provo on 22 May 1860 by Edson
Whipple. Bigler blessed and named Elizabeth Jane as a baby, but
Lot Smith, renowned Mormon frontiersman and a Latter-day
Saint hero of the recent Utah War, baptized Elizabeth Jane at
Bigler's invitation and Hector Haight, a founder of Farmington,

Salt Lake City Endowment House and Tabernacle, from Richard Burton, *The City of the Saints* (London, 1862). Reproduced by permission of the Huntington Library, San Marino, California.

confirmed her. Levi Thornton named and blessed Charles in January 1860, and Henry Hollist, both people of unknown connection to the family, baptized him in October 1868.[18] Eugene was baptized in August 1864 by his father. Henry Bigler asked Truman Leonard, a leading citizen of Farmington, to bless Jacob, the third son, in August 1865, and he was baptized in October 1873.

Henry and Jane themselves experienced a separate rite of passage for adult Latter-day Saints in 1867 when Jane was pregnant with the son who would be stillborn. The endowment and sealing that Henry and Jane had received in the Endowment House in 1856, a year after their marriage, would, they believed, ensure the continuation of their union beyond death and into eternity if they continued faithful and would also guarantee that their children would belong to them forever. The endowment was a system of instruction and covenants that set the framework for a righteous life and offered the promise, conditioned on continued worthiness, that a man could become a "king and a priest" to God while his wife or wives could become "queens and priestesses" to him. It was, in short, a theological system that terminated with godhood.

The second anointing, commonly known as "the fulness of the priesthood," was another step along that pathway and guaranteed godhood to the recipients. Unlike the endowment or temple marriage, it could not be actively sought but instead came at the invitation of a higher ecclesiastical officer. It was offered exclusively to Latter-day Saints of unquestionable integrity and commitment who had proven valiant in living the Mormon gospel and whose personal lives were unblemished by major sins. Lorenzo Snow, church president in 1901, stipulated that candidates "should be those who have made an exceptional record" and be "persons who will never apostatize."

On 3 April 1867, Bigler recorded the solemn, even sacred event: "To day I and my wife had our second anointings in an upper room in the Historians office in Salt Lake City Brother Daniel A. Miller and wife [Hannah Bigler Miller] got theirs at the same time. Brothers George A. Smith and Wilford Woodruff officiating in the ordinance."[19] This rite is an indication that Henry Bigler's spiritual standing among Mormon leaders was on solid footing in 1867. After all, he had successfully filled missions both in Virginia and abroad, willingly served in the Mormon Battalion, and seems to have had accepted every call which came his way.

In contrast to Bigler's careful recording of these personally significant events—the second anointing and the deaths of his loved ones—he makes only a single mention of the Civil War, then shattering the nation in ways that would permanently alter its political and social history. On 17 November 1860 Bigler almost casually wrote: "The Legislature of South Carolina past the law to secession" and, in his opinion, "war [will be] inaugurated the North against the South and the South against the North."[20] This apparent disinterest can be partially explained by the lack of news readily available in Farmington, which may have dampened his curiosity, but it more likely resulted from his overarching religious beliefs. The common Mormon view of the Civil War was that this conflict fulfilled prophecies by Joseph Smith and others, signaling the beginning of the collapse of the United States which would prepare the way for Christ's Second Coming. According to such a view, his duty remained the same: to faithfully fulfill his obligations as a member of the church and await instructions from his leaders that would be forthcoming at the appropriate time.

His reaction was not an anomaly among other Utah Mormons. Throughout the Civil War, Mormon attitudes were a curious mixture of professed loyalty, aloofness, and a sense of vindication. Joseph Smith had foretold the Southern insurrection in November 1832 during the Nullification Crisis triggered by South Carolina's disavowal of federal authority: "Verily, thus saith the Lord," Smith had proclaimed, "concerning the wars that will shortly come to pass, beginning at the rebellion of South Carolina, which will eventually terminate in the death and misery of many souls; . . . the time will come that war will be poured out upon all the nations, beginning at this place."[21] Henry Bigler did not remark that the beginning of the Civil War fulfilled one of Smith's prophesies, but others of his contemporaries did. When war actually broke out in 1861 the Mormon newspaper, the *Deseret News*, began to draw a clear connection between Smith's 1832 prophecy and current events.[22]

As residents of a territory, Utah's Mormons had no national voice. In 1857, presidential candidate Stephen A. Douglas called polygamy a "pestiferous, disgusting cancer," a view which Abraham Lincoln apparently shared, for during the presidential campaign of 1859–60, he stated, in reference to his opponent Douglas's concept of popular sovereignty for the western territories, "If it prove true, as is probable, that the people of Utah are in open rebellion to the United States . . . they ought to be somehow coerced to obedience."[23] Yet, in the Latter-day Saint view, the United States had failed to protect their rights in Missouri and Illinois, ignored their loyal service during the Mexican-American War, and denied them statehood in 1849–50 and again in 1861 and 1862. Estranged as Americans and reviled for their religious beliefs, it is little wonder that Mormons felt displaced in the United States. Most of them probably made the distinction Brigham Young did when, refuting the charge that Mormons were secessionists and disunionists, he thundered on 6 February 1862: "I am, so help me God, and ever expect to be a secessionist from their [the United States's] wickedness, unrighteousness, dishonesty, and unhallowed principles in a religious point of view; but am I or this people secessionists with regard to the glorious Constitution of our country? No."

The Civil War left Utah relatively untouched. Governor Alfred Cumming, the Georgia-born governor installed by Johnston's army, left Utah in May 1861 to offer his services to the Confederacy. A strong believer in states' rights, Cumming had proven acceptable to the Mormons. The new appointee, Stephen S. Harding, arrived in July 1861. Harding, an Indiana abolitionist, recognizing how truly powerless he was, claimed, "Brigham Young and the other leaders are constantly inculcating in the minds of [their] audience who sit beneath their teachings every sabbath that the Government of the United States is of no consequence, that it lies in ruins, that the prophecy of Joseph Smith is being fulfilled to the letter."[24] Meanwhile, Young unflinchingly boasted, "I am and will [continue to] be governor," not a stance to endear him to the federal structure, whatever its factual truth.[25] To keep his people focused on the kingdom, Young ordered the foundation walls of the Salt Lake Temple, buried at the approach of Johnston's army, uncovered on 18 December 1861; and the Mormon dream of erecting a mighty temple to God was rekindled.[26] In February 1862 celebrations commemorating the services of the Mormon Battalion were held in Salt Lake City and at Plain City, near Ogden.[27] Doubtless, Henry Bigler attended at least one of these events. In March 1862, Bigler's brother-in-law, John W. Hess, bishop of the Farmington Ward since 1855, was elected to the Territorial Senate, no doubt cause for celebration within the family.

Bigler attracted no particular attention among the residents of Farmington, either for good or for ill. Like most of his neighbors, he was a farmer. Many supplemented their farm income by moonlighting as cobblers, carpenters, coopers, or—like Bigler— seasonal school teachers. Reflecting the Mormon pattern of building a temporal as well as spiritual kingdom of God, Farmington residents were an industrious, religious people. Henry Bigler apparently never aspired to more elaborate pleasures than those of his own hearth nor visualized a more sophisticated form of livelihood than farming. Judging from the lack of contrary evidence, and sensing Bigler's fatherly devotion in the sparse journal entries for these years, he clearly seems to have found these years trying but fulfilling. The religious ritual of Mormonism dovetailed with

Bigler's personal values, and he must have diligently sought to impart the blessings of the faith to his children.

Furthermore, his record of missionary service, his Mormon Battalion friendships, and his brother-in-law bishop placed him solidly among the inner circle of Farmington's religious community. One indication of this favored standing is that on 10 March 1865 his stepson Willard received his endowment at Salt Lake City's Endowment House at the unusually youthful—though not unique—age of fifteen. At some point, he moved to Antioch, California, where he was located at the time of his mother's death. Elizabeth Jane, now known by the affectionate nickname of Lizzie, married Henry Lemon Wickel, in 1871, at age fifteen.

It was during this period of contented private life that Henry Bigler captured his place in history on 31 December 1870. He accidentally learned that the California gold discovery had been inaccurately dated and that James Marshall's role in the discovery had been questioned. Bigler wrote a letter to the editor of the San Francisco *Daily Evening Bulletin*, expressing himself modestly but with evident sincerity, and quoting his own 1848 diary to affirm that James Marshall had made the find: "I cheerfully give my testimony, although it is at a very late hour, because I feel that it is a duty I owe to Mr. Marshall, and perhaps to the public. . . . I was one of the men at work at Coloma at the time the gold was found by Mr. Marshall."28

Ultimately the letter came to the attention of California historian Hubert Howe Bancroft, who wrote to Bigler. It was the beginning of a long relationship between the Mormon patriarch and the California patrician. On 15 March 1872, Bancroft asked Henry Bigler to contribute his personal reminiscences. Bancroft suggested an immediate deadline, and Bigler wrote apologetically on 10 April in the middle of spring plowing and planting:

> Your circular of March 15th desireing me to contribute my recollection [and] personal reminiscences of my travels and adventures on the pacific co[a]st for The Pacific Encyclopedia was received several days since but owing to the press of buisness [*sic*], I have not been able [to write] sooner and even to the present I cannot do it Satisfactorily and to tell the truth I do not see how I can in any reasonbly time.

I would gladly do it if I could but my indigent circumstances seems to forbid it, it is true I have kept a kind of journal ever sence the days of my youth. I am now in my 57th year a Virginian and of dutch descent.[29]

Fortunately, Bancroft was willing to extend the deadline, and Bigler, five months from his fifty-seventh birthday, thus embarked on a new avocation: chronicler of the Mormon West. In May 1872, after completing spring work, Bigler wrote a ninety-eight-page narrative, entitled, either by himself or by his new friend, "Diary of a Mormon in California."[30] Making heavy use of his day books, but occasionally relying upon memory, Bigler narrated his history from Latter-day Saint conversion through the march of the Mormon Battalion. Self-conscious about his grammatical irregularities, Bigler pled, "Dear sir please excuse me for I expect you will laugh or sware at my awkward way of writing. I leave it to you to arrange and dress [it] up." He was so poor that he asked Bancroft to "send a few stamps & envelopes."

Bancroft liked what Bigler recounted, forwarded the requested items, and asked for more. Bigler, who was working twenty miles north of home in Brigham City, Box Elder County, as a tenant farmer, wrote back on 7 June, gratefully acknowledging receipt of the stamps and bringing his story up through his Mormon Battalion experiences. "I shall write oftener I have been disappointed in my calculations [regarding completion of the manuscript]," wrote Bigler, "I am and expect to be here all this summer."[31]

By working diligently in the evenings after he finished his day's labor, he had completed his account through the discovery of gold by 5 July 1872. "My journal tells me it was on the afternoon of the 24th day of January 1848 while I was at my drill buisy preparing to put in a blast when Marshall as useal went . . . towards the lower end of the race," wrote Bigler. The mill boss later returned carrying his old white hat in his arm and looking "wonderfully pleased." With a smile on his face, James Marshall announced, "Boys by g-d I believe I have found a gold mine."[32]

Although Bancroft tidied up Bigler's grammar, spelling, and punctuation, he did not alter either its organization nor its substance. His respect for Bigler seems to have been genuine, and he paid Bigler a well-deserved compliment in the *History of California* to which Bigler had contributed. Speaking of dating of the gold discovery, Bancroft wrote: "There are but two authorities to choose between, Marshall, the discoverer, and one Henry W. Bigler, a Mormon engaged upon the work at the time. . . . Marshall admits he does not know the date. . . . Bigler, on the other hand, was a cool, clear-headed, methodical man; it is from his journal that I get my date."[33]

Four years later in 1874, Bancroft's associate, John Shertzer Hittell, asked the Mormon to transcribe his January 1848 entries.[34] Hittell published this record and preserved the journal itself at the Society of California Pioneers in San Francisco. Still later, in 1886, George Q. Cannon asked Bigler to contribute reminiscences of his life, from his conversion to Mormonism through the discovery of gold at Sutter's Mill, to the Latter-day Saint publication *The Juvenile Instructor*, which Bigler did.

These contributions—both to Bancroft and Cannon—brought Bigler modest renown during his sixties and seventies, but he seems to have responded to requests as he did to callings: obediently trying to do his best to provide the material wanted in as workmanlike a fashion as possible. Simultaneously, however, he suffered a great sorrow. Jane developed an incurable cough during the winter of 1873–74, which steadily worsened, causing her to suffer severe pain in her right side. She did not improve with warmer weather but suffered through the spring and summer. Although Bigler sought the best medical knowledge available in Farmington, nothing helped; and in October 1874, it was obvious that she was dying.

With love and anguish he recorded her final day. She requested that he give one photograph of her to twenty-four-year-old Willard, then living in northern California, while Henry kept the other. Eighteen-year-old Lizzie, who had come from Idaho to nurse Jane all winter was to receive her clothes.

Jane died on 5 November 1874, thirteen days before their nineteenth wedding anniversary. She was thirty-nine years old. Two days later, Henry Bigler laid her to rest in the Farmington cemetery beside their infant daughter Emeline Elvira: "This has been a lonely day, I shall not attempt to describe my feelings," he penned mournfully that evening. The next few months were the

John S. Hittel. Courtesy of the California History Room,
California State Library, Sacramento.

most difficult of his entire life. He was unprepared to deal with his own sorrow, let alone the grief of his children. Fifteen-year-old Charles, twelve-year-old Eugene, and nine-year-old Jacob were devastated by Jane's death. Bigler records coming downstairs from his bedroom on the morning after Jane's death and seeing Eugene standing near his mother's coffin. The child's eyes were red and swollen as he bravely choked back the tears. "My heart bled for my motherless boy," Bigler lamented.[35]

Although he expresses no bitterness or anger at Jane's death, he was broken by it. He sent his sons to live temporarily with relatives, a common custom of the time even though it probably intensified the grief and disorientation of all concerned. Fifteen-year-old Charles went to live with Henry's sister, Hannah Bigler Miller, and her husband, Daniel, in Farmington. Nine-year-old Eugene went to "Mother Smith" (it is not clear who she was); while seven-year-old Jacob Edwin joined his sister Lizzie in Idaho.[36] Three months after her death, while sleeping alone in his house, Bigler awoke suddenly thinking that Jane had called him. "It was so plain and natural," he recalled, "that I answered and could not go to sleep for some time."

Mercifully, after a year of dull suffering, a church calling intervened, much to Bigler's relief. On Sunday, 14 November 1875, just a year after Jane's death, he received a letter from Brigham Young asking him to come to Salt Lake City to serve as an ordinance worker in the Endowment House. Bigler reported for duty on Monday, 29 November, only two weeks later; and the assignment was a godsend in relieving his grief.[37]

Like the temple, the Endowment House was considered a sacred structure. Entrance to it and service within it were conditioned on personal worthiness. This calling, therefore, which Bigler was expected to finance himself, both validated and extended his loyalty, his unshaken commitment, and his selfless service to the cause of building up Zion. At Salt Lake City he boarded with his cousin Bathsheba W. Bigler Smith, widowed earlier that year by the death of George A. Smith. Working with his sister, Hannah Bigler Miller, who still resided in Farmington, Bigler acted as a proxy in performing the Mormon rites of vicarious baptism, endowment, and sealing on behalf of deceased individuals, both his own ancestors and unrelated persons. He also acted as officiator in those same ceremonies for other participants. In this capacity, Bigler took the roles of several key players in the endowment pageant. Proxy ordinance work played an increasingly important major role in Henry Bigler's last quarter-century at the St. George Temple. In fact, from Bigler's Mormon perspective, it was this holy service, not his military, mining, or even mission experience, that became his lasting legacy.

On 30 October 1876, Brigham Young officially terminated ordinance work at the Endowment House. The St. George Temple was scheduled for dedication two months later on 1 January 1877, and from that point forward, all who wished to participate in Mormonism's most sacred rites were required to journey to southern Utah. The following day, Bigler wrote in his diary, "Today President Young told me he would like me to go to St. George and work in the St. George Temple." Reacting as Young probably knew he would, Bigler asked how soon he should leave. Brigham Young responded, "if the Lord was willing" Bigler should leave for southern Utah within one week.[38]

Within a week he had wrapped up his affairs in Salt Lake City and Farmington. "I bid my children good by praying in my heart for God to bless them and all who may befriend them," Bigler sorrowfully wrote.[39] Hurrying to catch his train on 6 November, it was "with a heavy heart" that Henry left his home of the past twenty years. He would never return, except for occasional visits.

Wilford Woodruff, ca. 1878. Used by permission, Utah State Historical Society, all rights reserved.

St. George Temple, ca. 1876. Used by permission, Utah State Historical Society, all rights reserved.

9

THE ST. GEORGE YEARS
1877–96

*There are 4 Temples one of which is finished the other three in the
course of erection and . . . all hell is beginning to boil over [and] the
Devil is to pay on account of the Endowments etc.*[1]

*A*lthough Bigler had passed through southern Utah five times
en route from and to California, the California trail cut off at
present-day Cedar City and St. George was over the edge of the
Great Basin, hidden behind its wrinkled black volcanic escarpments.
These walls had retarded settlement more than a decade after its near
neighbors, Cedar City and Parowan, had become well-established
towns in the early 1850s. Finally, in 1861 Bigler's old friend and kins-
man, George A. Smith, had led a company of resolute pioneers over
the battlements, pick-axing dugout trails in the sharp lava and easing
the wagons down with locked wheels. Reportedly, the community
was also named for Smith, although it was apostle Erastus Snow who
settled there and became the community's chief civic and ecclesiastical leader. Most of the settlers had been hand-picked by ecclesiastical
leaders and assigned to settle in Utah's Dixie, designated as the
Cotton Mission, under the same assignment as proselyting missionaries. Thus, Henry Bigler was joining other Latter-day Saints who
were very much like him—highly committed, fired by devotion, tem-
pered by hardship and adversity, self-sufficient, and persevering.[2]
When Bigler arrived on 22 November 1876, sixteen years after the
town's beginning, it had passed the perils of starvation and economic
collapse but it was not a wealthy community by any means.[3]

St. George's population in 1877, the year that the new temple was dedicated, stood at approximately thirteen hundred, making it by far the largest town in southern Utah. Washington County, of which St. George was the seat, numbered just over three thousand.[4] Its beautiful tabernacle, or main LDS meeting hall, of hand-hewed red sandstone had been completed in 1870.

Farmington was fertile and mild in contrast to the long, blazing summers and harshly arid desert of the south. Only the committed came. And only the triply committed stayed. As one example, the Saints of Dixie, including Henry Bigler, were determined practitioners of the Latter-day Saint communal life-style known as the United Order of Enoch. This practice, first instituted at Kirtland in the early 1830s, all but disappeared from mid-nineteenth-century Mormonism only to be resurrected in the Great Basin. In practice the Mormon United Order amounted to a cooperative movement aimed at increasing production, reducing costs, and making possible a superior organization of resources. It was purposely instituted, and later reinstituted, to heighten group unity and foster a spirit of "temporal oneness."[5]

Nineteenth-century Utah saw Mormon cooperatives spring up in the north at Brigham City, Hyrum, Logan, Ogden, and Salt Lake City, while in Dixie United Orders were established at Orderville and at St. George. About half of these orders lasted less than a year after their organization. St. George's order, established in 1874, was a prototype of the cooperative community. Participating families received "credits" for work performed. Each family was then allowed to make withdrawals from the cooperative in the form of consumer goods and services. At St. George the local tithing office served as bank and general store combined, collecting and dispensing contributions in this largely cashless society. Bigler joined the United Order, though he had precious few resources to commit to it; in fact, during his southern Utah years, he lived largely upon orders drawn from the tithing office.[6] The St. George United Order was dissolved in 1878. One reason was the difficulty of suppressing individualism to the extent required. Another was the generally inadequate financial base. Furthermore, the federal raid on polygamy had driven most of the ecclesiastical leaders underground, with almost immediate detrimental effects to the economic base of the Mormon community.[7]

St. George's Mormons practiced polygamy with the same quiet fervor. Between 25 and 30 percent of Farmington's households were polygamous by the last quarter of the nineteenth century, but the figure was nearly 40 percent for St. George.[8] As an escape from Salt Lake City's harsh winters, Young had established a winter home in southern Utah several years earlier. The Mormon leader had first proposed a temple for St. George in January 1871 at a meeting of local church leaders held in Erastus Snow's home. According to Latter-day Saint apostle and later church president John Taylor, Young saw in St. George a community of faithful Saints who deserved to have Utah's first temple. Besides, work on the Salt Lake Temple, intended from the outset as the showpiece of Zion, was inching along at a snail's pace and the church required a temple to house its sacred rites as soon as possible.[9]

The local Saints were enthusiastic about the project, despite the grueling burden it imposed on an already struggling community. At a stroke, the decision changed the isolated village of St. George into the region's most substantial community, a spiritual mecca for all nineteenth-century Mormons. Perhaps most compellingly, building the temple may have been an act of communal contrition and redemption. About thirty miles away, silent but not forgotten, was the site of the 1857 Mountain Meadows massacre, where by some estimates over 120 California-bound men, women, and children had been slain by misdirected Mormon militia and their Indian allies.[10]

On New Year's Day, 1877, "the Font room and the rooms in the basement story were dedicated by Brother Woodruff," Bigler wrote, "and the upper rooms so far as completed were dedicated by President Young."[11] This preliminary dedication made possible the practice of vicarious baptisms for deceased ancestors—one of the primary purposes of Mormon temples. Later, in April 1877, after all construction was completed, the final dedication was performed. The completion and final dedication of the St. George Temple fittingly marked the close of Brigham Young's kingdom-building career in the Mormon West. Four months later, he was dead. On 29 August 1877, Wilford Woodruff, the temple president and an apostle, received a telegram from Salt Lake City notifying him of the death of Brigham Young. We have lost "a kind and true friend, a wise counselor . . . a master mind of Utah," Bigler lamented.[12]

The leader Bigler had followed so faithfully since 1847 had left a visible legacy of Mormon villages, irrigation systems, chapels, and tabernacles dotted across the Great Basin. Brigham Young had launched many extensions of the Rocky Mountain Zion—San Bernardino, California; Carson Valley, Nevada; and Fort Limhi, Idaho—for the dual purposes of creating a buffer zone to safeguard the Saints' Great Basin kingdom and to further extend Mormonism's sphere of influence. Just the year before his death, a large colonization mission was undertaken to the Little Colorado River region of northeastern Arizona. Historically remembered as the "Great Colonizer," Young was, outside of the Mormon world as well as within, probably the best-known Latter-day Saint of Bigler's day.[13]

Perhaps more important, however, was the invisible legacy. During his presidency, a generation had been born, come of age, and raised children of their own in the Mormon faith, linked in mutually supportive families and bonded in wards that worked and socialized together. He had encouraged self-sufficiency, sacrifice, and identification with Mormonism's central values to counteract the inevitable influences of larger American society. More specifically, he had united them as a people against the increasing pressure of the federal government, determined to break the practice of plural marriage, the political monopoly of the Mormon Church, and its economic collectiveness, all traits considered highly un-American. Though his dream of establishing a homogenous, cooperative community failed, it left a legacy of idealism that has persisted to the present.

British-born John Taylor (1808–87), the ranking member of the Quorum of the Twelve Apostles, succeeded Young as president of the LDS Church. Life in St. George continued for Henry Bigler almost without interruption. However, Woodruff, now senior apostle, was required to assume greater responsibilities in overall church leadership; John D. T. McAllister (1827–1910), president of the St. George Stake, often acted in Woodruff's stead when the latter was away on church business. Until 1893 when David Henry Cannon, brother of Bigler's friend George Q. Cannon, was called to succeed Woodruff as temple president, Bigler frequently mentions McAllister in supervisory roles at the St. George Temple.[14]

The St. George Temple had an immediate impact upon Utah Mormonism in general as well as Henry Bigler in particular. Mormon couples came to St. George to have their marriages sealed, and family genealogists bent on performing the saving ordinances for their deceased ancestors came also. While statistics on temple attendance for the late nineteenth century are not available, Henry Bigler's journal leaves a clear indication of the enthusiasm which this first Mormon temple west of the Mississippi River provoked among believers. Returning from a visit to northern Utah to see his children in the fall of 1877, Bigler made his way south by rail from Salt Lake City to Nephi in central Utah where the train stopped and wagon travel began. En route, he noted several travelers on their way to St. George "to do work in the Temple for their Dead."[15]

Certainly, the temple was the focus of his life. In 1877, six temple rites were practiced: (1) adoption, (2) baptism for the dead (enabling them, according to LDS belief, to embrace the gospel in the next life if they so chose), (3) rebaptism for the living, either for a restoration of health or as a sign of renewed commitment to the gospel, (4) endowments for the living and the dead, (5) marriage sealings for the living and the dead, and (6) the second anointing.

Adoption sealed desirous Saints into the family of a Mormon priesthood holder of proven faithfulness. This practice was based on the belief that the adoptee's salvation would be assured within the postmortal "kingdom" of the adopter. Actively practiced in Nauvoo, the rite had been in abeyance since 1848 but revived markedly after 22 March 1877 when Woodruff adopted two couples to Brigham Young in the St. George Temple. Thereafter, thousands of persons were adopted at St. George and other LDS temples as they were subsequently constructed. Then, in April 1894, Woodruff announced a revelation-based change of policy: sealings (adoption) should only be done in lineal lines—children to parents.[16]

The first vicarious baptisms for the dead were performed on 9 January 1877, eight days after the dedication. Woodruff had himself baptized in behalf of 140 deceased persons. During the last two weeks of January alone, temple officiators John Lyman Smith and Anson P. Winsor baptized 927 persons on behalf of dead individuals, and over thirty thousand baptisms for the dead took place in the first year.[17]

Rebaptisms, or second baptisms, were practiced by late nineteenth century Mormons for at least two reasons: as a sign of renewed commitment to the faith and to benefit the sick and afflicted.[18]

The endowment ritual symbolically recreated events from biblical history in a dramatic form with ordinance workers acting the roles of key players. Events thus portrayed included the creation of the world; Adam and Eve's temptation, fall, and expulsion from the Garden of Eden; the apostasy from the gospel of Jesus Christ; and the bestowal of true priesthood authority upon worthy mortals through the ministration of the ancient apostles, Peter, James, and John.[19] Endowments for the living had been performed at the Nauvoo Temple and at Salt Lake City's Endowment House, but the ordinance was performed on behalf of deceased individuals for the first time on 11 January 1877 at the St. George Temple with Brigham Young presiding. Bigler's journal gives an unofficial count of 1,166 endowments for the living and 13,160 vicarious endowments performed in 1877.[20] The ceremony was identical for the living and for the dead; in the latter, a living individual assumed the name and represented a deceased person for ceremonial purposes.

Marital sealings of living persons under the auspices of priesthood authority united husbands and wives in a bond believed to survive beyond death for those couples who remained faithful throughout their mortal lives. This LDS concept emerged during the last years of Joseph Smith's lifetime and came to occupy a cherished spot within Mormondom. Not only were the marriages of living couples sealed in the St. George Temple, but the marital ties of deceased individuals were vicariously sealed as well, again with living individuals taking the names of and acting in behalf of the dead. According to Bigler, over five hundred sealings for the living and the dead were performed in 1877.[21]

Henry Bigler entered into the work of the temple wholeheartedly. As his diary evidences, he took these assignments seriously and kept very busy with them. "Tuesdays and Wednesdays of each week were set apart for baptisms for the Dead," he noted on 1 January 1877, "and Thursdays and Fridays of each week for the giving of Endowments and other ordinances."[22] One journal entry he made late in 1877 was repeated over and over with only slight variations for the next twenty-five years: "I worked all last week in the Temple."[23] In October 1877 Bigler was a witness at 258 vicarious baptisms for the dead and participated in an endowment ceremony which served eighty-four additional temple patrons.[24] In February 1878, after witnessing nearly a thousand baptisms for the dead, the sixty-two-year old Bigler dozed off in the temple and had a dream-vision of himself "standing in a large open pasture face towards the east with an outstretch[ed] hand as if I had salt, calling sheep and a large white flock came towards me there appeared to be thousands of sheep in the flock. I awoke, it all seemed to [have] hapened within a very few seconds."[25] This vision, which he interpreted as representing the departed souls vicariously offered the benefits of the Latter-day Saint gospel that day in the baptismal font, was very rewarding to him.

In addition to the time he spent in the temple assisting with ordinances, he also spent much of his spare time writing to relatives requesting the required genealogical information—birth and death dates of deceased relatives—so that their ordinances could be completed.[26] It is clear from his journal entries that his happiest temple experiences were completing ordinances for his own deceased relatives or friends. For instance, on 5 April 1878, he acted as proxy in an endowment ceremony "for my friend an old Hunter of Virginia by the name of Martin Cunningham." Several years later he performed endowment rites on behalf of his dead cousin, Daniel Mark Bigler, and his uncle, William Harvey. In January 1893, at age seventy-seven, Bigler records: "Went into the Font and was baptized for 21 of my dead among them W. E. Maikai, his father and a native by the name of Koa."[27] Koa was the Hawaiian who had drowned at Waialua, Oahu, in 1853, whom Bigler had committed himself to do this work for twenty-five years earlier. (See chapter 6.) It also gave him deep satisfaction to be endowed on behalf of W. E. Maikai, whose "house in Honolulu Oahu was my home while I was among the Sandwich Islanders." While these individuals might be assumed to have a strong interest in

Mormonism's tenets, Henry Bigler also acted for the eternal interests of a more famous acquaintance—John A. Sutter.[28]

He faithfully noted the various male roles he portrayed in the dramatized portion of the endowment along with other duties in regard to proxy baptisms and sealings:

> Sat. 19th [January 1878]. Worked this week in the Temple, and on the Endowment days I took the part of Peter.
>
> Sunday 17th [March 1878]. I worked all the past week in the Temple taking the part of peter and also officiating in other ordinances of the Endowments.
>
> Friday 12th [April 1878]. I took the part of james this week—today 127 went through [the Endowment ceremony], the largest company for several weeks past.
>
> Tuesday 12th [November 1878]. over 400 baptisms [for the dead]. I was witness part of the time.[29]

Perhaps reflecting his single-minded approach to this new calling, Bigler makes no mention in his diary of where he slept or how he lived, not even of which of St. George's four wards he moved into. His means, however, were clearly quite meager. He received a small monthly stipend for working in the temple of $62.50. In December 1877 he noted, "I went to the Temple to live having [been granted] that priviledge to do so."[30] This arrangement pleased Bigler and eased his financial burden immensely. Not only did he now have rent-free sleeping quarters, but "the House or the Temple will furnish my grub and I do my own cooking."[31] This arrangement lasted for five months when he received the use of a small house, in May 1878, presumably, a luxury available to him because the structure was located on the temple lot. Bigler observed happily, "This I have free of rent while I live there."[32]

He needed a separate residence for, with no mention of how they met or courted, the sixty-two-year-old Bigler had married again. On 6 March 1878, he wrote with a poetic flourish, "I took to my bosom Miss Ellinor Parthenia Emett, she being sealed to me for time and all eternity by Brother John D. T. McAllister, to be my Wife." Eleanor, almost thirty, had been born at Council Bluffs, Iowa, in 1848 and had been living with her parents, Moses and Catherine Emett, in the small community of Fort Hamblin west of

St. George. Catherine learned of the marriage after the fact, suggesting either that Eleanor kept the courtship from her parents for fear they may have interposed obstacles, or that the match was made almost impulsively.[33] Certainly, Bigler had not made housing arrangements. The couple lived with Eleanor's brother, James Emett, in St. George, for a month before the house near the temple block became available. In September 1879, Bigler purchased a two-story adobe house with "water right" for three hundred dollars.[34] This home was farther from the temple than Bigler's previous quarters, but the lot was large enough for a garden and some livestock.

Ten months after the wedding, on 25 January 1879, Eleanor gave birth to a daughter. One week later on 1 February Bigler named the child Maud and pronounced the customary father's blessing in his ward congregation. He "began to feel bad soon as the Babe was blessed," Bigler recorded in his earnest script, and "began to shed tears." Bigler feared Eleanor did not like the name. More importantly, remembering the devastating death of Emeline Elvira ten years earlier at Farmington (see chapter 8), he feared for Maud's well-being although she appeared healthy. Divining his feelings, Eleanor Bigler wrote him a brief but moving note: "Be comforted, your child shall live out the measure of her days. She will pass through many trials and tribulatons [sic] but will be faithful in the cause of God. She will be a mother to the poor and distressed in days to come and her name shall be handed down through many generations."[35] While Maud's tribulations, faithfulness, and compassion are unknown, she lived to age fifty-three, though she never married or had children.

Although Bigler says little in his journal about domestic joys in this last quarter-century of his life, he was obviously contented and grateful to be once again surrounded by a large family: "I have 6 children, 4 daughters & 2 sons, and when the next will come is to me unknown," Bigler wrote with pardonable complacence in an update to his old friend, Alexander Stephens, in 1891.[36]

His and Jane's four living children—Elizabeth Jane, Charles, Eugene, and Jacob—were adults now. Lizzie, Henry, and their eight children were living in Idaho. The three sons, all still single, were homesteading along Cassia Creek in southern Idaho. After moving to St. George, Bigler tried to make annual visits. Generally these visits were made in late summer and early fall when the St. George Temple was closed and Bigler could not only visit his children but also attend the semi-annual general conference of the church in October. On 30 August 1878 Bigler arrived in Farmington as a recently remarried man and happily noted that he "found all my children well and glad to see me." Two months later on the same visit, Bigler assumed the role of a doting grandfather as he "kept house for Henry and Lizzie while they went to the City to do a little trading."[37]

His purpose for making this prolonged visit was to sell his land in Farmington, "being told by Brother Woodruff that Pres. Young on leaving St. George had told him to keep me to work in the Temple." He offered the property to Ezra Clark, a local farmer and church leader, who suggested a price of one hundred dollars cash and two hundred bushels of wheat. Bigler "really felt he should give me about one hundred and fifty dollars more." But, acting upon Woodruff's earlier advice, that "my property [was] doing me no good," he agreed to Clark's offer. So, demonstrating more trust in Wilford Woodruff's counsel than any business acumen, Bigler "felt to sell and get a little something that mite do me a little good."[38] It is not clear whether anyone in his family was in a position to buy the land from him; certainly he could not afford to simply deed it over.

When he returned to St. George after this most recent trip, Bigler took thirteen-year-old Jacob with him for a year's stay.[39] Bigler seemed to make a conscious effort to share what was most important to him with Jacob. Within a month he took the boy to the temple where "Jacob was Baptized for his health and for his hearing as he is hard of hearing." The following May, Henry and Eleanor took Jacob to the Fourth Ward School House for a children's baptismal service. Jacob was baptized by Charles Cottam "for the Renewal of his Covenants and the Remission of his sins as he had not been since he was 8 years old."[40] Ever the true believer, Bigler must have sincerely felt these additional baptisms would improve his child's health and strengthen his commitment to the LDS gospel.

Henry Bigler was always poor, and often destitute. Certainly much of his poverty stemmed from his willingness to put religious duty ahead of economic interests. However, he also clearly lacked the temperament of a hard-nosed businessman; perhaps one trait reinforced the other. Through 1893 his Mexican-American War pension was eight dollars per month. In 1894, for an undisclosed reason but probably due to a governmental adjustment applying to all war veterans, he happily observed "an increase of pension" that raised this figure to "12 dollars a month." This, along with his temple stipend, gave him $74.50 per month to live on. So for Bigler's St. George years his annual income was around $894. But this clearly was not sufficient. In 1885, for instance, he ended the year $88.99 in the red. After his marriage, he had a home and lot valued at roughly three hundred dollars with some minor personal property, including a little livestock and furniture. All told, Henry Bigler's net worth for any given year between 1876 and 1900, when he was between sixty-one and eighty-five, probably never exceeded a thousand dollars. The mean figure for a man in Utah over sixty-five in 1870 was $2,304—nearer to $1,650 in St. George.[41]

Another indication of Bigler's persistent poverty is his fervent gratitude when a family member or friend gives him such necessities of life as clothing or food. Shortly after he and Eleanor wed, he noted in his diary, "last night Thomas Emitt [Emett] my wifes brother came and brought us some very nice fresh beef and a lot of tallow. I am very thankful and feel it is very kind in him and the next day he made me a present of a new pair of shoes." In 1889, when the seventy-four-year-old Bigler was visiting his son Charles, Charles encouraged him to "try on a coat & vest that was too little for him. They fit me very well and had not been worn but little. He told me to keep them. I thanked my son and took them."[42] The little incident shows a son's tact in helping his father without hurting the older man's pride.

Remarkably contented with what little he had, Bigler almost never complains about poverty, but his diary entry on 30 August 1878 is poignantly different. It was his first visit north after his move to St. George; his March marriage to Eleanor and his decision to sell his Farmington property had effected a redefinition as a St. George resident. As a man in transition, then, he visited the graves of his wife and daughter in the Farmington cemetery, finding them poorly maintained and overgrown with sagebrush. Bigler placed rude stone markers at the head and foot of the graves, then wrote feelingly: "I feel sorry that I am not able to put there respectable Tombstones." Returning eleven years later on 28 September 1889, he again found the graves overgrown with weeds and the temporary head and foot stones gone. "I could scarcely tell where my wife and child lies," he lamented in his journal. Just a few weeks earlier, visiting his children in Idaho, Henry Bigler had found Lizzie, Henry, and their eight children living in dire poverty. "I pitied her and was filled with sorrow and wished I was a rich man," he sadly observed.[43]

These entries, though atypical, document a life of uncomplaining but unremitting poverty. Perhaps on at least one level, his financial circumstances explain why he never became a polygamist. Certainly his unswerving commitment to Mormon practices, unquestioning obedience to the instructions of his leaders, and his selfless willingness to sacrifice personal gain for religious belief would all predict his acceptance of polygamy. Eleanor's father was a polygamist.[44] By 1880, over 30 percent of the men and two in five St. George households were polygamous.[45] Furthermore, St. George was a way station for Mormons fleeing southward into southern Arizona or northern Mexico to avoid federal prosecution for plural marriage, which had intensified during the 1880s to the point that nearly a thousand men and "a few" women had been jailed and an unknown number went "on the underground," or in hiding, to avoid the federal marshals.[46] Thus, the practice of plural marriage was something of a litmus test of total loyalty—and Bigler's loyalty to the church cannot plausibly fall under question.

It is true that a higher proportion of ward and stake ecclesiastical leaders were polygamists than lay members, and Bigler was never called to any significant local or regional office. Still, plenty of other men of comparatively humble social standing in Mormonism were much-married. More than a few of the known polygamists of southern Utah during the 1880s appear to have been men "of limited means and average position."[47] As a rule, St. George's polygamists were one-third wealthier than the town's monogamists, having a median net worth of $2,590.[48] Despite Bigler's obvious religious qualifications, he certainly could not have maintained more than one household.

Another reason may have been his age. Most Mormon men, at least those in St. George, married at around age twenty-four or twenty-five; polygamists took a second wife, on the average, between ages thirty-five and forty.[49] Bigler married Jane when he was forty, remained a widower for two years, and married Eleanor at age sixty-three. A third reason, though obviously speculative, may be a question of personality. Although it is obvious that he loved Jane, Eleanor, and his children deeply, he had delayed marriage far past the usual age. Perhaps his personality simply did not require intense or complex relationships. Or he may have been profoundly monogamist at heart. For whatever reason, he records a single and somewhat comical line in his journal in November 1877, when a friend, O. F. Due, wished to have three of his deceased female ancestors sealed to Bigler: "I don't know about having them sealed to me [for] they are all, I believe, Danish."[50] Whether the nationality of the women was really the issue, only the Dutch-descended Bigler knew for certain. For whatever cause, although by the terms of his two temple sealings he anticipated an afterlife in the company of two wives, Jane and Eleanor, he declined to increase their number by vicarious sealings to women he had not known personally during mortality.

And this suggests a final reason, which may have been a theological interpretation of plural marriage so personal that he simply did not or could not discuss it since it may have suggested a difference with the (admittedly shifting) position of the church on the centrality of the doctrine of plural marriage. In 1871, Brigham Young expressed the opinion, "A man may embrace [plural marriage] in his heart and not take the second wife and be justified before the Lord."[51] Perhaps Henry Bigler felt that he fit this category. Olive H. Stephan, Bigler's granddaughter, told me in 1989 that, according to family lore Bigler "never really believed" in polygamy.[52]

Whatever his thoughts on the matter, Bigler did not confide them to his diary. When he occasionally notes news items about antipolygamy legislation or federal enforcement activities, his sympathies are unquestioningly and completely with the beleaguered Mormon Church. In 1879 when the first case involving polygamy reached the U.S. Supreme Court on appeal (*Reynolds v. the United*

States), the Mormons were confidently expecting a positive decision based on the Constitutional guarantee of religious freedom. Bigler, in dismay, recorded the negative decision: "Brother Erastus Snow read a Tellegram he received yesterday announcing the strange news that judge Weight [Morris R. Waite] the Supreme judge of the United States had decided that the law of Sixty two against Polygamy was constitutional! . . . Judge [James B.] McKean of Salt Lake City is dead and buried as Br. Snow said He did not live to glory in the Decision against the Test Case of Polygamy; Dead and Damned." Then Bigler offered his judgment of the decision: "My own feelings are that the chief Justice of the United States has got his 'foot in it' if not soul and body unless he speedily repents."[53]

Needless to say, Bigler was not motivated by any personal concern since, as a monogamist, he was not susceptible either to the Morrill Act of 1862, the point at issue in the U.S. Supreme Court case, or to any of the new legislation which passed—the Edmunds Act in 1882 and the even stiffer Edmunds-Tucker Act in 1887. However, he identified wholeheartedly with the cause of his church and people against the federal government. On 4 August 1879 when Mormon leaders John Taylor, George Q. Cannon, Albert Carrington, and Brigham Young, Jr., were arrested for contempt of court, Bigler indignantly wrote: "4 of the Twelve Apostles of the Lamb has been indicted and condemned and sent to prison *for contempt?* or was it for doing their duty? . . . there are 4 Temples one of which is finished and the other three in course of erection and I suppose the seacret of the matter is all hell is beginning to boil over [and] the Devil is to pay on account of the Endowments etc." Seven years later when Bigler's friend George Q. Cannon was arrested by federal authorities for unlawful cohabitation (polygamy), Bigler's unflinching belief that the church, doing the will of God, was being unrighteously persecuted by the government officials, doing the will of the devil, had not altered: "I am sorry for brother George, I am sorry for our nation, . . . I am sorry that they have got him for his convictions altho he is an innocent man."[54]

In September 1890, church president Wilford Woodruff issued a manifesto stating, "Inasmuch as laws have been enacted by Congress forbidding plural marriages, which laws have been pronounced constitutional by the court of last resort, I hereby declare my intention to submit to those laws, and to use my influence with the members of the Church over which I preside to have them do likewise." Although a minority of the October 1890 general conference voted to accept Woodruff's declaration concerning plural marriage as "authoritative and binding" (the majority of those present abstained from voting), the Mormon practice of open polygamy had become a part of history.[55] Bigler does not comment on the Manifesto or his reaction to it, but the public concession had its desired effect. Late in 1895, the people of St. George learned that President Grover Cleveland "will issue a proclamation declaring Utah a sovereign state on the 4th day of January next." On 6 January 1896, St. George joined in the celebration with cannon, small arms fire, and a patriotic rally. Bigler wrote proudly, "This is a great day in St. George and throughout this county as our Territory is now the 45th State."[56]

Henry Bigler was eighty in 1896 and within four years of his death, no longer at an age when the church's political and cultural shifts significantly influenced his personal life. Because public polygamy could no longer be a demonstration of loyalty, the new agenda for the devout became an increased emphasis upon tithing (contributing one-tenth of one's income to the church), stricter observance of the Mormon health code known as the Word of Wisdom, and renewed efforts in proselyting among the living and genealogical research and temple work on behalf of the dead.[57] Despite advancing years, Bigler continued to participate in vicarious temple ordinances for deceased relations and friends, though less intensively than before, but actively collected genealogical information from many people in West Virginia and elsewhere. He ingenuously explained that he was preparing a personal history to avoid arousing apprehensions in his non-Mormon correspondents.[58]

Henry Bigler lived in St. George for nearly twenty-four years, between ages sixty-one and eighty-five. His service as a temple worker was deeply fulfilling to him, as was life with Eleanor and their six children. He endured the intensifying federal prosecution upon his people without abandoning his unwavering loyalty and proudly witnessed Utah's statehood. Despite his diligence and frugality, however, his unremitting poverty kept him from providing for his loved ones as he obviously wished. Beyond these personal and domestic concerns, however, was Henry Bigler's humble but significant participation in the growth of Mormonism and its rise as a regional power, paralleling the emergence and development of the American West. It is also clear that he had some grasp of the role he had played in that history, for at St. George Bigler emerged as a chronicler of Mormonism and the West.

CHRONICLER

*I have letters from both old acquaintances and strangers asking me
for information how the precious metal was found some has writen
for my photograph, some for my autograph . . . You see I have
become somewhat notorious.*[1]

*H*enry Bigler's sincere and modest effort to set the record
straight about James Marshall's role in the discovery of gold
in 1870 had two significant impacts upon Bigler's later life. First, he
realized that his historical information was valuable. Second, his
letter to the editor of a San Francisco newspaper ultimately connected him with professional historians Hubert Howe Bancroft and
John Shertzer Hittell. History soon became a source of immense
interest and entertainment to Bigler, providing a counterpoint to his
quiet life as a Utah farmer and Mormon temple worker.

A significant amount of information in newspapers came in
the form of letters from correspondents, and Bigler's contributions
were not only personally satisfying for him but warmly received by
the public. Writing of the importance of such letters in another
place but during the same era, historian John W. Blassingame
observes that such practices were "one of America's favorite pas-
times."[2] Between 1870 and 1900, Bigler contributed at least six letters to the editors of at least three different newspapers, the most
noteworthy being his 1870 letter to San Francisco's *Daily Evening
Bulletin* in which he first publicly mentioned the existence of his
gold discovery diary.

The bulk of this activity, from which Bigler emerged as a
popular spokesman for Mormonism and a valuable witness to

western American history, occurred in St. George between 1877 and 1887. Significantly, these letters went to non-Utah, non-Mormon newspapers, thus providing many readers who may have known little or nothing of Mormonism with a voice they accepted on historical matters. Bigler was a regular contributor to the newspapers of his native region, the *Telegram* of Clarksburg, West Virginia, and the Clarksburg *News*. His narratives included his experiences as a gold miner in California, with the built-in appeal of that dazzling national quest for wealth, his experiences as a Mormon missionary to the exotic and interesting Sandwich Islands, and his life as a participant in the settlement of the Utah Territory. To these readers, Bigler's was an informed voice from the Mormon West—that intriguing land of Brigham Young, polygamy, and such exotic practices as temple ceremonies.[3] While Bigler never explicitly mentions temple ordinances, other information regarding Mormon temples was available to the interested reader. The 1870 *Guide to Salt Lake City, Ogden, and the Utah Central Railroad*, for example, observed of the yet-unfinished Salt Lake Temple, "It is the centre of the hopes of many thousand devotees who cling to the Mormon faith throughout the world."[4] Bigler's personal link with the temple likely heightened reader interest. Historians Bancroft and Hittell retold his story in eastern periodicals and monumental history books.[5]

In 1885, at age seventy Bigler undertook another important project when George Q. Cannon, his old friend from Hawaii, asked him to recount his missionary experiences in the *Juvenile Instructor*, a faith-promoting publication for Mormon youth and teachers.[6] Writing under the Hawaiian form of his name, "Henele Pikale," Bigler wrote a twenty-part series entitled "Recollections of the Past," published during 1886.[7] This series began with his conversion to Mormonism, his Mormon Battalion experiences, and the discovery of gold, ending with his arrival in Utah in 1849. In places it is extracted almost verbatim from his journals, but Bigler clearly saw his history as a moral narrative with the dual purposes of not only describing historical events accurately but also inspiring and strengthening the faith of Latter-day Saint youth. For example, at one point he adds a story that does not appear in his journals but which reinforces the Word of Wisdom, which had received a great deal of attention in the speeches of Mormon general authorities at the semi-annual general conferences of 1883 and 1884. Writes Bigler: "After joining the Church, while I was reading the book of [Doctrine and] Covenants, I came to the revelation on the Word of Wisdom. At the time I was using tobacco; that is, I smoked cigars. I has just bought a bunch of one hundred; I picked them up, walked to the door, and I scattered them to the four winds."[8] Clearly, this experience did not become significant to Henry Bigler until after his ecclesiastical leaders started to advocate strict adherence to the health code. As another example of his concern to strengthen the faith of his young readers, Bigler wrote of his first impression of Joseph Smith, "I felt and fully believed he was all the Elders [who converted him in Virginia] had said he was."[9]

Writing in the 1880s as he described the forced abandonment of Nauvoo in 1846, Bigler reflected the official position taken by Brigham Young and other ecclesiastical leaders that the loss of Nauvoo was no calamity. He quoted his old friend, George A. Smith, who, in February 1846 when the last endowments were performed at the Nauvoo Temple, reassuringly stated to his family, in Bigler's presence, "Now let the mob work; the Priesthood is secure on the earth. The temple has answered the end for which it was built."[10] In telling of the discovery of gold, Bigler told the familiar and glamorous story of James Marshall's find but also reinforced the official view which discouraged Mormon participation in gold-seeking by depicting the hardships and meager returns of mining: "I sat in one position all bent over for hours, picking up the valuable particles. All at once I could not see, and as I arose to my feet I yelled with pain; I reeled and staggered and it seemed as though my back was broken."[11] Although he does not claim that quick wealth would not have been welcome, he did make it clear that life in the gold fields was anything but idyllic. His *Juvenile Instructor* narrative bemoaned the high prices of the gold rush California— "One pair of white shirts, $40; one hickory shirt, $5; one pair of socks, $3."[12] As his reminiscences and *Juvenile Instructor* writings clearly show, by his later years Henry Bigler recognized the value his story had as a faith-promoting epic.

Bigler was not the only nineteenth-century American who had interesting experiences, of course. He was, however, one of a limited number to preserve and ultimately share his colorful life with interested readers. What reasons may have prompted Bigler to keep a systematic diary for much of his life and then encouraged him to share it with others? Several factors suggest themselves.

First, he was born in a state with a renowned historical heritage—Virginia. That sense of the past was a part of his cultural background. Bigler wrote to several acquaintances between 30 June 1879 and 14 February 1880, trying to secure a copy of Alexander Wither's 1831 *Chronicles of Border Warfare*. On 19 February 1880, he noted with satisfaction, "The book has at last come."[13] This history recounted the settlement of northwestern Virginia, the area's Indian wars, and reflections by the region's pioneers. As a local history, it undoubtedly had personal significance to Bigler as he worked steadily through his life story.

Second, Bigler's conversion to Mormonism undoubtedly played a major part in shaping his tendency toward keeping a journal. Joseph Smith had appointed a scribe, Willard Richards, to record the church's history in the form of Smith's daily diary as early as 1841 and appointed an official church historian in 1843.[14] This preoccupation with a group heritage was passed on to the Saints in the form of articles about earlier episodes of church history that appeared in Mormon newspapers in Nauvoo. Bigler's long-time friend and cousin by marriage, George A. Smith, became church historian in 1854 and held that office until his death in 1870. Although Bigler records no conversations with Smith on the importance of personal or institutional history, it seems likely that Bigler valued them highly, perhaps linking them to his religious life. As nineteenth-century Mormons wrote their personal histories, many wrote, not as private expressions, but as semi-public documents, attempting to explain to their children or to nonbelieving relatives or the public at large why they believed as they did.[15]

Nor should the psychological validation provided by creating and interpreting one's life in the permanent form of a written journal or memoir be overlooked. Such a document not only preserves cherished memories but also fixes the writer's identity or place in history.[16] For Bigler, writing about his own life was not simply an expression of his faith in Mormonism but also a legacy to his family. As he explained to his friend from Sutter's Mill,

Alexander Stephens, in 1891: "I am now writing my own history. I have kep[t] a sort of journal ever since the Church left Nauvoo in 1846, but in writing my history I give some account of the day and time before the gospel found me, also genealogy of my ancestors on both sides . . . this I do for the benefit of my children after I am gone."[17] For a man who had little to bequeath in the way of worldly goods, a personal history reflecting his faith in Mormonism was a substantial inheritance.

Although Bigler's poverty was a check on his writing, he also struggled with feelings of technical inadequacy. In 1872, in the midst of preparing his memoirs for California historian H. H. Bancroft, Bigler pleaded, "Please excuse me for I fear you will laugh or sware at my awkward way of writing." But Bancroft replied with a reassurance so important that Bigler recorded it in his journal, "Despite the faults of your spelling and grammar, your diary will take a place among the valuable documents of California history; and taken as a whole, you have no need to feel ashamed of your literary work."[18]

Bigler's had been a humble life with little chance for recognition, and his simple pleasure in the modest amount of fame that came his way is endearing. He was obviously pleased to be a spokesman at public occasions. For example, the annual celebrations of Pioneer Day, commemorating the arrival of Brigham Young and the Mormon vanguard in Salt Lake Valley on 24 July 1847, usually honored venerable Saints. By request, the sixty-eight-year-old Bigler delivered an address on his Mormon Battalion experience to the St. George celebration in 1883. It is interesting for the alternative view it presents from his contemporary diary: "You may imagin[e] if you can the feelings we then had in having to part with dear ones. Husbands leaving their wives & children to obey a cruel [government] mandate if not wicked . . . because it was a duty we owed to our country and to God." He explained that "in 1846 many of the Saints had feared that the government was setting a trap to destroy the Mormon church by taking so many of the able-bodied men into the Battalion," and comforted his listeners by pointing out the operation of divine providence: "Like the Edmunds bill and the law of 62 it failed to accomplish its design." Now, as then, he prophesied, "there is no fears as regards the

Sectarian priests, Editors, politicians or even by the Cong. of the United States having the power to bring down the Latter-day Saints." This reminiscence contains no hint of Brigham Young's eagerness to cooperate with the government nor Bigler's own reluctant but unquestioned obedience to Young's instructions. Rather it was shaped to the 1880s collective self-image of the Saints, then beleaguered by intense federal prosecution for polygamy, and shows the Mormons as not only a God-fearing but a highly patriotic people. They no doubt enjoyed seeing themselves as loyally patriotic, though persecuted, Americans; and Bigler willingly cooperated in this construction of communal memory.[19]

As another example, while journeying to Salt Lake City on 2 April 1893 to attend general conference, he found himself the center of attention among his fellow travelers. "I met a number on the train who knew me and treated me with becoming respect," Bigler modestly noted in his diary.[20]

Clearly the high point of public recognition came for him in 1898 during the fiftieth anniversary of the discovery of gold. Early in 1897, John S. Hittell wrote Bigler that the Society of California Pioneers, with which Hittell had been affiliated for three decades, planned a gala the following January; Bigler promptly wrote back suggesting that the society invite the four survivors of Marshall's work crew to participate—himself, James S. Brown, William Johnston, and Azariah Smith. On 21 December 1897, Bigler received the hoped-for invitation from Hittell: "This evening the Celebrating Committee of the Pioneer Society adopted a resolution to invite you to the Golden Jubilee of California as an honored guest of the Society."[21] First-class transportation from Utah to California, along with ten days' lodging at a San Francisco hotel, would be paid for by the society. Bigler was to travel to the Golden Jubilee via Pullman sleeping car and receive fifty dollars to cover incidental expenses, both events which created a sensation in his quiet life.

Despite this generosity, Bigler's poverty left him ill-equipped even for the expenses which remained, so he approached the LDS Church leadership in Salt Lake City for additional funds. On 10 January the welcome news that the church would help came via telegram: "We have appropriated enough to furnish you a suit of clothes and give you ten or fifteen dollars pocket money besides."

Group photograph of "Marshall's Companions" on the occasion of California's 1898 Golden Jubilee. Left to right, Henry W. Bigler, William Johnston, Azariah Smith, and James S. Brown. Courtesy of the California History Room, California State Library, Sacramento.

The dispatch was signed by Bigler's long-time friend George Q. Cannon, now second counselor in the First Presidency.[22] Bigler left home for the Jubilee on 13 January 1898. After journeying four days through snow and cold by what he termed "private conveyance," Bigler must have been delighted to catch the Utah Southern Railroad at Milford, nearly a hundred miles north of St. George. After arriving in Salt Lake City, Bigler continued on to Farmington to spend the night with his sister, Hannah Bigler Miller, and visit old friends. There he met his three traveling companions, and the elderly Mormons took the Southern Pacific Railroad from Ogden, arriving at San Francisco on 22 January.[23] After making the previous trip by horseback and on foot, the ease of the train trip must have been a delight to the eighty-two-year-old Bigler.

James S. Brown was probably best known of the four after Bigler because of his 1894 publication of his reminiscences,

Reproduced by permission of the Huntington Library, San Marino, California.

California Gold, An Authentic History of the First Find. While Henry Bigler professed to respect Brown and "cannot believe he would tell anything he did not believe was true," still, Bigler candidly told Hittell that Brown's "account of the find is full of inaccuracys." He felt, however, that "it would not become me to criticise and say much as it might seem I wanted to have the honor of making known how and when the first find was made."[24]

A welcoming committee from the Society of California Pioneers greeted Bigler and the others upon their arrival. Bigler was delighted when Mary M. Greer, a relative of Hittell's, welcomed him, "Mr. Bigler, I am pleased to meet you. I know your history [as] I have read your journal," then pinned a badge on him, identifying him as a dignitary at the festivities.[25]

The party stayed at the Russ House, a palatial San Francisco hotel with three hundred rooms, electric lighting, and an elegant dining salon. That evening the four Mormons granted interviews to members of the local press and other well-connected San Franciscans. The reporter for the *San Francisco Chronicle* noted that Mr. Bigler, "a very interesting and plain mannered old man [who] likes to talk of his early experience in California," had an active mind and an excellent memory. In fact, Bigler captured the attention of the reporter so thoroughly that next day's headline read, "H. W. Bigler Tells about the Days of Sutter's Mill at Coloma."[26]

On 24 January 1898, described by Bigler as a "cold and disagreeable" day, a parade, composed of local dignitaries, fraternal orders, civic groups, and civil servants (such as firemen), and honored guests, including Bigler and his friends, wound through San Francisco's business district. "Many wanted to know which was Mr. Bigler," Bigler noted proudly. "I being the one who gave the true date of the discovery all wanted to see me."[27] In the following days, the elderly Mormons visited Golden Gate Park, where Bigler, still a backwoodsman at heart, found the grizzly bear weighing over two thousand pounds the most impressive sight. They also visited the Union Iron Works, a ship building facility that employed three thousand workers. Later Brown, Johnston, Smith, and Bigler had their photograph taken at Pioneer Hall, the headquarters of the Society of California Pioneers.[28]

On 30 January, their last Sunday in San Francisco, the Mormons attended religious services at the local LDS congregation, where each spoke and also delivered some final remarks at the closing ceremonies of the Jubilee. Each received keepsakes from the society along with the unexpected gift of fifty dollars in gold from F. J. Parsons, one of the leading organizers of the Golden Jubilee.[29]

Bigler and Smith left for Utah on 31 January. Johnston, who had lost his ticket, stayed until it was found, while Brown lingered for a few days, seeking an opportunity to lecture on the gold discovery or to preach Mormonism.[30] The Golden Jubilee celebration brought Henry Bigler acclaim and must have heightened his sense of importance. Also, it gave him the opportunity to relive history in the company of some of the men who shared this moment with him.

On his way home, Bigler called on the First Presidency in Salt Lake City who, he reported, "blessed me." It is unclear if he meant he received a formal priesthood blessing by the laying on of hands or simply expressed gratitude for the audience in these terms. He had become acquainted with President Wilford Woodruff when Woodruff presided over the St. George Temple. George Q. Cannon was an old friend; and, although there is no previous record of Bigler's knowing second counselor Joseph F. Smith, who also served a Hawaiian mission during the late 1850s, his nineteen-year-old daughter, Maud, went to Salt Lake City two months later to work as a hired girl for the Smith family.[31]

Back home in St. George, life resumed its quiet tenor. The local newspapers make no mention of the trip, nor does Bigler record reporting his visit in public or private gatherings. Maud's departure on 1 April 1898 "makes me lone some," Bigler wrote, "and I pray the Lord to bless her and be with her." His loneliness lessened three weeks later when eighteen-year-old Eleanor returned "hail and hearty" from Provo, where she had been attending Brigham Young Academy since August 1897.[32]

The visit to San Francisco was the highlight of Henry Bigler's never-very-public life. In the closing two years of his life, his journal contains events that breathe domestic concerns and a continuation of the quiet but unmovable spiritual commitments that had brought him to Mormonism sixty-four years earlier. For example, on 7

August 1898, Bigler and Eleanor blessed eleven-year-old Adelbert, who had a severe toothache: "His mother had done everything in vain to ease him, he came to me crying, I told him to tell his mother to anoint his face and tooth with consecrated oil [then] he wanted me to administer to him . . . I arose and told his mother to lay on hands with me which she did praying the Lord to ease our boy. He went to bed and slept soundly all night."[33] The matter-of-fact manner in which Bigler relates this incident speaks volumes about the simplicity and strength of his faith. On 11 July 1892 at age seventy-seven, he recorded an administration to three-year-old Myrtle, then suffering from a high fever: "I administered to [her] by the anointing of oil and laying on of hands and when I went home [from the temple] in the evening . . . the fever had in a great measure left [her]. I was thankful to God to find my child so smart."[34]

On 2 September 1898, Bigler sadly recorded: "We have word this afternoon that President Woodruff is dead, that he departed this life this morning at 7 oclock in San Francisco."[35] Eleven days later on 13 September, Henry Lunt, the seventy-four-year-old St.George Stake patriarch, came to Bigler's house to give a patriarchal blessing to departing missionary Joseph Eldridge, a man whose connection to the Bigler family is unknown. LDS patriarchs, following a pattern established with Joseph Smith, Sr., the prophet's father, were spiritual older men set apart to give patriarchal blessings, believed to contain inspired direction for individual lives. Bigler had never received such a blessing. Lunt, after completing Eldridge's blessing, "came into my room and said he wanted to bless me if I had no objections. I told him I had none [so] he laid his hands on my head and gave me a first rate blessing." Undoubtedly with Woodruff's recent death in mind, Lunt promised Henry Bigler he would go to his grave "like a shock of corn fully ripe and not taste death more than Brother Woodruff and [that Bigler] was beloved of the Lord."[36]

This blessing seems to have been literally fulfilled. Bigler was spared a lingering, debilitating illness and does not mention any physical ailments in his diary. On 24 November 1898, he had all of his grandfather Jacob Bigler's children sealed to their father as well as doing similar temple work for other ancestors. On 9 January 1899 when the ordinance workers at the St. George

Temple commemorated the first baptisms for the dead at that temple twenty-two years earlier, Bigler proudly observed, "The work done on that day [9 January 1877] shows that I confirmed 180 persons for the Dead as kept by the [temple] Recorders."[37]

Henry Bigler was now eighty-four. It is probable that his health was failing, although his last recorded temple ordinance was on 10 August 1899, when he had "all of Grand Father Harveys children sealed to [him] and his two wives."[38] On 19 October 1899 he received a "cordial invitation" to participate in the fiftieth anniversary of California's statehood to be held at San Jose in December. Regretfully, Bigler declined this offer because he felt "too old to travel far from home."[39]

On 15 July 1900, he responded to a letter from a W. E. Ashburn of West Virginia that challenged his explanation of the Mormon doctrine of baptism by immersion. In obvious irritation, Bigler wrote:

> You make a great fuss over what I said that no one can be saved unless baptized by immersion by one having authority. I say so still. Your language on that subject is insulting and abusive in the extream. . . . You have preached quite a sermon to prove that a person can be saved without baptism now I will preach you a short sermon that people must be baptized in order to be saved. . . . I refer you to Mark 16: 15, 16, Acts 2: 37 and 39, Acts 8: 36–39. . . . I still believe that baptism by emersion to be valid must be done by one having authority or it is of no account.[40]

Ashburn apparently responded with a hostile rejoinder, and the still-vigorous Bigler, only three months before his death, wrote again, reaffirming the necessity of baptism by immersion by the proper authority and warning: "You may turn and twist the scriptures as you please, but you will find in the end at the bar of God you have been wresting them to your own destruction."[41] It is appropriate that virtually his last written words were a stirring defense of his faith.

Bigler died quietly and relatively quickly of pneumonia at St. George, Utah, on the morning of 24 November 1900, attended by Eleanor and at least three of his children. Two days later, the *Los Angeles Evening Express* noted the passing of Henry William

Bigler, "the man who made the first record of the great California gold discovery in 1848," and Salt Lake City's *Deseret Evening News* eulogized him as "one of the notable characters of Western America." This obituary briefly recalled his service with the Mormon Battalion, his presence at Sutter's Mill when gold was discovered, two missions to the Hawaiian Islands during the 1850s, and his years of service as an ordinance worker at the St. George Temple. "As a pioneer in Utah," the article observed, "he has been an active, energetic man, well and favorably known." Bigler would also have appreciated the eulogy's closing sentence, "He goes down to the grave . . . with an honorable record before all who have known him." About twenty years later, Andrew Jenson, assistant church historian, praised him as "an unassuming, humble, useful man, beloved by everyone who knew him."[42]

History tends to focus on the comparatively rare figures who occupy positions of social or political prominence, while those like Bigler, who make up the fabric of history, remain in the background. Many who receive no public attention during their lives lack any kind of private record to counter the public blankness. Here, however, Henry Bigler proves an exception. His journals and autobiography are a window through which to view stories of a host of lesser-known Latter-day Saints of the nineteenth century.

Biographer Jerome G. Manis suggests the concept of "great little persons" to describe the unrecorded or underrecorded "individuals whose lives or actions have had important consequences."[43] Bigler's life story parallels the Mormon experience from the 1840s on, typical in many ways of the average Mormon's story. He embraced the Latter-day Saint gospel, heeded Joseph Smith's call to gather to Zion, suffered persecution and dislocation, served as a missionary, reared a family, and helped build a community; and then, as his final act of commitment, he labored over twenty-three years as an ordinance worker in the sacred rituals of Mormonism.

Henry Bigler's family and his religion were his life. He can accurately be described as a Mormon "true believer"—a militant defender of the cause he followed, marked by single-hearted allegiance and self sacrifice. Often, according to Eric Hoffer, a true believer is "a man of fanatical faith who is ready to sacrifice his life for a holy cause."[44] While it is difficult to see Henry Bigler as a fanatic, he certainly was willing to give his all for Mormonism. Hoffer's true believer is also a practical "man of action"—a label which clearly fits Bigler. Social, political, or economic discontent, commonly accompanied by a feeling of powerlessness, are, according to Hoffer, other traits of the true believer.[45]

Henry Bigler, whose patience with poverty, scanty education, and lack of worldly ambition would have marginalized him in most societies, found a secure and honored place in Mormonism for his single-hearted allegiance following his 1837 conversion. The wish to be a true Saint "however great the cross," to an extent unusual in the many facets that represent most human personalities, explains Henry Bigler. This desire led him to sacrifice any opportunity for wealth, to postpone marriage and children, and to commit the last quarter-century of his life to financially unremunerative religious labor. Yet according to his Mormon beliefs, his achievements were heroic. As Hoffer points out, the true believer is "capable of releasing a powerful flow of activity" into the cause holding his allegiance. Such commitment is possible because "the true believer is apt to see himself as one of the chosen, the salt of the earth."[46] Bigler, like his cobelievers, saw himself engaged in a mighty work—preaching the gospel to the living and redeeming even the dead.

Notes

Introduction

1. Eric Hoffer coined the phrase "true believer" to identify those who willingly sacrifice themselves during the most active phases of building a new movement. This description fits Bigler, although he never reached the final stage of Hoffer's model, a fanatical defense of the cause. *The True Believer: Thoughts on the Nature of Mass Movements* (New York, 1951), x. Robert Lawrence Kuhn's and George Thomas Geis's portrait of the "partisan . . . unshakable in mind and deed, zealous in fervor and intensity, . . . ready to sacrifice for the good of the organization" offers another model similar to that of Hoffer's. Robert Lawrence Kuhn and George Thomas Geis, *The Firm Bond: Linking Meaning and Mission in Business and Religion* (New York, 1984), 82.
2. Erwin G. Gudde, *Bigler's Chronicle of the West: The Conquest of California, Discovery of Gold, and Mormon Settlement as Reflected in Henry William Bigler's Diaries* (Berkeley, 1962), 135.
3. Hubert H. Bancroft, *History of California*, 7 vols. (San Francisco, 1884–90), 6:32 n.

Chapter 1
The Making of a Mormon, 1836–38

1. Henry William Bigler, autobiography, ca. 1898, 13, (hereafter cited as Autobiography), Archives, Historical Department of the Church

of Jesus Christ of Latter-day Saints, Salt Lake City, Utah (hereafter cited as LDS Archives).

2. Bathsheba Wilson Bigler Smith, autobiography, ca. 1875–1906, 1, Family History Library, Church of Jesus Christ of Latter-day Saints, Salt Lake City, Utah; hereafter cited as Family History Library.

3. Norman Burns, "The Bigler Family: Descendants of Mark Bigler Who Immigrated to America in 1773," typescript, 1960, 1, Family History Library; Bernard Bailyn, *The Peopling of British North America: An Introduction* (New York, 1986), 22.

4. Autobiography, 4; Franklin Keith Brough, *Freely I Gave: The Life of Jacob G. Bigler* (Wichita, Kansas, 1958), 3; Henry P. Haywood, *History of Harrison County* (Morgantown, West Virginia, 1910), 17–18, 275, 344–45.

5. Jack Sandy Anderson, "The Levi Shinn House," *West Virginia History* 29 (January 1968): 138–40; Hamill Kenny, *West Virginia Place Names* (Piedmont, West Virginia, 1945), 574.

6. Autobiography, 3, 5.

7. Ibid., 11–12.

8. Ibid., 8, 9.

9. Ibid., 9.

10. Ibid., 6, 11; Otis K. Rice, *West Virginia: A History* (Lexington, Kentucky, 1985), 223–24.

11. Sidney L. Ahlstrom, *A Religious History of the American People* (New Haven, 1972), 320–21.

12. Rice, 267–308.

13. Autobiography, 13; Manuscript History of the Virginia Conference, LDS Archives.

14. Autobiography, 14.

15. Leonard J. Arrington and Davis Bitton, *The Mormon Experience: A History of the Latter-day Saints* (New York, 1979), 27–29.

16. John Steele, "Extracts from the Journal of John Steele," *Utah Historical Quarterly* 6 (January 1933): 3.

17. Lorenzo Dow Young, "Biography of Lorenzo Dow Young," *Utah Historical Quarterly* 14 (January 1946): 33–34.

18. Joseph Smith, *History of the Church of Jesus Christ of Latter-day Saints, Period 1, History of Joseph Smith, the Prophet, By Himself,* 7 vols., 2d ed. rev. (Salt Lake City, 1976), 1:16. This version of Joseph Smith's account was canonized and now forms part of the Pearl of Great Price, one of the LDS scriptures. Hereafter *History of the Church,* cited by volume and page number.

19. Autobiography, 15.

20. Ibid., 15–17. He was referring to the ordinance of vicarious baptism for the dead, discussed in more detail in chaps. 2 and 9.

21. Ibid., 17.

22. Mormon millenarianism differed from that of the Shakers or John Humphrey Noyes's Oneida community in New York. Both movements professed that Christ had already come, while the Mormons anticipated it in the near future. Although they shared this perspective with the Millerites, they differed in not pinning their hopes on an exact date. See Jonathan Butler, "From Millerism to Seventh-day Adventism: 'Boundlessness to Consolidation,'" *Church History* 55 (March 1986): 50–64; David L. Rowe, "A New Perspective on the Burned-Over District: The Millerites in Upstate New York," *Church History* 47 (December 1978): 408–20; Grant Underwood, "Millenarianism and the Early Mormon Mind," *Journal of Mormon History* 9 (1982): 41–52.

23. Richard L. Jennings, "The City in the Garden: Social Conflict in Jackson County, Missouri," in F. Mark McKiernan, Alma R. Blair, and Paul M. Edwards, eds., *The Restoration Movement: Essays in Mormon History* (Lawrence, Kansas, 1973), 99–119; Warren A. Jennings, "The Expulsion of the Mormons from Jackson County, Missouri," *Missouri Historical Review* 64 (October 1969): 41–63; and R. J. Robertson, "The Mormon Experience in Missouri, 1830–1839," *Missouri Historical Review* 68 (April 1974): 280–98.

24. Autobiography, 19.

25. John D. Lee, quoted in Fawn M. Brodie, *No Man Knows My History: The Life of Joseph Smith*, 2d ed. (New York, 1982), 125.

26. Autobiography, 20–21.

27. Ibid., 22.

28. Ibid., 23–24; Brough, 6–8.

29. Stephen C. LeSueur, *The 1838 Mormon War in Missouri* (Columbia, Missouri, 1987), 150–51.

30. Autobiography, 23.

31. Ibid., 23–24.

32. Davis Bitton and Leonard J. Arrington, *Mormons and Their Historians* (Salt Lake City, 1987), 15, 23.

33. Henry W. Bigler to Alexander Stephens, 5 April 1891, Special Collections, Merrill Library, Utah State University, Logan, Utah.

34. Robert Bruce Flanders, "Nauvoo Revisited," in *The Restoration Movement*, 149; see also Marvin S. Hill, *Quest for Refuge: The Mormon Flight from American Pluralism* (Salt Lake City, 1989).

Chapter 2
On the Forge, 1839–45

1. Autobiography, 26.
2. Roger D. Launius and John E. Hallwas, eds., *Kingdom on the Mississippi Revisited* (Urbana, 1996), 1.
3. *History of the Church*, 3:301.
4. Ibid., 3:260; James B. Allen and Glen M. Leonard, *The Story of the Latter-day Saints* (Salt Lake City, 1976), 141; Robert Bruce Flanders, *Nauvoo: Kingdom on the Mississippi* (Urbana, 1965), 25–26.
5. Autobiography, 24, 29.
6. Ibid., 24.
7. Ibid., 25.
8. Flanders, 37–38; see also Dennis Rowley, "Nauvoo: A River Town," *BYU Studies* 18 (winter 1978): 255–72; David E. Miller and Della S. Miller, *Nauvoo: The City of Joseph* (Santa Barbara, California, 1974), 27; M. Guy Bishop, Vincent Lacey, and Richard Wixon, "Death at Mormon Nauvoo, 1843–45," *Western Illinois Regional Studies* 9 (fall 1986): 70–83.
9. Autobiography, 25.
10. Lyons was junior in both age and authority. Bigler had been ordained to the Melchizedek priesthood, of which "elder" was the first rank (seventy and high priest were the two higher offices), while Lyons was ordained to the Aaronic, or "lesser," priesthood in which the offices were, in ascending order, deacon, teacher, and priest.
11. Autobiography, 25.
12. Ibid., 26.
13. *History of the Church*, 4:11; Samuel George Ellsworth, "A History of Mormon Missions in the United States and Canada, 1830–1860" (Ph.D. diss., University of California, Berkeley, 1951), chap 2.
14. Autobiography, 26.
15. Ibid., 27.
16. *History of the Church*, 4:472; Flanders, 47.
17. Autobiography, 27.
18. Charlotte Haven, "A Girl's Letters from Nauvoo," *Overland Monthly* 16 (July–December 1890): 620–21.
19. Michael Guy Bishop, "The Celestial Family: Early Mormon Thought on Life and Death, 1830–1846" (Ph.D. diss., Southern Illinois University, Carbondale, 1981), 37–38.
20. *Times and Seasons* 5 (15 January 1844): 412.
21. Ibid., 5 (1 January 1844): 329.

22. Stephen Post, journal, 12 November 1842, Stephen Post Papers, LDS Archives.

23. Danel Bachman, "A Study of the Mormon Practice of Plural Marriage before the Death of Joseph Smith" (M.A. thesis, Purdue University, 1975); Lawrence Foster, *Religion and Sexuality: The Shakers, the Mormons, and the Oneida Community* (1981; reprint ed., Urbana, 1984); Linda King Newell and Valeen Tippetts Avery, *Mormon Enigma: Emma Hale Smith* (Garden City, New York, 1984); Richard S. Van Wagoner, *Mormon Polygamy: A History*, 2d ed. (Salt Lake City, 1989).

24. *Times and Seasons* 3 (1 August 1842): 868–69; see also Flanders, 93–97.

25. Autobiography, 27.

26. Brodie, 314–15; Flanders, 265.

27. Autobiography, 27; *History of the Church*, 5:136–37.

28. Autobiography, 27–28; *History of the Church*, 5:193.

29. Henry W. Bigler, "Henry William Bigler's Journal, Book A," 1846–50, typescript of three volumes in one, 5, Special Collections and Manuscripts Department, Harold B. Lee Library, Brigham Young University, Provo, Utah; hereafter cited as Journal, typescript.

30. Journal, typescript, 5–6.

31. Autobiography, 29.

32. Journal, typescript, 7.

33. Autobiography, 30.

34. Ibid.

35. Ibid., 30–31.

36. Ibid., 30.

37. Ibid., 31.

38. In Roger D. Launius, "American Home Missionary Society Ministers and Mormon Nauvoo: Selected Letters," *Western Illinois Regional Studies* 8 (spring 1985): 26.

39. Autobiography, 31.

40. Journal, typescript, 11.

41. D. Michael Quinn, "LDS Church Authority and New Plural Marriages, 1890–1904," *Dialogue: A Journal of Mormon Thought* 18 (spring 1985): 9–105.

42. Autobiography, 32.

43. Journal, typescript, 11–12.

44. See Marshall Hamilton, "From Assassination to Expulsion: Two Years of Distrust, Hostility and Violence," in Launius and Hallwas, eds., 214–30.

45. Autobiography, 32.
46. Journal, typescript, 12.
47. B. H. Roberts, *A Comprehensive History of the Church of Jesus Christ of Latter-day Saints, Century I*, 6 vols. (Salt Lake City, 1930; 1965 printing), 2:93–95; M. Guy Bishop, "Eternal Marriage in Early Mormon Marital Beliefs," *The Historian* 53 (autumn 1990): 77–88.
48. David John Buerger, "The Development of the Mormon Temple Endowment Ceremony," *Dialogue: A Journal of Mormon Thought* 20 (winter 1987): 33–76; Mark F. Leone, "The Mormon Temple Experience," *Sunstone* 3 (September–October 1979): 6–10.
49. Autobiography, 34.
50. Ibid.
51. Richard S. Van Wagoner and Steven C. Walker, *A Book of Mormons* (Salt Lake City, 1982), 270.

Chapter 3
Marching to the Pacific, 1846–48

1. Autobiography, 40.
2. Ibid., 35; *History of the Church*, 7:581.
3. Journal, typescript, 19. See also Susan W. Easton, "Suffering and Death on the Plains of Iowa," *BYU Studies* 21 (fall 1981): 431–39.
4. Journal, typescript, 35–36.
5. Ibid., 37.
6. Ibid., 39.
7. William L. Barney, *The Passage of the Republic: An Interdisciplinary History of Nineteenth Century America* (Lexington, Massachusetts, 1987), 164.
8. Seymour V. Connor and Odie B. Faulk, *North America Divided: The Mexican War, 1846–48* (New York, 1971), 21–24, 26–32; Robert W. Johannsen, *To the Halls of Montezuma: The Mexican War in the American Imagination* (New York, 1985), 7–8.
9. David Lavender, *The Great West* (Boston, 1965), 226.
10. Stephen E. Ambrose, *Undaunted Courage: Meriweather Lewis, Thomas Jefferson, and the Opening of the West* (New York, 1996), 94.
11. John S. D. Eisenhower, *So Far from God: The U.S. War with Mexico 1846–48* (New York, 1989), 195.
12. In Daniel Tyler, *A Concise History of the Mormon Battalion in the Mexican War* (1881; 4th ed., Glorieta, New Mexico, 1980), 113–14; see

also Norma Baldwin Ricketts, *The Mormon Battalion: U.S. Army of the West, 1846–1848* (Logan, Utah, 1996); W. Ray Luce, "The Mormon Battalion: A Historical Accident?" *Utah Historical Quarterly* 42 (winter 1974): 27–38; Eisenhower, 195.

13. Autobiography, 39. On the enlistment of the Mormon Battalion, see Ricketts, *The Mormon Battalion*, 5–6.

14. John F. Yurtinus, "'Here Is One Man Who Will Not Go, Dam 'um: Recruiting the Mormon Battalion in Iowa Territory," *BYU Studies* 21 (fall 1981): 476.

15. In John F. Yurtinus, "A Ram in the Thicket: The Mormon Battalion in the Mexican War," 2 vols. (Ph.D. diss., Brigham Young University, 1975), 1:39–40.

16. Autobiography, 40.

17. Ibid.

18. Tyler, 120, 124, 126; for the roster of the Mormon Battlalion, including Bigler's own Company B, see Ricketts, *The Mormon Battalion*, 21–28.

19. Tyler, 128–29.

20. Ibid., 134; see also Autobiography, 41. When the battalion arrived at Fort Leavenworth in early August, "several were shaking with chills and fever." Three heavy rainstorms they had encountered en route had caused these malaria-like symptoms. Ricketts, *The Mormon Battalion*, 35.

21. Autobiography, 41.

22. Tyler, 128.

23. Journal, typescript, 41; Ricketts, *The Mormon Battalion*, 37.

24. Journal, typescript, 41–42.

25. Ibid.

26. See Ricketts, *The Mormon Battalion*, 40.

27. Tyler, 143.

28. Journal, typescript, 42.

29. Ibid., 28.

30. Eugene E. Campbell, "The Mormon Gold Mining Mission of 1849," *BYU Studies* 1 (autumn 1959–winter 1960): 19–31.

31. Journal, typescript, 33, 45.

32. Ibid., 28. John Steele of Company D wrote, "The storm came with such violence that nothing could withstand its power." Ricketts, *The Mormon Battalion*, 42.

33. Journal, typescript, 33.

34. Autobiography, 43.

35. Ibid., 45.
36. James Pace, journal, 7 August 1846 to 7 October 1847, 9, holograph, LDS Archives.
37. Henry Standage, journal, 1846–47, typescript, Mormon File, Henry E. Huntington Library, San Marino, California. Pettegrew quote from Ricketts, *The Mormon Battalion*, 49.
38. Journal, typescript, 32–33, 36.
39. Tyler, 145–46.
40. Ibid.
41. Philip St. George Cooke, "Official Journal of the March of Lieutenant Colonel Philip St. George Cooke from Santa Fe, in New Mexico, to San Diego, in Upper California," *Report from the Secretary of War to the United States Senate, March 19, 1849* (Washington, D.C., 1849), 2, 3.
42. Ibid., 2; Tyler, 169–70.
43. Autobiography, 47.
44. Ibid., 48.
45. Journal, typescript, 47.
46. Autobiography, 50.
47. Ibid., 48.
48. Journal, typescript, 47.
49. Robert Stanton Bliss, diary, 1846–48, 6 November 1846, holograph, San Diego Historical Society, San Diego, California.
50. Journal, typescript, 45.
51. Henry Green Boyle, journal, 1824–88, 14 November and 3 December 1847, Special Collections and Manuscripts Department, Harold B. Lee Library, Brigham Young University, Provo, Utah; photocopy of holograph at the Huntington Library.
52. Cooke, 21–22.
53. Journal, typescript, 45, 47.
54. Standage, journal, 11 December 1846. See also Ricketts, *The Mormon Battalion*, 94.
55. Journal, typescript, 57–58.
56. Tyler, 371.
57. Ibid., 222–23.
58. Ibid., 233.
59. Cooke, 65.
60. Boyle, journal, 16 January 1847; Journal, typescript, 56.
61. Cooke, 72.
62. Journal, typescript, 56.
63. Boyle, journal, 27 January 1847.

64. Journal, typescript, 60.
65. See M. Guy Bishop, "'We Are Rather Weaker in Righteousness Than in Numbers': The Mormon Colony at San Bernardino, California, 1851–1857," in Carl Guarneri and David Alvarez, eds., *Religion and Society in the American West* (Lanham, Maryland, 1987), 171–96.
66. Journal, typescript, 60.
67. Cooke, 84–85.
68. Bliss, diary, 30 January 1847.
69. Journal, typescript, 62.
70. Zephyrin Engelhardt, *San Luis Rey Mission* (San Francisco, 1921), 3–14.
71. Journal, typescript, 63.
72. Ibid.
73. Tyler, 264, 266.
74. Ibid., 256–57; Cooke, 72.
75. Journal, typescript, 67–68; Gudde, *Bigler's Chronicle of the West*, 57; Tyler, 286–87.
76. Journal, typescript, 65, 67.
77. Standage, journal, 25 and 18 April 1847.
78. Pace, journal, 24 April 1847, 41.
79. Journal, typescript, 68.
80. Ibid.

Chapter 4
Sutter's Mill, 1848

1. Gudde, *Bigler's Chronicle of the West*, 66–67.
2. "Diary of H. W. Bigler in 1847 and 1848," ed. John S. Hittel, *Overland Monthly* 10 (September 1887): 239. Also helpful for understanding this portion of Bigler's battalion experience is J. Roderic Korns and Dale L. Morgan, eds., *West from Fort Bridger: The Pioneering of Immigrant Trails across Utah, 1846–1850*, revised and updated by Will Bagley and Harold Schindler (Logan, Utah, 1994), especially 278–301.
3. Journal, typescript, 3.
4. Ibid., 72.
5. Dale L. Morgan, *Jedediah Smith and the Opening of the West* (Lincoln, 1953), 117.
6. Journal, typescript, 72.
7. Bliss, 22 July 1847; *Overland Monthly*, 239.

8. Journal, typescript, 72.
9. *Overland Monthly*, 239.
10. Journal, typescript, 79.
11. Gudde, *Bigler's Chronicle of the West*, 59.
12. Ibid., 69.
13. Harvey Clinton McReady, "New Hope: A Mormon Colony in Central California" (M.A. thesis, Brigham Young University, 1976), 54. He may have exaggerated. Bancroft reported "ten or twelve colonists and several houses" in April 1847. Bancroft, *History of California*, 6:11–12.
14. Allen and Leonard, 244.
15. Journal, typescript, 81.
16. *Overland Monthly*, 240.
17. Helen Putnam Van Sicklen, ed., *New Helvetia Diary: Record of Events Kept by John A. Sutter and His Clerks at New Helvetia, California, from September 9, 1845 to May 25, 1848* (San Francisco, 1939), 72.
18. See Bancroft, *History of California*, 6:28; Jean-Nicholas Perlot, *Gold Seeker: Adventures of a Belgian Argonaut during the Gold Rush Years*, ed. Howard R. Lamar (New Haven, 1985), 5n; Andrew F. Rolle, *California: A History*, 3d ed. (Arlington Heights, Illinois, 1978), 162; James P. Zollinger, *Sutter: The Man and His Empire* (New York, 1939).
19. Journal, typescript, 82.
20. *Overland Monthly*, 240.
21. Journal, typescript, 85..
22. Ibid.
23. Journal, typescript, 85–86.
24. C. F. McGlashan, *History of the Donner Party: A Tragedy of the Sierra* (Stanford, California, 1940), xii–xiii, xxii; Bernard DeVoto, *The Year of Decision: 1846* (Boston, 1942), 350–58.
25. Gudde, *Bigler's Chronicle of the West*, 74.
26. *Overland Monthly*, 240.
27. Ibid., 240–41.
28. Ibid., 241.
29. Bancroft, *History of California*, 6:29; John Walton Caughey, *The California Gold Rush* (Berkeley, 1975), 6; Theressa Gay, *James W. Marshall: The Discoverer of California Gold* (Georgetown, California, 1967); Aubrey Neasham, "Sutter's Sawmill," *California Historical Society Quarterly* 26 (June 1947): 110.
30. *Overland Monthly*, 241; J. Kenneth Davies, *Mormon Gold: The Story of California's Mormon Argonauts* (Salt Lake City, 1984), 357.

31. Gudde, *Bigler's Chronicle of the West*, 87–88.
32. Neasham, 113–14; Norma Baldwin Ricketts, *Mormons and the Discovery of Gold* (Sacramento, 1982), 15.
33. Gudde, *Bigler's Chronicle of the West*, 84.
34. William C. Grant, diary, United States Military Academy Library, West Point, New York; Ricketts, *The Mormon Battalion*, 15; Gudde, *Bigler's Chronicle of the West*, 84.
35. James W. Marshall, as quoted in *Hutchings California Magazine* 2 (November 1857): 201.
36. *Overland Monthly*, 242.
37. John S. Hittell, James W. Marshall, and Edwin G. Waite, *The Discovery of Gold* (Palo Alto, 1968), 24.
38. Gudde, *Bigler's Chronicle of the West*, 87–88. Compare David L. Bigler, ed., *The Gold Discovery Journal of Azariah Smith* (Logan, Utah, 1996), 108. Smith was making only weekly entries (on Sundays), thus he records the happenings of the 24th on 30 January.
39. D. Bigler, 108, n. 39.
40. Gudde, *Bigler's Chronicle of the West*, 89.
41. Ibid.
42. Van Sicklen, 113.
43. *Overland Monthly*, 241.
44. Ibid., 243. Compare D. Bigler, 109–10.
45. Ibid.
46. Van Sicklen, 113.
47. *Overland Monthly*, 241, 244. Azariah Smith also appears to have been bitten by the "gold bug." He records hunting gold on six different occasions between 14 February and 7 April. See D. Bigler, 110–12.
48. *Overland Monthly*, 241–42.
49. Davies, 21.
50. Ibid., 22–23.
51. *Overland Monthly*, 243.
52. Ibid., 244–45.
53. Van Sicklen, 138, 129. *Overland Monthly*, 244.
54. *Overland Monthly*, 245.
55. Caughey, 39–43; Rodman W. Paul, *California Gold: The Beginning of Mining in the Far West* (Cambridge, 1947), 22–23; Rolle, 195.
56. On the Salt Lake Cutoff, see Korns and Morgan, 277–306. Henry Bigler's journey along this route is mentioned intermittently throughout these pages.
57. *Overland Monthly*, 245; Journal, typescript, 106.

Chapter 5
Reluctant Argonaut, 1849–50

1. Henry W. Bigler, journal, Book B, 10 October 1849–15 November 1850, 114, Huntington Library; hereafter cited as Book B, by page number or date.

2. Gudde, *Bigler's Chronicle of the West*, 129; Brigham Madsen, *Gold Rush Sojourners in Great Salt Lake City 1849 and 1850* (Salt Lake City, 1983), 1.

3. Book B, 109–10.

4. Thirtieth Quorum of Seventies, Records 1839–76, November 1850, LDS Archives.

5. In Eugene E. Campbell, "The Mormon Gold Mining Mission of 1849," *BYU Studies* 1 (autumn 1959–winter 1960): 2; see also Davies, 60–62; Leonard J. Arrington, *Brigham Young: American Moses* (New York, 1985), 181–82.

6. Journal, typescript.

7. Orson F. Whitney, *History of Utah*, 4 vols. (Salt Lake City, 1892), 1:386–87.

8. Davies, 109–10.

9. Ibid.

10. LeRoy R. Hafen and Ann W. Hafen, eds., *Journals of the Forty-Niners Salt Lake to Los Angeles: With Diaries and Contemporary Records of Sheldon Young, James S. Brown, Jacob Y. Stover, Charles C. Rich, Addison Pratt, Howard Egan, Henry W. Bigler, and Others* (Glendale, California, 1954), 142–43; Campbell, 23.

11. Irene M. Bates, "Uncle John Smith, 1781–1854: Patriarchal Bridge," *Dialogue: A Journal of Mormon Thought* 20 (fall 1987): 84–86; Davies, 163–64.

12. Book B, 112–13.

13. Ibid, 113.

14. Ibid., 114.

15. Ibid., 113.

16. Ibid., 114–15. For a more typical reaction, see the eager anticipation recorded by two other diarists who also set out for California in 1849, William C. Johnston, *Experiences of a Forty-Niner* (New York, 1973), 20–22; and Friedrich Gerstaecker, *California Gold Mines*, foreword by Joseph A. Sullivan (Oakland, 1946), 1–9. The account of Bigler's and Keeler's trip to California is taken from Journal, typescript, 114–46.

17. Davies, 161; Hafen and Hafen, 141.

18. Book B, 116.

19. Ibid., 116; William Lewis Manley, *Death Valley in '49* (1894; reprint ed., Bishop, California, 1977), 105; George Koenig, *"Beyond This Place There Be Dragons": The Routes of the Tragic Trek of the Death Valley 1849ers through Nevada, Death Valley, and to Southern California* (Glendale, California, 1984), 25.

20. Koenig, 25. For additional discussions of this ill-fated adventure, see Hafen and Hafen, 34–36; Charles Kelly, "On Manley's Trail to Death Valley," *Desert Magazine* 2 (February 1939): 6–8; Richard E. Lingenfelter, *Death Valley and the Amargosa: A Land of Illusion* (Berkeley and Los Angeles, 1986); Manley, 18; Clifford L. Stott, *Search for Sanctuary: Brigham Young and the White Mountain Expedition* (Salt Lake City, 1984), 11–12.

21. Hafen and Hafen, 149.

22. Ibid., 121; emphasis theirs.

23. Book B, 3 November 1849; Kelly, 41; and Koenig, 30. This rock is near the current Utah-Nevada border about twenty-five miles due east of Caliente, Nevada. Charles Kelly saw the carving in 1938, and George Koenig saw it in the early 1980s. Other trail historians have reported seeing it within the past decade.

24. Book B, 8 November 1849.

25. Ibid., 18 November 1849.

26. Ibid., 9 November 1849.

27. Ibid., 16 November 1849.

28. For background on this party, see Hafen and Hafen, 210–11; James Edsell Serven, "The Ill-Fated '49er Train," *The Historical Society of Southern California* 62 (March 1960): 29–40. Smith fought on the Union side in the Civil War, was wounded at Antietam, and died at Los Angeles in 1904. Margaret Long, *The Shadow of the Arrow* (Caldwell, Idaho, 1950), 301.

29. Book B, 5 December 1849.

30. Ibid., 18 December 1849.

31. Ibid., 25 December 1849.

32. Ibid., 18 November 1849.

33. Hafen and Hafen, 66–69, 77–78.

34. Book B, 18 November 1849.

35. Ibid., 31 December 1849.

36. Paul, 24–25.

37. Caughey, *The California Gold Rush*.

38. Book B, 25 September 1850.

39. Ibid., 23 September 1850. This silence is so unusual for Bigler, otherwise a model of consistency, that it supports J. Kenneth Davies's

hypothesis that these Mormon miners may have been counseled *not* to record their experiences in the gold fields. Davies, 227. Corroborating evidence is the fact that Bigler's associates, George Q. Cannon, William Farrer, and James Keeler, were also daily diarists for extended periods of their lives and had all kept diaries of the journey from Utah to California; these diaries were also silent for the months they were mining.

40. Erwin G.Gudde, *California Gold Camps: A Geographical and Historical Dictionary of Camps, Towns, and Localities where Gold Was Found and Mined; Waystations and Trading Centers* (Berkeley, 1975); Gudde, *Bigler's Chronicle of the West*, 131.

41. Book B, 25 September 1850.

42. Gudde, *Bigler's Chronicle of the West*, 131.

43. Book B, 25 September 1850.

44. Ibid.

45. Ibid., 22 October 1850.

46. Ibid., 29 and 30 October 1850; Roger W. Lochkin, *San Francisco 1846–1856: From Hamlet to City* (New York, 1974), 67.

47. Conway B. Sonne, *Ships, Saints, and Mariners: A Maritime Encyclopedia of Mormon Migration* (Salt Lake City, 1987), 104–5. Sonne and Bigler disagree by two days on when the vessel cleared port.

Chapter 6
The Sandwich Islands, 1850–54

1. Autobiography, 60.

2. John A. Andrew III, *Rebuilding the Christian Commonwealth: New England Congregationalists* (Lexington, Kentucky, 1976); Nathan O. Hatch, "Millennialism and Popular Religion in the Early Republic," in *The Evangelical Tradition in America*, ed. Leonard I. Sweet (Macon, Georgia, 1984); Ralph S. Kuykendall, *The Hawaiian Kingdom*, 3 vols. (Honolulu, 1980 ed.), 1:100–116; Clifton Jackson Philips, *Protestant America and the Pagan World: The First Half Century of the American Board of Commissioners for Foreign Missions, 1810–1860* (Cambridge, 1969).

3. Kuykendall, 1:24–25.

4. Gavan Daws, *Shoal of Time: A History of the Hawaiian Islands* (Honolulu, 1974), 64.

5. R. Lanier Britsch, *Moramona: The Mormons in Hawaii* (Laie, Hawaii, 1989), 11.

6. Ibid., 80–81.

7. George Q. Cannon, *My First Mission*, vol. 1 in the Faith Promoting Series (Salt Lake City: Juvenile Instructor Office, 1879), 4–8; typed extracts from the St. George, Utah, *Union* (hereafter *Union* extracts), 15–16, in Henry William Bigler Collection, Huntington Library.

8. Journal, typescript, 13 December 1850; see also George Q. Cannon, diaries, 1849–54, 13 December 1850, LDS Archives; hereafter cited as Cannon, by date; Britsch, *Moramona*, 4.

9. Journal, typescript, 15 December 1850.

10. Ibid.

11. Hawaiian Mission Children's Society, *Missionary Album: Portraits and Biographical Sketches of the American Protestant Missionaries to the Hawaiian Islands*, sesquicentennial ed., 1820–1870 (Honolulu, 1969), 14–16; Kuykendall, 1:104–6; Cummins E. Speakman, Jr., *Mowee: An Informal History of the Hawaiian Island* (San Rafael, California, 1981), 105–6.

12. Kanehoa [John Young] to Minister of the Interior, 21 December 1850, Minister of the Interior Papers, Hawaii State Archives. Young's letter is misdated.

13. Journal, typescript, 22 December 1850; Cannon, 22 December 1850; Keeler, 22 December 1850.

14. Cannon, 4 January 1851.

15. Journal, typescript, 29 December 1850.

16. G. Cannon, *My First Mission*, 14.

17. Ibid., 58–61; Britsch, *Moramona*, 5; Journal, typescript,19 January 1851; Keeler, 19 January 1851. Years after the fact, both Bigler and Cannon affirmed that Cannon's linguistic ability was the result of a miracle (see *Union* extracts, 26), but Cannon's diary does not report a miraculous event, only endless hours of study (see his *My First Mission*, 58–61).

18. Henry W. Bigler to William Farrer, 26 June 1852, Hawaiian Mission Letters, 1851–54, LDS Archives; Book B, 28 August 1853.

19. Journal, typescript, 13 January 1851.

20. Ibid., 2 Febuary 1851; Hafen and Hafen, 193.

21. Journal, typescript, 9 April 1851.

22. Clark had previously filled two successful missions to Great Britain but had apparently been unable to withstand the temptations of Polynesia's sexual freedom. He was excommunicated by Addison Pratt and the Mormon missionaries in Tubuai in the Society Islands, and committed suicide at San Bernardino, California, in December 1853. Phillip Bessom Lewis eventually became the second president

of the Hawaiian Mission (1851–55). Andrew Jenson, *Latter-day Saint Biographical Encyclopedia: A Compilation of Biographical Sketches of Prominent Men and Women in the Church of Jesus Christ of Latter-day Saints*, 4 vols. (Salt Lake City, 1901–36), 3:672, 4:338–39; Donald Robert Shaffer, "A Forgotten Missionary: Hiram Clark, Mormon Itinerant, British Emigration Organizer, and First President of the L.D.S. Hawaiian Mission, 1795–1853" (M.A. thesis, California State University, Fullerton, 1990).

23. Autobiography, 161; Britsch, *Moramona*, 20–21; Henry W. Bigler, Book D, Huntington Library, 14 February 1853 (hereafter cited as Book D, by date); Francis Asbury Hammond, journal, 2 February 1852, LDS Archives.

24. Station Report, Lahaina, 1851, Hawaiian Mission Children's Society Library, Honolulu, Hawaii. These reports were filed annually from 1851 to 1859.

25. Farrer, 15 December 1850; Keeler, 19 January 1851.

26. G. Cannon, *My First Mission*, 30.

27. Kuykendall, 1:47; Hawaiian Mission Children's Society, *Missionary Album*, 15.

28. Book B, 24 January 1853.

29. Ibid., 26 January 1853.

30. Hawaiian Mission Children's Society, *Missionary Album*, 92–93.

31. Book B, 24 January 1853.

32. Ibid., 8 and 10 February 1853.

33. Ibid., 14 February 1853.

34. Ibid., March 1853.

35. Ibid., 6 and 17 April 1853; Thomas Karren, diary, 17 April and 14 May 1853, LDS Archives. See Station Report for Lahaina, Maui, 1853, and for Wailua, Oahu, 1853; Book B, 6 and 17 April, 21 May, and 12 June 1853. There is no record of any interest among Hawaiian converts in plural marriage, even though native marriage patterns had always been "very flexible" and laws against polygamy were not instituted until after the coming of the Protestant missionaries (see Book D, 17 April 1853); Patricia Grimshaw, "New England Missionary Wives, Hawaiian Women, and the 'Cult of True Womanhood,'" *Hawaiian Journal of History* 19 (1985): 81–82; Jane L. Silverman, "To Marry Again," *Hawaiian Journal of History* 17 (1983): 64.

36. Book B, 31 March 1853.

37. Hawaiian Mission Children's Society, *Missionary Album*, 154–55; Book B, 1 April 1853.

38. Book B, 15 April 1853. For a fuller discussion of the Mormon practice of vicarious baptism, see chap. 9. Simply put, Mormon doctrine identifies baptism as an ordinance mandatory for salvation. Baptism for the dead was a potentially saving ordinance (contingent upon the departed spirit's acceptance of the ordinance) for those who, for whatever reason, had not had an opportunity to receive an LDS baptism during mortality.

39. Book D, 21 July 1853.

40. Ibid., 20 and 22 July 1853.

41. Ralph S. Kuykendall and A. Grove Day, *Hawaii: A History* (New York, 1948), 127; Laura Fish Judd, *Sketches of Life in the Hawaiian Islands from 1828 to 1861*, ed. Dale L. Morgan (Chicago, 1966), 310–11; Station Report, Koloa, Kauai, 1853; Book D, 16 November 1853; see also M. Guy Bishop, "To Overcome the 'Last Enemy': Early Mormon Perceptions of Death," *BYU Studies* 26 (summer 1986): 63–80.

42. Henry W. Bigler to Brigham Young, Heber C. Kimball, and Willard Richards, 7 January 1854, Brigham Young Collection, LDS Archives. The letter is catalogued in Brigham Young's incoming correspondence as addressed to Young only.

43. Book D, 24 July 1853.

44. Ibid., 25 July 1854.

45. Ibid., 25 and 28 July 1854.

46. Ibid., 22 June 1854.

47. Autobiography, 212–13.

48. Ibid., 213.

Chapter 7
Marriage and Return to Hawaii, 1855–58

1. Autobiography, 223.

2. Ibid., 217.

3. Ibid., 219.

4. Ibid., 218.

5. Ibid.

6. Ibid., 219.

7. Autobiography, 222, 5 February 1857. On the Latter-day Saint practice of blessing children, see M. Guy Bishop, "Preparing to 'Take the Kingdom': Childrearing Directives in Early Mormonism," *Journal of the Early Republic* 7 (fall 1987): 275–90.

8. Autobiography, 222, 28 February 1857.
9. Ibid., 223, 3 April 1857.
10. Ibid., 223.
11. Ibid.
12. Henry W. Bigler, journal, Book G, 14 May 1857, Huntington Library; hereafter cited as Book G, by date.
13. Ibid., 16 May 1857.
14. Ibid., 1 July 1857; Autobiography, 230, 11 July 1857. From this point until the end of his mission, Bigler copied the entries from his journal, Book G, into his autobiography, where they may be found with insignificant variations.
15. Book G, 14 July 1857.
16. Ibid., 15 July 1857; parentheses his.
17. Ibid., 22 July 1856.
18. Thirty-two-year-old Charles Wesley Wandell had joined the church in New York at the age of seventeen. He spent some time in Nauvoo but passed into disaffection after the death of Joseph Smith in 1844. Leaving his wife and children in New York, he voyaged around the Horn to San Francisco in 1849, presumably in search of wealth; instead, he found Pratt's mission party and was rebaptized only nine days after their arrival on 20 July 1851. He immediately began proselyting and was promptly appointed mission clerk. Pratt assigned him to proselyte in Australia with John Murdock, and Wandell's later career is checkered. Ambitious and competent, he broke with the church, possibly chagrined and embarrassed by having staunchly defended the church against charges of polygamy only to have the practice made public in 1852. He later affiliated with the Reorganized Church of Jesus Christ of Latter Day Saints and became a powerful preacher of that gospel in Australia. Marjorie Newton, *Southern Cross Saints: The Mormon Church in Australia* (Independence, Missouri, 1992), 26–27, 100–104.
19. Book G, 7 August 1857. Parley P. Pratt had been murdered earlier in 1857 at Van Buren, Arkansas, by the husband of a woman Pratt had converted, then taken to Utah with him. Breck England, *The Life and Thought of Orson Pratt* (Salt Lake City, 1985), 203–4; Steven Pratt, "Eleanor McLean and the Murder of Parley P. Pratt," *BYU Studies* 15 (winter 1975): 225–56.
20. Book G, 4 and 6 September 1857.
21. Ibid., 7 and 24 September 1857.
22. Ibid., 4 October 1857; also Autobiography, 236–37.

23. R. Lanier Britsch, "The Lanai Colony: A Hawaiian Extension of the Mormon Colonial Idea," *Hawaiian Journal of History* 12 (1971): 68–83.

24. Book G, 4 October 1857. In October 1864, long after Bigler's departure, Francis A. Hammond, who had served with Bigler in 1857–58, and George Nebeker were called as co-presidents of the mission. Brigham Young asked them to find "a suitable place or places for the gathering of the Hawaiian Saints." After attempting to secure land on Kauai, in January 1854, Hammond purchased Laie planation on north Oahu from Thomas T. Dougherty for $14,000. Young, accustomed to "settling land that was virtually free," initially objected to the price; but Laie had two advantages: it was near Honolulu but not too close and already had a nucleus of seventy Saints. Britsch, *Moramona*, 63, 72–73.

25. See, for example, Book G, 11 October 1857.

26. Book G, 4 October 1857; Paul H. Peterson, "The Mormon Reformation" (Ph.D. diss., Brigham Young University, 1981).

27. Ibid., 5 and 6 October 1857.

28. Lynne Watkins Jorgensen, "John Hyde, Jr., Mormon Renegade," *Journal of Mormon History* 17 (1991): 120–44.

29. Book G, 11 October 1857.

30. Ibid., 13 October and 9 December 1857.

31. Ibid., 13–14 November 1857.

32. Ibid., 7 January 1858; Autobiography, 249.

33. Bigler copied this letter into his diary when he received it more than ten weeks later. See Book G, 20 November 1857. Young sent similar letters to most of the church's missionaries. For the impact of this crisis upon LDS missionary work, see Norman F. Furniss, *The Mormon Conflict 1850–59* (New Haven, 1960).

34. Book G, 20 November 1857.

35. Ibid., 27 November 1857.

36. Ibid., 3 October 1857.

37. Ibid., 23 December 1857.

38. Ibid., 24 April 1858.

39. For an account of the move south, see Furniss, chap. 8.

40. Book G, 25 April 1858.

41. Ibid., 9 December 1857, 25 April 1857, 29 April 1858.

42. Ibid., 30 April 1858.

43. Ibid., 1, 9, and 10 May 1858.

44. Station Report, Hana (Maui) 1859.

45. Britsch, *Moramona*, 56–57; Samuel W. Taylor, "Walter Murray Gibson: Great Mormon Rascal," *The American West* 1 (spring 1964): 18–27.

46. Henry W. Bigler and John S. Woodbury to Brigham Young, 21 May 1858, San Francisco, Incoming Correspondence, Brigham Young Collection, LDS Archives.

Chapter 8
Family and Farming, 1859–76

1. Autobiography, 275. This event occurred in February 1875, about three months after the death of Jane Whipple Bigler. Their two youngest sons had been staying with daughter Lizzie and her husband in Idaho, and Bigler's loneliness was undoubtedly acute.
2. Ibid., 254.
3. Quoted in Book G, 19 May 1858.
4. Glen Milton Leonard, "A History of Farmington, Utah, to 1890" (M.A. thesis, University of Utah, 1966), 71.
5. Quoted in Book G, 19 May 1858.
6. Autobiography, 255, 257.
7. Book G, 30 July 1858.
8. Ibid., 31 July 1858.
9. Ibid., 10 August 1858.
10. Ibid.
11. Furniss, 168–75.
12. Henry W. Bigler, untitled record with miscellaneous genealogical entries, unpaginated, Huntington Library (hereafter cited as Genealogy Journal).
13. Ibid. Jacob Bigler died on 3 September 1859 and was buried at Farmington. The vicarious sealing which he requested was performed in Salt Lake City's Endowment House on 22 April 1869 (see Genealogy Journal).
14. Autobiography, 268.
15. Genealogy Journal.
16. Book G, 5 August 1869.
17. Genealogy Journal.
18. Elizabeth Jane's ordinance was performed on 13 May 1866 when she was nine and a half. See ibid.
19. Autobiography, 270.
20. Ibid., 266.
21. *History of the Church* 1:301.
22. See E. B. Long, *The Saints and the Union: Utah Territory during the Civil War* (Urbana, 1981), 26.

23. Both quoted in ibid., 9.
24. Ibid., 119.
25. Quoted in Hubert Howe Bancroft, *History of Utah, 1540–1886* (San Francisco, 1889; reprint, Las Vegas, 1982), 605.
26. *Deseret News*, 18 December 1861.
27. Ibid., 29 January and 12 February 1862.
28. *(San Francisco) Daily Evening Bulletin*, 31 December 1870.
29. Henry W. Bigler to Hubert Howe Bancroft, 10 April 1872, C-D 45:1, Bancroft Library, University of California at Berkeley.
30. Henry W. Bigler, "Diary of a Mormon in California," August–September 1848, composed in 1872, Bancroft Library.
31. Bigler to Bancroft, 7 June 1872, C-D 45:4.
32. Ibid., 5 July, C-D 45:9.
33. Bancroft, *History of California*, 6:32n.
34. *Quarterly of the Society of California Pioneers* 11 (1925): 19. Hittell came to California in 1849 hoping, like a host of others, to find gold. Failing in that quest, he soon opted for pursuits more given to his temperament and talents and took an editorial position on San Francisco's *Alta California*. Hittell wrote articles about the history of his adopted state for this newspaper. As a historian Hittell provided invaluable service to the Society of California Pioneers by collecting valued records such as Bigler's account of the gold discovery. *The Society of California Pioneers, Centennial Roster*, 7.
35. Autobiography, 276.
36. Ibid., ca. November 1874, 274–75.
37. Ibid., 277.
38. Ibid., 31 October 1876, 277.
39. Ibid, 6 November 1876, 278.

Chapter 9
The St. George Years, 1877–96

1. Henry W. Bigler, journal, Book A, 4 August 1879, Huntington Library; hereafter cited as Book A, by date.
2. Larry M. Logue, *A Sermon in the Desert: Belief and Behavior in Early St. George, Utah* (Urbana, 1988), chap. 1; and Melvin T. Smith, "Forces That Shaped Utah's Dixie: Another Look," *Utah Historical Quarterly* 47 (spring 1979): 111–29.
3. Autobiography, 22–23 November 1876, 278; Logue, *A Sermon in the Desert*, chap. 1; Allen and Leonard, 266–67; Leonard J. Arrington,

Great Basin Kingdom: An Economic History of the Latter-day Saints, 1830–1900 (1958; reprint ed., Lincoln, 1966), 217–22; and Leonard J. Arrington, "The Mormon Cotton Mission in Southern Utah," *Pacific Historical Review* 25 (August 1956): 221–38. On the naming of the city, see Albert E. Miller, *The Immortal Pioneers: Founders of the City of St. George* (St. George, Utah, 1946), 1–3.

4. "Population of Washington County, Utah (1890–1940)," typescript, Washington County Library, St. George, Utah.

5. See Arrington, *Great Basin Kingdom*, 315; for an in-depth overview of the St. George United Order, see Leonard J. Arrington, Feramorz Y. Fox, and Dean L. May, *Building the City of God: Community and Cooperation among the Mormons*, 2d ed. (Urbana, 1976, 1992), chap. 8.

6. Arrington, *Great Basin Kingdom*, 330–31; Logue, *A Sermon in the Desert*, 18; Book A, 1882–91.

7. Logue, *A Sermon in the Desert*, 116; Nels Anderson, *Desert Saints: The Mormon Frontier in Utah* (Chicago, 1942), 379–80.

8. Larry M. Logue, "A Time of Marriage: Monogamy and Polygamy in a Utah Town," *Journal of Mormon History* 11 (1984): 9; and Lowell "Ben" Bennion, "The Incidence of Mormon Polygamy in 1880: 'Dixie' versus Davis Stake," *Journal of Mormon History* 11 (1984): 37.

9. Kirk M. Curtis, "History of the St. George Temple" (M.A. thesis, Brigham Young University, 1964), 24.

10. Juanita Brooks, *The Mountain Meadows Massacre* (Norman, 1962); and her *John Doyle Lee: Zealot, Pioneer Builder, Scapegoat* (1972; reprint ed., Salt Lake City, 1984). Lee, an adopted son of Brigham Young, bore a responsibility for the massacre that should have been more widely shared. Repudiated by Brigham Young and eventually excommunicated in an act of distancing the church leader from the vigilante, Lee was tried in a federal court and executed on the site of the massacre 23 May 1877, four months after Bigler reached St. George; he makes no comment on the execution.

11. Book A, 1 January 1877.

12. Autobiography, 279.

13. Arrington, *Brigham Young*; and Lester E. Bush, Jr., "Brigham Young in Life and Death: A Medical Overview," *Journal of Mormon History* 5 (1978): 79–104. For the Arizona venture, see Charles S. Peterson, *Take Up Your Mission: Mormon Colonizing along the Little Colorado River* (Tucson, 1973).

14. See Book A, October [n.d.] 1877.

15. Ibid., 19 November 1877.

16. Gordon Irving, "The Law of Adoption: One Phase of the Development of the Mormon Concept of Salvation, 1830–1900," *BYU Studies* 14 (spring 1974): 303–6, 312.

17. James G. Bleak, "Annals of the Southern Utah Mission," facsimile, Huntingon Library, 682; John Daniel Thompson McAllister, journal, 1 January–14 February 1877, holograph, LDS Archives.

18. In 1853, Brigham Young admonished the Saints who had just crossed the plains "to go ahead and be baptized [again] for the remission of sins and start afresh." *Journal of Discourses*, 1:324. Three years later, he urged the Saints to be rebaptized "to renew your covenants." Ibid., 4:44. Henry's son Jacob was baptized in the temple font for his hearing.

19. Mark S. Leone, "The Mormon Temple Experience," *Sunstone* 3 (September–October 1979): 10.

20. David H. Cannon, diary, 11 January 1877, holograph, LDS Archives; Book A, 31 December 1877. I thank Gregory A. Prince of Gaithersburg, Maryland, who shared some of his research notes on this topic.

21. See Bishop, "Eternal Marriage in Early Mormon Marital Beliefs," 81–88; Book A, 31 December 1877.

22. Book A, 1 January 1877.

23. Ibid., 2 December 1877.

24. Ibid., 30 October 1877.

25. Ibid., 5 February 1878.

26. See ibid., 1877–86, passim; and Henry W. Bigler, memorandum and letter copybook, Huntington Library.

27. Book A, 5 April 1878, 3 and 17 November 1891, and 17 January 1893.

28. Ibid., 29 June 1893 and 22 October 1889.

29. Ibid., 12 November 1878.

30. Ibid., 11 December 1877.

31. Ibid.

32. Ibid., 4 May 1878.

33. Ibid., 6–12 March 1878. Bigler spells his wife's name Eleanor/Ellinor Emett/Emitt/Emmitt. I am grateful to Mrs. Olive Heppler Stephan of Salt Lake City, Utah, a granddaughter of Henry and Eleanor Bigler, for providing genealogical information.

34. Ibid., 1 April and 4 May 1878, 20 September 1879.

35. Ibid., 25 January and 1 February 1879.

36. These children were Maude, born 25 January 1879; Eleanor, born 21 September 1880; Edna Catherine, born 9 November 1882; Henry, born 24 November 1884; Adelbert, born 23 June 1887; and Myrtle

Ivy, born 13 March 1889. Genealogy Journal, 27 May 1895; Henry W. Bigler to Marshall Depue, letter copybook; and Bigler to Stephens.

37. Book A, 30 August and 11 October 1878.

38. Ibid., 19 and 21 October 1878.

39. Ibid., 11 October 1878.

40. Ibid., 19 November 1878 and 1 May 1879.

41. Ibid., 31 December 1885, 14 October 1889, 11 October 1893, and 11 January 1894; and Logue, *A Sermon in the Desert*, 124. While a farmer in northern Utah (ca. 1870), probably the financial high point of Bigler's life, his relative wealth was $1,000 in real estate and $300 in personal property. See J. R. Kearl, Clayne L. Pope, and Larry T. Wimmer, *Index to the 1850, 1860 and 1870 Censuses of Utah* (Baltimore, 1981), 31. It is very difficult to imagine his net worth increasing as a temple worker of limited means. I thank Dr. D. Gene Pace of Alice Lloyd College, Pippa Passes, Kentucky, for assistance in determining Bigler's comparative financial worth.

42. Ibid., 21 April 1878 and 12 August 1889.

43. Ibid., 9 August 1889.

44. Bigler noted a visit from "Father Emmitt and wives" on 12 December 1893.

45. Logue, *A Sermon in the Desert*, 49.

46. Richard Van Wagoner, *Mormon Polygamy: A History*, 2d ed. (Salt Lake City, 1989), 119.

47. Bennion, 41.

48. Logue, *A Sermon in the Desert*, 55; Arrington, *Great Basin Kingdom*, 238.

49. Logue, *A Sermon in the Desert*, 54; Bennion, 29.

50. Book A, 20 November 1877.

51. Wilford Woodruff, *Wilford Woodruff's Journal, 1833–1898*, typescript, ed. Scott G. Kenny. 9 vols. (Midvale, Utah, 1983–85), 7:131. However, two years later, Young reportedly believed that "a man who did not have but one wife in the Resurrection that woman will not be his but [be] taken from him & given to another." Quoted in Van Wagoner, 114n. Van Wagoner speculates that in later life Brigham Young's position on polygamy "fluctuated."

52. Mrs. Stephan made this statement in casual conversation with me in November 1989 at her home in Salt Lake City. When I sought further clarification two years later, Mrs. Stephan explained, "I really can't document my grandfather's definite beliefs about polygamy—I just remember my mother [Eleanor Bigler Heppler] saying something about it, but I don't know if he didn't actually

believe in it, or he just didn't choose to marry more than one woman." Olive Heppler Stephan to Guy Bishop, 15 December 1991. Whether or not Henry Bigler personally accepted polygamy, he certainly accepted the practice as divinely ordained and defended it staunchly, as his missionary activity in Hawaii shows. Indeed, to do anything else would have been strikingly out of character.

53. Van Wagoner, 109–11; Book A, 9 January 1879. McKean was a virulent anti-Mormon appointed by President U. S. Grant in 1871 as chief justice of the Utah Territorial Court. He had worked incessantly to crush plural marriage and rendered the original decision in the Reynolds case.

54. Cannon, vigorously sought in early 1886 by U.S. Marshal E. A. Ireland, had been captured along with apostle Erastus Snow and two others while attempting to flee the Utah Territory. Cannon later forfeited his $25,000 bond when he did not appear for trial. He chose instead to return to the Mormon underground in hope of avoiding prosecution. To the Mormons of his time, including Bigler, Cannon was unjustly persecuted and had obeyed a higher law when he fled from the courts. For Bigler's comment on this incident see Book A, 16 February 1886. See also Gustive O. Larson, *The Americanization of Utah for Statehood* (San Marino, California, 1971), 146–51.

55. See Foster, 223; Van Wagoner, 139–52; Edward Leo Lyman, *Political Deliverance: The Mormon Quest for Utah Statehood* (Urbana, 1986), 296; and D. Michael Quinn, "LDS Church Authority and New Plural Marriages, 1890–1904," *Dialogue: A Journal of Mormon Thought* 18 (spring 1985): 9–105. The text of the Manifesto is canonized as Official Declaration-1 in the Doctrine and Covenants, an official Mormon scripture. Information on the voting of the general conference comes from Quinn, 48; his article documents the extent of officially authorized post-Manifesto plural marriages.

56. See Lyman, especially chaps. 8 and 9. For reactions in St. George to statehood, see *The Union* 28 December 1895 and Autobiography, 324.

57. For an excellent overview of this post-Manifesto refocusing within Mormonism, see Thomas G. Alexander, *Mormonism in Transition: A History of the Latter-day Saints, 1896–1930* (Urbana, 1986), 3–15. For parallel movements in St. George, see Logue, *A Sermon in the Desert*, 120–21.

58. For examples, see Bigler, memorandum and letter copybook.

Chapter 10
Chronicler

1. Bigler to Stephens.
2. John W. Blassingame, *The Slave Community: Plantation Life in the Antebellum South* (New York, 1980), ix.
3. For an analysis of the appeal and terror of exotic religions in nine-teenth-century America, see David Brion Davis, "Some Themes of Counter-Subversion: An Analysis of Anti-Masonic, Anti-Catholic, and Anti-Mormon Literature," *Mississippi Valley Historical Review* 67 (September 1960): 205–24. Davis asserts that Americans had long been told that "Mormons were undermining political and economic freedom in the West," that the Mormon hierarchy was as fearsome as the Catholic Pope, and that Mormon revelations and rituals were "preposterous hoaxes" (205, 207, 216).
4. *Guide to Salt Lake City, Ogden, and the Utah Central Railroad* (Salt Lake City, 1870), 8, copy at the Huntington Library.
5. Bancroft, *History of California*, 6:31–32; *Overland Monthly*, 233–45.
6. Cannon had begun this periodical in 1866, and it became the quasi-official publication of the church's Deseret Sunday School Union. Following the lead of the American Sunday School Union, founded by evangelic Protestants of the 1830s in hopes of supplying religious reading material to the nation's youth, Cannon believed that the *Juvenile Instructor* might serve a similar purpose for young Mormons. It offered faith-promoting articles, memoirs of Mormon founders and Utah pioneers, and general guidance for the youth and their teachers. In 1900 the LDS Church purchased the periodical from the Cannon family and formalized its status with the Sunday School. See Allen and Leonard, 336, 461; Alexander, 136. On the American Sunday School Union, see Timothy L. Smith, *Revivalism and Social Reform: American Protestantism on the Eve of the Civil War,* (New York: 1965). 39–42; and Sydney L. Ahlstrom, *A Religious History of the American People*, 425.
7. Henele Pikale (Henry Bigler), "Recollections of the Past," *Juvenile Instructor* 21 (1 January–15 December 1886).
8. Bigler, "Recollections of the Past," *Juvenile Instructor* 21 (1886): 14. Ironically, Bigler's journal throughout the St. George years frequently notes his purchase of coffee, also prohibited by the Word of Wisdom. For the development of the Word of Wisdom, see Alexander, 259.
9. See Autobiography, 19; *Juvenile Instructor* 21 (1886): 31. In 1898, during a special party in the St. George Tabernacle for the community's "Old

Folks" over sixty, an unidentified person asked everyone who had known Joseph Smith personally to stand. Henry Bigler was proud to be one of the twenty-seven who responded. Autobiography, 353.

10. "Recollections of the Past," *Juvenile Instructor* 21 (18 March 1886): 82.

11. Ibid., 21 (1 November 1886): 329.

12. Ibid., 21 (15 November 1886): 343.

13. Henry W. Bigler, miscellaneous journal, 19 February 1880, Huntington Library.

14. Bitton and Arrington, *Mormons and Their Historians*, 7.

15. A partial indication of the Mormon fascination with personal records is Davis Bitton, *Mormon Diaries and Autobiographies* (Provo, Utah, 1977), an annotated bibliography, still valuable though incomplete and outdated, of nearly three thousand extant Mormon diaries.

16. Neal Lambert, "The Presentation of Reality in Nineteenth-Century Mormon Autobiography," *Dialogue: A Journal of Mormon Thought* 11 (summer 1978): 63–64.

17. Bigler to Stephens.

18. Bigler to Bancroft, 12 May 1872, C-D 45:3.

19. Bigler to Bancroft, 24 July 1883; Clyde A. Milner II, in "The Shared Memories of Montana's Pioneers," *Montana: The Magazine of Western History* 37 (winter 1937): 4, observes a parallel experience among another community of Westerners: "Some elements of these memoirs, regardless of their accuracy, take on great emblematic significance . . . and thus seem to represent a collectively remembered past."

20. Henry W. Bigler, daybook, 1892–93, 2 April 1893, Huntington Library.

21. Autobiography, 21 December 1897—7 January 1898, 341–43 provides a record of Bigler's correspondence from the historical society regarding this gala event.

22. Ibid., 344.

23. Ibid.

24. Henry W. Bigler to John S. Hittell, 7 February 1897, letter copybook. While some historians give the Bigler and Brown accounts equal validity, Bancroft, Hittell, and, more recently, Erwin G. Gudde correctly give primacy to Bigler's because it is the only contemporary account. Bancroft observed, "There are but two authorities to choose between, Marshall, the discoverer, and one Henry W. Bigler, a Mormon engaged upon the work at the time. . . . Marshall

admits that he does not know the date." Bancroft, *History of California*, 6:32, n18. John S. Hittell, in his editorial remarks accompanying the presentation of the "Diary of H. W. Bigler in 1847 and 1848" in the *Overland Monthly* 10 (July–December 1887) called Bigler's diary "the conclusive authority" for dating the gold discovery (333). See also Gudde, *Bigler's Chronicle of the West*, 94. Brown's account, while reasonably accurate, differed from Bigler's in that James S. Brown, who recorded the event in retrospect, confused the activities of Marshall and others in the moments and hours immediately after the find was made.

25. Autobiography, 345.
26. *San Francisco Chronicle*, 23 January 1898, 31; Autobiography, 345; for a contemporary description of the Russ House, see *San Francisco: The Metropolis of Western America*, 187.
27. Autobiography, 345.
28. Ibid., 346–47.
29. Ibid., 347.
30. Ibid.
31. Ibid., 348–49. The First Presidency Appointment Books (LDS Church Archives) do not list Bigler's visit, so he may have dropped in without a formal appointment.
32. Ibid., 349.
33. Ibid., 350. Nineteenth-century Mormon women routinely anointed the sick with consecrated oil and pronounced blessings of healing, a function now reserved almost exclusively to male priesthood holders. Anointing the afflicted part of the body was also a nineteenth-century custom; such anointings are now limited to the crown of the head, although consecrated olive oil is still used, as it has been from the time of Joseph Smith.
34. Bigler, miscellaneous journal, 11 July 1892.
35. Autobiography, 350.
36. Ibid., 351. On the role of LDS patriarchs, see Arrington and Bitton, *The Mormon Experience*, 187.
37. Autobiography, 352, 354, and 357.
38. Ibid., 357. This man was Basil Harvey, the father of Bigler's mother, Elizabeth, who had been such an outspoken foe of Mormonism while alive that he threatened to burn the Book of Mormon. Bigler dreamed later that he was concerned about his salvation.
39. Ibid., 358. Other Mexican-American War veterans were among the honored guests. See *The Pioneer* (San Jose, California), 15 January 1900.

40. Henry W. Bigler to W. E. Ashburn, 15 July 1900.

41. Letter to Ashburn, 11 August 1900.

42. *Los Angeles Evening Express*, 26 November 1900; *Deseret Evening News*, 26 November 1900; Jenson, 3:599.

43. Jerome G. Manis, "Great Little Persons," *Biography* 12 (winter 1989): 18. For a consideration of the ways in which Bigler fits this model, see M. Guy Bishop, "A Great Little Saint: A Brief Look at the Life of Henry William Bigler." *BYU Studies* 30 (fall 1990): 27–38.

44. Hoffer, *The True Believer*, xii.

45. Ibid., 12–13.

46. Ibid., xi, 98.

BIBLIOGRAPHY

Primary Sources

Bigler, David L., ed. *The Gold Discovery Journal of Azariah Smith*. Logan: Utah State University Press, 1996.

Bigler, Henry William. Autobiography, ca. 1898. Archives, Historical Department of the Church of Jesus Christ of Latter-day Saints, Salt Lake City, Utah (hereafter cited as LDS Archives). In 1890 California historian John S. Hittell presented Bigler with a large, new journal in which he wrote a retrospective autobiography copied from his original journals and daybooks. Internal sources indicate that Henry Bigler wrote (compiled) this work about 1898. It retrospectively covers his life from 1815 and continues to 1899 with dated entries.

———. Book A. A retrospective autobiography and journal with a diary of almost daily entries from 1846 through 1899. Henry E. Huntington Library, San Marino, California (hereafter cited as Huntington Library).

———. Book B. A daybook (approximately 100 pages) with dated entries from 10 October 1849 to 15 November 1850. Huntington Library.

———. Book D. A daybook (approximately 240 pages) with dated entries from 31 March 1853 to 20 March 1857. Huntington Library.

———. Book G. A journal (approximately 200 pages) with dated entries from 14 May 1857 to 13 January 1859. Huntington Library.

———. Daybook, 1892–93. Huntington Library.

———. "Diary of a Mormon in California." Bancroft Library, University of California, Berkeley, California. A long, autobiographical letter to Hubert H. Bancroft followed by dated entries covering the period August–September 1848.

———. "Diary of H. W. Bigler in 1847 and 1848." Ed. John S. Hittell, *Overland Monthly* 10 (September 1887): 233–45. This was drawn from Bigler's original diary, Book A.

———. Genealogical journal, untitled record with miscellaneous genealogical entries, unpaginated. Huntington Library.

———. "Henry Bigler's Journal Book A: Autobiography of H. W. Bigler," ca. February 1846 to November 1850. Special Collections and Manuscripts Department, Harold B. Lee Library, Brigham Young University, Provo, Utah. Although both are called "Book A," this typescript copy should not be confused with the Huntington Library and *Overland Monthly* version above.

———. Letter to Alexander Stephens, 5 April 1891. Special Collections, Merrill Library, Utah State University, Logan, Utah.

———. Letters to Hubert Howe Bancroft, 1872–1883, C-D 45, Bancroft Library, University of California, Berkely.

———. Letter to Brigham Young, Heber C. Kimball, and Willard Richards, 7 January 1854. Brigham Young Collection, Incoming Correspondence, LDS Archives.

———. Memorandum and letter copybook. Huntington Library.

———. Miscellaneous journal. Huntington Library.

Bigler, Henry William and John S. Woodbury. Letter to Brigham Young, 21 May 1858, Brigham Young Collection, Incoming Correspondence, LDS Archives.

Bleak, James G. "Annals of the Southern Utah Mission." Facsimile, Huntington Library.

Bliss, Robert Stanton. Diary, 1846–48. Holograph, San Diego Historical Society, San Diego, California.

Boyle, Henry Green. Journal, 1824–88. Mormon File, Huntington Library.

Cannon, David. H. Diary. Holograph, LDS Archives.

Cannon, George Q. *My First Mission.* Vol. 1 in the Faith Promoting Series. Salt Lake City: Juvenile Instructor Office, 1879.

———. Diaries, 1849–54. LDS Archives.

Cooke, Philip St. George. "Official Journal of the March of Lieutenant Colonel Philp St. George Cooke from Santa Fe, New Mexico, to San Diego, in Upper California." In *Report from the Secretary of War to the United States Senate, March 19, 1849.* Washington, D. C.: Government Printing Office, 1849.

Grant, William C. Diary. Typescript, United States Military Academy, West Point, New York.

Guide to Salt Lake City, Ogden, and the Utah Central Railroad. Salt Lake City: Deseret Book Company, 1870. Copy at the Huntington Library.

Hammond, Francis Asbury. Journal. LDS Archives.

Hawaiian Mission Letters, 1851–54. LDS Archives.

Kanehoa [John Young]. Letter to Minister of the Interior, 21 September 1850, Hawaii State Archives, Honolulu.

Karren, Thomas. Diary. LDS Archives.

Keeler, James. Journal, 1855–59. LDS Archives.

Manuscript History of the Virginia Conference. LDS Archives.

McAllister, John Daniel Thompson. Journal, 1877. Holograph, LDS Archives.

Pace, James. Journal. Holograph, LDS Archives.

"Population of Washington County, Utah (1890–1940)." Typescript, Washington County Library, St. George, Utah.

Post, Stephen. Journal, 12 November 1842. LDS Archives.

Smith, Bathsheba Wilson Bigler. Autobiography. Family History Library, Church of Jesus Christ of Latter-day Saints, Salt Lake City, Utah.

[Smith, Joseph, Jr.]. *A History of The Church of Jesus Christ of Latter-day Saints.* 2d ed. revised. 7 vols. Ed. B. H. Roberts. Salt Lake City: Deseret Book, 1978.

Standage, Henry. Journal, 1846–47. Typescript, Mormon File, Huntington Library.

Station Reports, 1851–59. Hawaiian Mission Children's Society Library, Honolulu.

Thirtieth Quorum of Seventies Records, 1839–76. LDS Archives.

Books

Ahlstrom, Sidney L. *A Religious History of the American People.* New Haven: Yale University Press, 1972.

Alexander, Thomas G. *Mormonism in Transition: A History of the Latter-day Saints.* Urbana and Chicago: University of Illinois Press, 1986.

Allen, James B. and Glen M. Leonard. *The Story of the Latter-day Saints.* 2d ed. Salt Lake City: Deseret Book Co., 1976, 1994.

Ambrose, Stephen E. *Undaunted Courage: Meriweather Lewis, Thomas Jefferson, and the Opening of the West.* New York: Simon and Shuster, 1996.

Anderson, Nels. *Desert Saints: The Mormon Frontier in Utah.* Chicago: University of Chicago Press, 1942.

Andrew, John A., III. *Rebuilding the Christian Commonwealth: New England Congregationalists.* Lexington: University of Kentucky Press, 1976.

Arrington, Leonard J. *Brigham Young: American Moses.* New York: Alfred A. Knopf, 1985.

———. *Great Basin Kingdom: An Economic History of the Latter-day Saints, 1830–1900.* 1958; reprint ed., Lincoln: University of Nebraska Press, 1966.

Arrington, Leonard J. and Davis Bitton. *The Mormon Experience: A History of the Latter-day Saints.* New York: Alfred A. Knopf, 1979.

Arrington, Leonard J., Feramorz V. Fox, and Dean L. May. *Building the City of God: Community and Cooperation among the Mormons.* Urbana: University of Illinois Press, 1976, 1992.

Bailyn, Bernard. *The Peopling of North America: An Introduction.* New York: Alfred A. Knopf, 1986.

Bancroft, Hubert H. *History of California.* 7 vols. San Francisco: The History Book Company, 1884–90.

———. *Reproduction of Hubert Howe Bancroft's History of Utah 1540–1886.* San Francisco: The History Book Company, 1889; reprint, Las Vegas: Nevada Publications, 1982.

Barney, William L. *The Passages of the Republic: An Interdisciplinary History of Nineteenth Century America.* Lexington: D. C. Heath and Company, 1987.

Bitton, Davis. *Mormon Diaries and Autobiographies.* Provo, Utah: Brigham Young University Press, 1977.

Bitton, Davis and Leonard J. Arrington. *Mormons and Their Historians.* Salt Lake City: University of Utah Press, 1987.

Blassingame, John W. *The Slave Community: Plantation Life in the Antebellum South.* New York: Oxford University Press, 1980.

Britsch, R. Lanier. *Moramona: The Mormons in Hawaii.* Laie, Hawaii: The Institute for Polynesian Studies, 1989.

Brodie, Fawn M. *No Man Knows My History: The Life of Joseph Smith.* 2d ed. New York: Alfred A. Knopf, 1982.

Brooks, Juanita. *John Doyle Lee: Zealot, Pioneer Builder, Scapegoat.* 1972; reprint ed., Salt Lake City and Chicago: Howe Brothers, 1984.

———. *The Mountain Meadows Massacre.* Norman: University of Oklahoma Press, 1962.

Brough, Franklin Keith. *Freely I Gave: The Life of Jacob G. Bigler.* Wichita, Kansas: Grit Publishing Co., 1958.

Burns, Norman. "The Bigler Family: Descendents of Mark Bigler Who Immigrated to America in 1773." 1960. Typescript copy at the Family

History Library, Church of Jesus Christ of Latter-day Saints, Salt Lake City, Utah.

Bushman, Richard L. *Joseph Smith and the Beginnings of Mormonism.* Urbana and Chicago: University of Illinois Press, 1987.

Caughey, John Walton. *The California Gold Rush.* Berkeley: University of California Press, 1975.

Connor, Seymour V. and Odie B. Faulk. *North America Divided: The Mexican War, 1846–48.* New York: Oxford University Press, 1971.

Coy, Owen C. *In the Diggings in 'Forty-Nine.* Los Angeles: California State Historical Society, 1948.

Davies, Kenneth. *Mormon Gold: The Story of Califonia's Mormon Argonauts.* Salt Lake City: Olympus Publishing Company, 1984.

Daws, Gavan. *Shoal of Time: A History of the Hawaiian Islands.* Honolulu: University of Hawaii Press, 1974.

DeVoto, Bernard. *The Year of Decision: 1846.* Boston: Houghton Mifflin Company, 1942.

Eisenhower, John S. D. *So Far from God: The U.S. War with Mexico 1846–48.* New York: Doubleday, 1989.

England, Breck. *The Life and Thought of Orson Pratt.* Salt Lake City: University of Utah Press, 1985.

Englehardt, Zephyrin. *San Luis Ray Mission.* San Francisco: James H. Berry Company, 1921.

Flanders, Robert Bruce. *Nauvoo: Kingdom on the Mississippi.* Urbana: University of Illinois Press, 1965.

Foster, Lawrence. *Religion and Sexuality: The Shakers, the Mormons, and the Oneida Community.* 1981; reprint ed., Urbana and Chicago: University of Illinois Press, 1984.

Furniss, Norman F. *The Mormon Conflict 1850–59.* New Haven: Yale University Press, 1960.

Gay, Theressa. *James W. Marshall: The Discoverer of California Gold.* Georgetown, California: Talisman Press, 1967.

Gerstaeker, William and Friedrich. *California Gold Mines.* Foreword by Joseph A. Sullivan. Oakland, California: Biobooks, 1946.

Gudde, Erwin G. *Bigler's Chronicle of the West: The Conquest of California, Discovery of Gold, and Mormon Settlement as Reflected in Henry William Bigler's Diaries.* Berkeley and Los Angeles: University of California Press, 1962.

———. *California Gold Camps: A Geographical and Historical Dictionary of Camps, Towns, and Localities where Gold Was Found and Mined; Waystations and Trading Centers.* Berkeley and Los Angeles: University of California Press, 1975.

Hafen, LeRoy R. and Ann W., eds. *Journals of the Forty-Niners Salt Lake to Los Angeles: With Diaries and Contemporary Records of Sheldon Young, James S. Brown, Jacob Y. Stover, Charles C. Rich, Addison Pratt, Howard Egan, Henry W. Bigler, and Others.* Glendale, California: Arthur H. Clark Company, 1954.

Hawaiian Mission Children's Society. *Missionary Album: Portraits and Biographical Sketches of the American Protestant Missionaries to the Hawaiian Islands, 1820–1870.* Sesquicentennial ed. Honolulu: 1969.

Haywood, Henry P. *History of Harrison County.* Morgantown, West Virginia: Acme Publishing Company, 1910.

Hill, Marvin S. *Quest for Refuge: The Mormon Flight from American Pluralism.* Salt Lake City: Signature Books, 1989.

Hittell, John S., James W. Marshall, and Edwin G. Waite. *The Discovery of Gold.* Palo Alto: Lewis Osborn, 1968.

Hoffer, Eric. *The True Believer: Thoughts on the Nature of Mass Movements.* New York: Harper, 1951.

Jensen, Andrew. *Latter-day Saint Biographical Encyclopedia: A Compilation of Biographical Sketches of Prominent Men and Women in the Church of Jesus Christ of Latter-day Saints.* 4 vols. Salt Lake City: Andrew Jensen History Company, 1901–36.

Johannsen, Robert W. *To the Halls of Montezuma: The Mexican War in the American Imagination.* New York: Oxford University Press, 1985.

Johnston, William C. *Experiences of a Forty-Niner.* New York: Arno Press, 1973.

Judd, Laura Fish. *Honolulu: Sketches of Life in the Sandwich Islands from 1828 to 1861.* Ed. Dale L. Morgan. Chicago: Lakeshore Press, 1966.

Kearl, J. R., Clayne L. Pope, and Larry T. Wimmer. *Index to the 1850, 1860 and 1870 Censuses of Utah.* Baltimore: Genealogical Publishing Company, 1981.

Kenny, Hamill. *West Virginia Place Names.* Piedmont, West Virginia: The Place Names Press, 1945.

Koenig, George. *"Beyond This Place There Be Dragons": The Routes of the Tragic Trek of the Death Valley 1849ers through Nevada, Death Valley, and to Southern California.* Glendale, California: Arthur H. Clark Company, 1984.

Korns, J. Roderic and Dale L. Morgan, eds. *West from Fort Bridger: The Pioneering of Immigrant Trails across Utah, 1846–1850.* Revised and updated by Will Bagley and Harold Schindler. Logan: Utah State University Press, 1994.

Kuhn, Robert Lawrence and George Thomas Geis. *The Firm Bond: Linking Meaning and Mission in Business and Religion*. New York: Praeger Publishers, 1984.

Kuykendall, Ralph S. *The Hawaiian Kingdom*. 3 vols. Honolulu: University of Hawaii Press, 1980.

Kuykendall, Ralph S. and A. Grove Day. *Hawaii: A History*. New York: Prentice-Hall, 1948.

Larsen, Gustive O. *The Americanization of Utah for Statehood*. San Marino: Huntington Library, 1971.

Launius, Roger D. and John E. Hallwas, eds. *Kingdom on the Mississippi Revisited*. Urbana and Chicago: University of Illinois Press, 1996.

Lavender, David. *The Great West*. Boston: Houghton Mifflin Company, 1965; 1987.

LeSueur, Stephen C. *The 1838 Mormon War in Missouri*. Columbia: University of Missouri Press, 1987.

Lingenfelter, Richard E. *Death Valley and the Amargosa: A Land of Illusion*. Berkeley and Los Angeles: University of California Press, 1986.

Lochkin, Roger W. *San Francisco 1846–1856: From Hamlet to City*. New York: Oxford University Press, 1974.

Logue, Larry M. *A Sermon in the Desert: Belief and Behavior in Early St. George, Utah*. Urbana and Chicago: University of Illinois Press, 1988.

Long, E. B. *The Saints and the Union: Utah Territory during the Civil War*. Urbana and Chicago: University of Illinois Press, 1981.

Long, Margaret. *The Shadow of the Arrow*. Caldell, Idaho: Caxton Printers, 1950.

Lyman, Edward Leo. *Political Deliverance: The Mormon Quest for Utah Statehood*. Urbana and Chicago: University of Illinois Press, 1986.

Madsen, Brigham D. *Gold Rush Sojourners in Great Salt Lake City 1849 and 1850*. Salt Lake City: University of Utah Press, 1983.

Manley, William Lewis. *Death Valley in '49*. 1894; reprint, Bishop, California: Chalfant Press, 1977.

McGlashan, C. F. *History of the Donner Party: A Tragedy of the Sierra*. Stanford: Stanford University Press, 1940.

McKiernan, F. Mark, Alma R. Blair, and Paul M. Edwards, eds. *The Restoration Movement: Essays in Mormon History*. Lawrence, Kansas: Coronado Press, 1973.

Miller, Albert E. *The Immortal Pioneers: Founders of the City of St. George*. St. George, Utah: Albert E. Miller, 1946.

Miller, David E. and Della S. *Nauvoo: The City of Joseph*. Santa Barbara: Peregrine Smith, 1974.

Morgan, Dale L. *Jedediah Smith and the Opening of the West*. Lincoln: University of Nebraska Press, 1953.

Newell, Linda King and Valeen Tippetts Avery. *Mormon Enigma: Emma Hale Smith*. Garden City, New York: Doubleday & Co., Inc., 1984.

Newton, Marjorie. *Southern Cross Saints: The Mormon Church in Australia*. Independence, Missouri: Independence House, 1992.

Paul, Rodman W. *California Gold: The Beginning of Mining in the Far West*. Cambridge: Harvard University Press, 1947.

Perlot, Jean-Nicholas. *Gold Seeker: Adventures of a Belgian Argonaut during the Gold Rush Years*. Ed. Howard R. Lamar. New Haven: Yale University Press, 1985.

Peterson, Charles S. *Take Up Your Mission: Mormon Colonization along the Little Colorado River*. Tucson: University of Arizona Press, 1973.

Phillips, Clifton Jackson. *Protestant America and the Pagan World: The First Half Century of the American Board of Commissioners for Foreign Missions, 1810–1860*. Cambridge: Harvard University Press for the East Asian Research Center, 1969.

Rice, Otis K. *West Virgina: A History*. Lexington: University of Kentucky Press, 1985.

Ricketts, Norma Baldwin. *The Mormon Battalion: U.S. Army of the West*. Logan: Utah State University Press, 1996.

———. *Mormons and the Discovery of Gold*. Sacramento: Primm Printing, 1982.

Roberts, B. H. *A Comprehensive History of the Church of Jesus Christ of Latter-day Saints, Century I*. 6 vols. 1930; reprint, Provo, Utah: Brigham Young University Press, 1965.

Rolle, Andrew F. *California: A History*. 3d ed. Arlington Heights, Illinois: Harlan-Davidson, Inc., 1978.

Smith, Timothy L. *Revivalism and Social Reform: American Protestantism on the Eve of the Civil War*. New York: Harper and Row, 1965.

Sonne, Conway B. *Ships, Saints, and Mariners: A Maritime Encyclopedia of Mormon Migration*. Salt Lake City: University of Utah Press, 1987.

Speakman, Cummins E., Jr. *Mowee: An Informal History of the Hawaiian Island*. San Rafael, California: Pueo Press, 1981.

Stott, Clifford L. *Search for Sanctuary: Brigham Young and the White Mountain Expedition*. Salt Lake City: University of Utah Press, 1984.

Tanner, Annie Clark. *A Biography of Ezra Thompson Clark*. Salt Lake City: Tanner Trust Fund, University of Utah Library, ca. 1981.

Tyler, Daniel. *A Concise History of the Mormon Battalion in the Mexican War*. 4th ed. Glorietta, New Mexico: The Rio Grande Press, 1980.

Van Sicklen, Helen Putnam, ed. *New Helvetia Diary: A Record of Events Kept by John A. Sutter and His Clerks at New Helvetia, California, from September 9, 1845 to May 25, 1848*. San Francisco: Grabhorn Press, 1939.

Van Wagoner, Richard S. *Mormon Polygamy: A History*. 2d ed. Salt Lake City: Signature Books, 1989.

Van Wagoner, Richard S. and Steven C. Walker. *A Book of Mormons*. Salt Lake City: Signature Books, 1982.

Whitney, Orson F. *History of Utah*. 4 vols. Salt Lake City: George Q. Cannon and Sons, 1892.

Woodruff, Wilford. *Wilford Woodruff's Journal, 1833–1898*. 9 vols. Typescript, ed. Scott G. Kenney. Midvale, Utah: Signature Books, 1983–85.

Zollinger, James P. *Sutter: The Man and His Empire*. New York: Oxford University Press, 1939.

Articles

Anderson, Jack Sandy. "The Levi Shinn House," *West Virginia History* 29 (January 1986): 138–40.

Arrington, Leonard J. "The Mormon Cotton Mission in Southern Utah," *Pacific Historical Review* 25 (August 1956): 221–38.

Bates, Irene. "Uncle John Smith, 1781–1854: Patriarchal Bridge," *Dialogue: A Journal of Mormon Thought* 20 (fall 1987): 79–89.

Bennion, Lowell "Ben." "The Incidence of Mormon Polygamy in 1880: 'Dixie' versus Davis Stake," *Journal of Mormon History* 11 (1984): 37.

Bishop, M. Guy. "Eternal Marriage in Early Mormon Marital Beliefs," *The Historian* 53 (autumn 1990): 77–88.

———. "A Great Little Saint: A Brief Look at the Life of Henry William Bigler," *BYU Studies* 30 (fall 1990): 27–38

———. "Preparing to 'Take the Kingdom': Childrearing Directives in Early Mormonism," *Journal of the Early Republic* 7 (fall 1987): 275–90.

———. "To Overcome the 'Last Enemy': Early Mormon Perceptions of Death," *BYU Studies* 26 (summer 1986): 63–80.

———. "'We Are Rather Weaker in Righteousness Than in Numbers': The Mormon Colony at San Bernardino, California, 1851–1857." In *Religion and Society in the American West*, ed. Carl Guarneri and David Alvarez (Lanham, Maryland: University Press of America, 1987): 171–96.

Bishop, M. Guy, Vincent Lacey, and Richard Wixon. "Death at Mormon Nauvoo, 1843–45," *Western Illinois Regional Studies* 9 (fall 1986): 70–83.

Britsch, R. Lanier. "The Lanai Colony: A Hawaiian Extension of the Mormon Colonial Idea," *Hawaiian Journal of History* 12 (1971): 68–83.

Buerger, David John. "The Development of the Mormon Temple Endowment Ceremony," *Dialogue: A Journal of Mormon Thought* 20 (winter 1987): 33–76.

Bush, Lester, Jr. "Brigham Young in Life and Death: A Medical Overview," *Journal of Mormon History* 5 (1978): 79–104.

Butler, Jonathan. "From Millerism to Seventh-day Adventism: 'Boundlessness to Consolidation,'" *Church History* 55 (March 1986): 50–64.

Campbell, Eugene E. "The Mormon Gold Mining Mission of 1849," *BYU Studies* 1 (autumn 1959–winter 1960): 19–31.

Davis, David Brion. "Some Themes of Counter-Subversion: An Analysis of Anti-Masonic, Anti-Catholic, and Anti-Mormon Literature," *Mississippi Valley Historical Review* 67 (September 1960): 205–24.

Easton, Susan W. "Suffering and Death on the Plains of Iowa," *BYU Studies* 21 (fall 1981): 431–39.

Grimshaw, Patricia. "New England Missionary Wives, Hawaiian Women and the 'Cult of True Womanhood,'" *Hawaiian Journal of History* 19 (1985): 81–82.

Hatch, Nathan O. "Millenialism and Popular Religion in the Early Republic." In *The Evangelical Tradition in America*, ed. Leonard I. Sweet (Macon, Georgia: Mercer University Press, 1984).

Haven, Charlotte. "A Girl's Letters from Nauvoo," *Overland Monthly* 16 (July–December 1890): 620–21.

Irving, Gordon. "The Law of Adoption: One Phase of the Mormon Concept of Salvation, 1830–1900," *BYU Studies* 14 (spring 1974): 303–6.

Jennings, Richard L. "The City in the Garden: Social Conflict in Jackson County, Missouri." In *The Restoration Movement: Essays in Mormon History*, ed. F. Mark McKiernan, Alma Blair, and Paul M. Edwards (Lawrence, Kansas: Coronado Press, 1973).

Jennings, Warren A. "The Expulsion of the Mormons from Jackson County, Missouri," *Missouri Historical Review* 64 (October 1969): 41–63.

Jorgensen, Lynne Watkins. "John Hyde, Jr., Mormon Renegade," *Journal of Mormon History* 17 (1991): 120–44.

Kelly, Charles. "On Manley's Trail to Death Valley," *Desert Magazine* 2 (February 1939): 6–8.

Lambert, Neal "The Presentation of Reality in Nineteenth-Century Mormon Autobiography," *Dialogue: A Journal of Mormon Thought* 11 (summer 1978): 63–64.

Launius, Roger D. "American Home Missionary Society Ministers and Mormon Nauvoo: Selected Letters," *Western Illinois Regional Studies* 8 (spring 1985): 16–45.

Leone, Mark F. "The Mormon Temple Experience," *Sunstone* 3 (September–October 1979): 6–10.

Logue, Larry M. "A Time of Marriage: Monogamy and Polygamy in a Utah Town," *Journal of Mormon History* 11 (1984): 9.

Luce, W. Ray. "The Mormon Battalion: A Historical Accident?" *Utah Historical Quarterly* 42 (winter 1974): 27–38.

Manis, Jerome G., "Great Little Persons," *Biography* 12 (winter 1989): 18.

Milner, Clyde A., II. "The Shared Memories of Montana's Pioneers," *Montana: The Magazine of Western History* 37 (winter 1987): 4.

Neasham, Aubrey. "Sutter's Sawmill," *California Historical Society Quarterly* 26 (June 1947): 110.

Pratt, Steven. "Eleanor McLean and the Murder of Parley P. Pratt," *BYU Studies* 15 (winter 1975): 225–56.

Quinn, D. Michael. "LDS Church Authority and New Plural Marriages, 1890–1904," *Dialogue: A Journal of Mormon Thought* 18 (spring 1985): 9–105.

Robertson, R. J. "The Mormon Experience in Missouri, 1830–1839." *Missouri Historical Review* 68 (April 1974): 280–98.

Rowe, David L. "A New Perspective on the Burned-Over District: The Millerites in Upstate New York," *Church History* 47 (December 1978): 408–20.

Rowley, Dennis. "Nauvoo: A River Town," *BYU Studies* 18 (winter 1978): 255–72.

Serven, James Edsell. "The Ill-Fated '49er Train," *Historical Society of Southern California* 62 (March 1960): 29–40.

Silverman, Jane L. "To Marry Again," *Hawaiian Journal of History* 17 (1983): 64.

Smith, Melvin T. "Forces That Shaped Utah's Dixie: Another Look," *Utah Historical Quarterly* 47 (spring 1979): 111–29.

Steele, John. "Extracts from the Journal of John Steele," *Utah Historical Quarterly* 6 (January 1933): 3.

Taylor, Samuel W. "Walter Murray Gibson: Great Mormon Rascal," *The American West* 1 (spring 1964): 18–27.

Underwood, Grant. "Millenarianism and the Early Mormon Mind," *Journal of Mormon History* 9 (1982): 41–52.

Young, Lorenzo Dow. "Biography of Lorenzo Dow Young," *Utah Historical Quarterly* 14 (January 1946): 33–34.

Yurtinus, John F. "Here Is One Man Who Will Not Go, Dam 'um: Recruiting the Mormon Battalion in Iowa Territory," *BYU Studies* 21 (fall 1981): 476.

Periodicals and Newspapers

Deseret Evening News, Salt Lake City.

Hutchings California Magazine. Sacramento, California.

Journal of Discourses. 27 vols. London and Liverpool: LDS Booksellers Depot, 1855–86.

Los Angeles Evening Express The Pioneer, San Jose, California.

Quarterly of the Society of California Pioneers, San Francisco, California.

Times and Seasons. Nauvoo, Illinois.

The Union. St. George, Utah.

Theses and Dissertations

Bachman, Danel. "A Study of the Mormon Practice of Plural Marriage before the Death of Jospeh Smith." M.A. thesis, Purdue University, 1975.

Bishop, Michael Guy. "The Celestial Family: Early Mormon Thought on Life and Death, 1830–1846." Ph.D. diss., Southern Illinois University at Carbondale, 1981.

Curtis, Kirk M. "History of the St. George Temple." M.A. thesis, Brigham Young University, 1964.

Ellsworth, Samuel George. "A History of the Mormon Missions in the United States and Canada, 1830–1860." Ph.D. diss., University of California at Berkeley, 1951.

Leonard, Glen Milton. "A History of Farmington, Utah, 1890." M.A. thesis, University of Utah, 1966.

McReady, Harvey Clinton. "New Hope: A Mormon Colony in Central California." M.A. thesis, Brigham Young University, 1976.

Peterson, Paul H. "The Mormon Reformation." Ph.D. diss., Brigham Young University, 1981.

Shaffer, Donald Robert. "A Forgotten Missionary: Hiram Clark, Mormon Itinerant, British Emigration Organizer, and First President of the L.D.S. Hawaiian Mission, 1795–1853." M.A. thesis, California State Univerity, Fullerton, 1990.

Yurtinus, John F. "A Ram in the Thicket: The Mormon Battalion in the Mexican War." 2 vols. Ph.D. diss., Brigham Young University, 1975.

INDEX